US SUPER CARRIER

All makes and models

First published in May 2020

A catalogue record for this book is available from the British Library.

ISBN 978 1 78521 667 1

Library of Congress control no. 2019949568

Published by Haynes Publishing,
Sparkford, Yeovil, Somerset BA22 7JJ, UK.
Tel: 01963 440635
Int. tel: +44 1963 440635
Website: www.haynes.com

Haynes North America Inc.,
859 Lawrence Drive, Newbury Park,
California 91320, USA.

Printed in Malaysia.

Senior Commissioning Editor: Jonathan Falconer
Copy editor: Michelle Tilling
Proof reader: Penny Housden
Indexer: Peter Nicholson
Page design: James Robertson

Acknowledgements

The author would like to give his sincere thanks to Captain Kyle Higgins (Commanding Officer) and the crew of the USS *Dwight D. Eisenhower* (CVN-69) for granting myself and photographer Patrick Bunce access to the ship for research and image purposes. Special thanks also go to Lieutenant Commander Ben Tisdale (Public Affairs Officer) and Lieutenant Junior Grade Lewis Aldridge (Assistant Public Affairs Officer) for arranging the mechanics of the visit, and to the following carrier personnel for their time and assistance:

- Lieutenant Commander Jitindra W. Sirjoo (Handler)
- Lieutenant Benjamin R. Farnham
- Aviation Boatswain's Mate (Handling) Second Class Leanna M. Rose
- Aviation Boatswain's Mate (Handling) Third Class Mia G. Lapan
- Aviation Boatswain's Mate (Handling) Third Class Omar E. Buendia
- Commander Andrew McClune (CDC Officer)
- Commander Dean Schoenrock (Gun Boss)
- Commander Raymond Stromberger (Navigator)
- Boatswain's Mate Chief Andrew Wood
- Commander Rhonda Wallace (Ship's Doctor)
- Commander Frank Gasperetti (Chief Engineer)
- Lieutenant Commander Timothy Hill (Assistant Supply Officer)
- Commander Rob Radak (Safety Officer)
- Captain Jon Bradford (Executive Officer)
- Commander Jason Witt (Air Operations Officer)
- Machinist Mate 1st Class Daniel Ostarello
- Machinist Mate 2nd Class Jonathon Timpson
- Damage Controlman 2nd Class Marissa Macaluso

I would also like to thank Commander Richard Hecht, Chief Petty Officer Michael Cole and Lieutenant Junior Grade Marc Rockwellpate for processing the initial administration and practicalities to make our visit possible.

Final thanks go Michelle Tilling, for her careful editing, and to Jonathan Falconer of Haynes Publishing, for making numerous accommodations during the writing of this book.

US SUPER CARRIER

All makes and models

Operations Manual

"CVN-69"

Insights into the design, departments, flight operations and daily life of the US Navy's greatest warships

Dr Chris McNab

Contents

OPPOSITE **An F/A-18E Super Hornet assigned to the 'Tomcatters' of Strike Fighter Squadron (VFA) 31 approaches the flight deck of USS *Theodore Roosevelt* (CVN-71) on 31 December 2019, when the carrier was conducting routine training in the eastern Pacific Ocean.** *(US Navy photo by Mass Communication Specialist 2nd Class Alex Corona/Released)*

Introduction

Few man-made objects in the modern world represent power projection as emphatically as the supercarriers of the US Navy. Emerging in the aftermath of the Second World War in the *Forrestal* and *Enterprise* classes, the supercarrier concept has become most potently embodied in the great *Nimitz*-class vessels, ten of which have been commissioned since 1975. It is these warships, plus the now emerging supercarriers of the *Gerald R. Ford* class, that form the lethal heart of the US Navy's Carrier Strike Groups (CSGs), previously referred to as Carrier Battle Groups (CBGs).

US supercarriers have been referred to as 'floating cities', and with some justification. They are quite simply the largest warships that have ever taken to the seas – vast works of tactical, organisational, social and physical engineering that occupy the summit of military ingenuity and ambition. Some headline statistics amply illustrate the point. The typical *Nimitz*-class supercarrier has an overall length of 1,092ft

BELOW USS *Ronald Reagan* (CVN-76), left, and the amphibious assault ship USS *Boxer* (LHD-4) and ships from the *Ronald Reagan* Carrier Strike Group and the *Boxer* Amphibious Ready Group are here seen under way as part of security and stability operations in the US Seventh Fleet area of operations. *(US Navy photo by Mass Communication Specialist 2nd Class Erwin Jacob V. Miciano/Released)*

(332.8m) and an overall beam of 250ft 8in (76.4m), the structure capped by a flight deck that covers 4½ acres (1.8 hectares). From the keel to the top of the mast, the ship towers 252ft (76.8m). The total displacement is in excess of 101,600 tons (100,000 long tons). The scale of the carrier means that it can house a total complement of 6,012 personnel, including the air wing, who crew and maintain some 85–90 fixed-wing and rotary aircraft, which between them can deliver more than 150 combat sorties per day. The Westinghouse A4W nuclear powerplants that provide the ships with their propulsion and power give the vessels a truly unlimited oceanic range; indeed, the ships are capable of operating continuously without refuelling for 20–23 years. The *Gerald R. Ford*-class vessels, as we shall see, are of even greater scale and scope. Given their capabilities

and size, the supercarriers occupy the very pinnacle of naval power.

This book provides a detailed insight into the structure, organisation, equipment, operation and combat potential of the US *Nimitz*-class and *Gerald R. Ford*-class supercarriers. Given that the warships are, at the time of writing, operational vessels, there are some limitations on the information that can appear. Yet drawing on both open access sources, some little known in the public domain, plus the kind assistance of the US Navy, especially the crew of the USS *Dwight D. Eisenhower* who graciously received myself and the photographer aboard their ship, we can explore life both above and below decks. In the process, we explore extraordinary physical and human structure that will continue to embody US military might for years to come.

ABOVE USS *John C. Stennis* (CVN-74) steams through the Atlantic Ocean in October 2019. The carrier was commissioned in 1995. *(US Navy photo by Mass Communication Specialist 3rd Class Skyler Okerman/ Released)*

Chapter One

History of the supercarrier

The six years of the Second World War reconfigured naval warfare at a fundamental level. At the start of the conflict, naval might was largely represented by capital battleships, bristling with turreted long-range guns. At war's end just six years later, such vessels appeared as little more than obsolete, cumbersome targets, their position utterly overthrown by the perfection of two very different types of fighting vessel – submarines and aircraft carriers.

OPPOSITE The *Nimitz*-class aircraft carrier USS *Carl Vinson* (CVN-70) transits past Waterman Point on its way to Naval Base Kitsap-Bremerton in the state of Washington. *(US Navy photo by Mass Communication Specialist 2nd Class Wyatt L. Anthony)*

In terms of aircraft carriers, in 1945 the US Navy had an unassailable lead in both the size of the carrier fleet and the combat capability of the individual vessels, which were larger and more potent than those of any of their rivals (Japanese carriers had been progressively wiped out between 1942 and 1945).

Post-war modernisation

Prior to and during the war, the United States' formidable industrial machine had produced more than 100 carriers of various types and classes. Following the commissioning of the first US carrier, the USS *Langley* (CV-1), on 20 March 1922, the most significant US carrier classes of the 1920s and 1930s were the *Lexington* and *Yorktown*, many of which would not survive the war. But in terms of

in-war production, the *Essex* class was the most significant, 24 of which would enter service between 1942 and 1946. The other major carrier type was the prolific *Independence* class – no fewer than nine of which were commissioned in 1943 alone.

The capabilities of these carriers were impressive for the time, and their contribution to the Allied victory, especially in the Pacific Theatre of Operations (PTO), was central. The USS *Essex* (CV-9), for example, had a length of 820ft (249.9m), a displacement of 36,960 US tons (33,529 tonnes) at full load, a complement of 2,600 officers and men and an air wing of more than 90 combat aircraft. Yet as early as 1940, the US Navy was investigating the possibilities for producing a larger class of carrier. The output of this design challenge was the *Midway* class of carriers, three of which were commissioned between September 1945 and October 1947. These vessels – *Midway* (CVB-41), *Franklin D. Roosevelt* (CVB-42) and *Coral Sea* (CVB-43) – upscaled the combat capability of US naval aviation, measuring 968ft

BELOW The USS *Franklin* (CV-13), an *Essex*-class carrier, lists heavily following Japanese bomb strikes sustained during an air raid off the Japanese mainland on 19 March 1945. *(NARA)*

(295m) overall, displacing 45,000 tons (40,823 tonnes) and operating an air wing of up to 130 aircraft, 30 more than an *Essex*-class carrier. The complement of the ships had climbed to 4,104, although the size was not matched by ergonomic considerations – the internal layout of the *Midway* class was cramped and uncomfortable for the crew.

The *Midway* class emerged in the immediate aftermath of the Second World War, which was in many ways an unpromising time for ambitious military investment. Although new tensions with the Soviet Union were becoming apparent, the US military embarked on a massive programme of post-conflict demilitarisation. Financial constraints loomed large over big-budget capital warship development, not least because the US Navy found itself fighting over central funds with the US Air Force (USAF). Both the Navy and the Air Force in the 1950s saw themselves at the vanguard of American strategic reach, especially in the emerging nuclear age. The Air Force's long-range strategic bomber fleet and the Navy's nuclear-capable air wing had inevitable areas of overlap that caused frictions and competition, and with immediate

consequences for the Navy's carrier fleet – three of the planned *Midway*-class vessels were cancelled. But the cancellation of the *Midway* vessels was only partly due to budgetary constraints. There was also a technological challenge to be addressed, one that would force a rethink on the very design principles behind carriers.

The late 1940s and the 1950s saw the advent of the jet age. Although US carriers would continue to operate some breeds of prop-driven aircraft – notable examples including the Douglas AD Skyraider and the Grumman AF-2 Guardian – jet-powered fighters, strike aircraft and bombers were emphatically the future of carrier aviation. Early types of jet carrier aircraft were the Douglas F3D Skyknight (principally used as a fighter and electronic countermeasures (ECM) aircraft), the Grumman F9F Panther fighter, the North American FJ Fury (the first jet fighter to operate from a carrier in squadron strength), the North American AJ Savage (a hybrid radial engine/turbojet heavy attack aircraft), the McDonnell FH-1 Phantom fighter, the McDonnell F2H Banshee reconnaissance aircraft and the Douglas A-3

ABOVE F6F-3 Hellcats aboard USS *Yorktown* (CV-10) in August 1943. The low take-off speed of prop aircraft obviated the need for catapult launch equipment. *(US Navy)*

Skywarrior (which had some significance for the supercarrier programme). The introduction of jet aircraft on to carriers demanded that the following challenges be addressed:

■ Longer take-off distances/the requirement for catapult assistance.
■ Longer landing distances/the requirement for heavy arresting gear.
■ Stronger decks to take the increased aircraft weight.
■ Decks reconfigured for the different safety issues presented by jet aircraft (dangers from both the air intakes and the thrust exhausts).
■ Greater aviation fuel storage requirements.

To develop a carrier fleet suited to the jet age, the US Navy had two options: 1) modernise existing carriers or 2) build new generations of carriers designed for jet aviation from the outset.

For the modernisation option, the focus naturally fell upon the many *Essex*-class vessels still in service, plus the three of the *Midway* class. The *Essex* class also includes what has been referred to as the *Ticonderoga* class. The USS *Ticonderoga* (CV-14) was commissioned on

RIGHT Despite being built during the Second World War, the *Essex*-class USS *Intrepid* (CV-11) stayed in service until the 1970s, courtesy of major upgrades. Here we see the before-and-after images following SCB-125 modifications in the 1950s. *(US Navy)*

8 May 1944. An *Essex*-class carrier, it featured a new extended bow, as did all subsequent iterations of that class. These extended-bow vessels are therefore referred to as the *Ticonderoga* class. The *Essex/Ticonderoga* class went through two major upgrade programmes in the 1940s and 1950s. The first of these was Ship Characteristics Board (SCB) Program 27 in 1947–55, the specifications of which were actually installed first in the new-build *Oriskany* (CV-34), laid down on 1 May 1944 but not commissioned until 25 September 1950, its construction having been suspended between August 1946 and August 1947. Fourteen further *Essex*-class vessels received the upgrade and were recommissioned between January 1951 and September 1955. The modifications to the carriers were substantial and included the following (here we also collect all the sub-modifications delivered under SCB-27A and SCB-27C):

■ Reinforced flight deck to take the weight of heavier jet aircraft, including the AJ Savage (maximum take-off weight 51,580lb/23,396kg). Other deck modifications included (SBC-27C) a deck-cooling system, jet-blast deflectors and an emergency recovery barrier. All deck-mounted guns were also removed to improve total available flight-deck space.
■ More powerful H8 slotted tube hydraulic catapults or (SBC-27C) C-11 steam catapult, the latter delivering 70,000lb (31,181kg) at 108 knots (200km/h).
■ Installation of the Mk 5 arresting gear.
■ Installation of more powerful elevators.
■ Redesigned island, being taller in but shorter in length (to maximise deck space) with gun armament removed and a single radar and communications mast.
■ A 50% increase in fuel storage space, to 300,000 US gallons (1,135,624 litres), with more powerful fuel-pumping capabilities.
■ Extensive safety modifications, including an advanced fog/foam firefighting system and air crew ready rooms located beneath the armoured flight deck.
■ Armour belt removed to reduce weight, with torpedo hull blisters fitted to compensate.

Even as the SCB-27 programme was entering its final months, the Navy implemented another

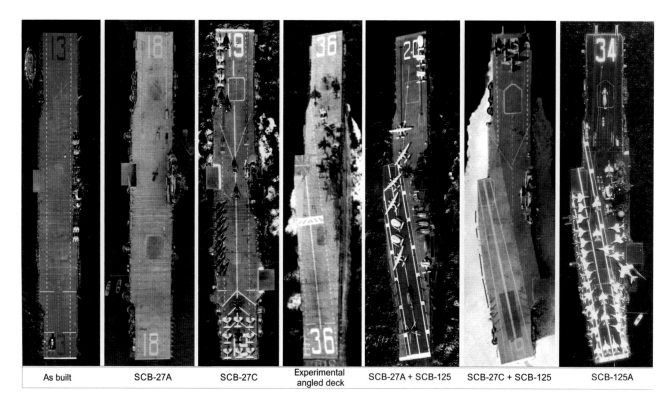

| As built | SCB-27A | SCB-27C | Experimental angled deck | SCB-27A + SCB-125 | SCB-27C + SCB-125 | SCB-125A |

upgrade, SCB-125, which was applied to 14 *Essex*-class carriers between 1954 and 1959, running concurrently with the SBC-27C upgrades. The emphasis of this programme was principally on improving the carriers' seakeeping qualities and also the efficiency of flight deck operations. Two major structural changes were therefore implemented. The installation of a 'hurricane bow' – meaning a bow that went all the way up to the flight deck, completely enclosing the hangar deck – enhanced the carriers' speed and handling. Yet most visibly striking was the addition of an angled flight deck on the port side. This feature, one borrowed from British Royal Navy carriers, was to become standard on their US counterparts, and transformed carrier operations. The specific advantages of the angled flight deck are explained in Chapter 3, but here we can summarise briefly by saying that having two decks provided far greater flexibility in the organisation of landings, take-offs and

ABOVE This useful photograph shows modernisations received by the *Essex*-class carriers between, on the far left, the USS *Franklin* (CV-13) in 1944, as delivered, and the USS *Oriskany* (CV-34), far right, following SCB-125A upgrades in 1974. *(US Navy)*

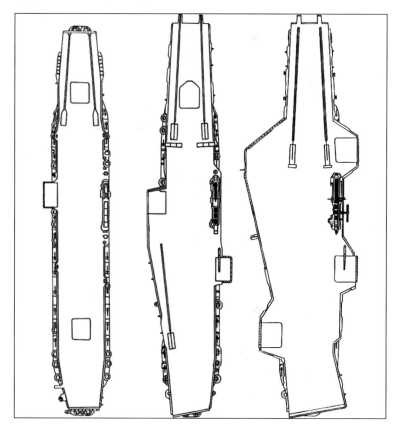

RIGHT The changing form of US carriers. Here we see deck plans for the USS *Midway* (CV-41). From left to right: 1) as completed, in 1945; 2) following her SCB-110 refit, in 1957; 3) following her SCB-110.66 refit, in 1970. *(US Navy)*

aircraft parking, plus some major benefits in
safety and storage. The SBC-27C vessels that
went into the SBC-125 programme also had
their No. 3 elevators moved to the starboard
deck edge (previously they had been on the
centreline). The last of the SBC-125 upgrades,
USS *Oriskany*, also had aluminium flight deck
cladding, the Mk 7-1 arresting gear and the
more powerful C-11-1 steam catapults fitted.

The *Midway*-class carriers also received
upgrade investment to cope with the new
generations of heavy jet bombers either
entering service or planned for the future.
The modifications were conducted as part of
the SCB-110 programme and they included
major enhancements such as the angled
flight deck, an enlarged foredeck, the fitting
of three C-11 steam catapults, the mirror
landing system pioneered by the British (see
Chapter 4), improved elevators, a hurricane
bow and far more generous fuel storage.
In addition, the *Midway*-class islands were
enhanced, particularly in terms of internal
accommodation, and electronic navigation and
surveillance systems were upgraded to the
latest standards. *Coral Sea* was the last of the
class to receive an upgrade, via SCB-110A in
1957, which was actually more extensive than
SCB-110. Yet on 11 February 1966, *Midway*
entered San Francisco Bay Naval Shipyard
for SCB-101.66 modernisation, which made it
the mightiest specimen of its class. In a huge

four-year development that cost $202 million
(which was $114 million more than originally
costed), the flight deck was increased in size
from 122,000 to 174,000sq ft (11,300 to
16,200m^2), elevators were given greater lift
capacity, new catapults and arresting gear
were installed and the ship was fitted with a
centralised air conditioning plant. While the
broader and longer flight deck gave a more
comfortable expanse of real estate for the
aircraft operations, the major weight increase
of the carrier (which now had a displacement
of 69,873 tons/63,388 tonnes full load, as
opposed to 45,000 tons/40,823 tonnes at
commissioning) had a detrimental impact
upon seakeeping, the deck now being 'wetter'
and the flight operations more susceptible to
problems in rough sea conditions.

Despite their major upgrades and continual
refinements, which kept some of the ships in
service until the early 1990s, the *Essex* and
Midway carriers had limited futures in terms of
the US Navy's bolder plans for the strategically
influential fleet. Even these beefy vessels
would be unable to cope with some of the
nuclear-capable long-range carrier bombers
in development, some of which were intended
to have an operational weight of 100,000lb
(45,454kg). The Navy therefore began to
develop proposals and designs for a new breed
of naval aviation warship, one that would carry a
bold title – *supercarrier*.

The first supercarriers

The turning point in US Navy carrier design was the USS *United States* (CVA-58). Although this ship had a failed birth, it laid the conceptual keel for all supercarriers that followed. Driven hard during the 1940s by supercarrier advocate Admiral Marc Mitscher, one of the landmark figures of US carrier warfare, plans for the next generation of US carriers were persuasive enough to convince President Harry Truman, on 29 July 1948, to approve construction of five such vessels, the funding for these granted in the Naval Appropriations Act of 1949. The lead ship of the new class would be the USS *United States*, whose primary function was to deploy long-range nuclear bomber aircraft, although it would also have a major contingent of strike aircraft for tactical operations.

United States represented a revolutionary design on multiple levels. It would be far larger than anything that preceded it – 1,093ft (330m) overall length and a 190ft (58m) beam on the flight deck, the warship displacing 83,350 tons (76,614 tonnes) at full load. Propulsion came from eight Foster-Wheelhouse boilers and four Westinghouse geared steam turbines, generating a power output of 280,000shp (153,000kW) and a maximum speed of 33 knots (61km/h). Most striking in the design drawings is the flush deck – it did not feature an island, just an open expanse of deck area.

Those command spaces and functions that could not be facilitated below the flight deck were intended to be given to a command ship that would follow the carrier closely during operations. The air wing was to consist of up to 18 heavy bombers and 54 other aircraft (principally fighters/strike aircraft), supported by 2,480 air wing officers and crew within a total ship's complement of 3,019. It was a carrier the likes of which had never been seen before.

Even as construction began on the *United States* – keel laying started on 18 April 1949 – the ship was sailing into political high seas. Budgetary conflicts between the USAF and the US Navy resulted, on 23 April, just five days after the keel laying, in the Secretary of Defense, Louis Johnson, cancelling the *United States*-class programme altogether. This left the US Navy reeling, and with force reductions to its *Essex*- and *Midway*-class carriers, it was faced with a problematic future in terms of its strategic role in the gathering Cold War.

Nevertheless, recognising that existing classes of carrier were simply inadequate to operate new generations of carrier aircraft, particularly the 70,000lb (31,751kg) Douglas A-3 Skywarrior, the Navy began pursuing a new class of carrier design, one with scaled-down ambition compared to the *United States*, but which still represented a major step forward compared to the Second World War generations of carriers.

ABOVE This artist's vision of the USS *United States* (CVA-58), by Bruno Figallo in October 1948, illustrates how unusual was the design proposition. Note the complete absence of the island and the single catapult angled to port. *(US Navy)*

The outcome of this investment was the birth of the supercarrier generation – the *Forrestal* class. The first of the four, the USS *Forrestal* (CVA-59), was laid down in July 1952, and from the outset represented a seismic shift in naval aviation deployment. With an overall length of 1,039ft (317m), it was only 66ft (20m) short of the *United States* design and had a deep-load displacement of 77,800 tons (79,200 tonnes). It incorporated two crucial British innovations – the angled flight deck and steam catapults – and it also included the Fresnel Lens Landing System to enhance the precision of aircraft recovery operations (see Chapter 4). Unlike the *United States*, the *Forrestal* reintroduced a carrier

island, although this was developed with minimal dimensions to make the most of flight deck space. The total air complement (as designed) for the *Forrestal* was 32 A-3 Skywarrior bombers and 12 F3H Demon fighters. The ship was powered by geared steam turbines producing the total power output of 260,000shp (194,000kW), and with 7,800 tons (7,940 tonnes) of fuel on board the ship had an operational range of 10,000nm (18,520km) at 20 knots (37km/h). The total ship's complement was 4,500 men.

Between 1955 and 1957, four of the *Forrestal*-class carriers were commissioned: *Forrestal* (CVA-59), *Independence* (CVA-62), *Ranger* (CVA-61) and *Saratoga* (CVA-60). They would stay in service until the 1990s, undergoing frequent upgrades and modifications in response to new aircraft types and the emergence of other technological advances. Indeed, given the rate of change in post-war aviation, the question of the *Forrestal* class's successor soon arose, accompanied by all the usual heat and light of disagreement. Some argued for carriers of reduced size and cost, but eventually it was decided to produce an improved version of the *Forrestal* class, such that the extent of the modifications would effectively place it in a different class. The principal changes were in flight deck layout, which was widened in the centre to give it a greater surface area, and the location of the island was also placed further aft, with, on the starboard side, one elevator aft of the island and two forward; previous *Forrestal* carriers had a reverse arrangement. The air wing of the carrier had, as designed, also changed fairly radically from previous members of the class, with more than 90 aircraft aboard, primarily A-4 Skyhawks, A-3 Skywarriors, F-4 Phantoms and F-8 Crusaders. The complement of sailors had crept up to the 5,500 mark. Note also that in the process of widening the flight deck, the top-weight of the carriers increased significantly, and

LEFT The explosion and fire aboard the USS Forrestal (CVA-59) on 29 July 1967, caused by the malfunction and accidental firing of a Zuni rocket on a F-4B Phantom, killed 134 sailors and injured 161. The accident resulted in major changes to naval carrier firefighting procedures and equipment. *(US Navy)*

to compensate the *Forrestal* class's extensive anti-aircraft gun armament was removed, the compensation being the installation of two twin Terrier surface-to-air (SAM) systems plus the protective firepower of surrounding surface ships.

Three of the 'Improved *Forrestal* class' were built and commissioned in the early to mid-1960s: *Kitty Hawk* (CVA-63), *America* (CVA-66) and *Constellation* (CVA-64). In fact, such was the breadth of the changes that the ships were also called the *Kitty Hawk* class. A further conventional carrier was launched during the 1960s, the USS *John F. Kennedy* (CVA-67). *John F. Kennedy* was the last of the Navy's conventionally powered

supercarriers, commissioned on 7 September 1968. Her design was partly indebted to the *Kitty Hawk* class, and partly to the nuclear-powered USS *Enterprise* (CVAN-65), which, having launched before *John F. Kennedy*, had stepped in and taken the last number in the sequence of the *Kitty Hawk* class. CVA-67 was, therefore, a class of its own, a major combat vessel that served on in the US Navy until its decommissioning in 2007.

BELOW USS *Kitty Hawk* (CV-63) steams in formation during Exercise Valiant Shield, 2007. *(US Navy photo by Mass Communication Specialist Seaman Stephen W. Rowe/Released)*

The US Navy's conventional aircraft carriers, both supercarriers and modernised *Essex*-class vessels, formed a critical component of American naval power projection from the 1950s right through to the 1990s and 2000s, seeing intensive combat service in many theatres, especially during the Vietnam War and in various Middle Eastern conflicts. But the 1960s was also the decade when the world saw the advent of the nuclear-powered carrier, and it would be these vessels that came to dominate the force architecture of the modern US Navy.

From *Enterprise* to *Nimitz*

On 30 September 1954, USS *Nautilus* (SSN-571) was commissioned into Navy service – the first nuclear-powered operational submarine in history. As the Cold War grew ever more guarded and tense, the world's oceans became a strategic chessboard, with moves played deep beneath the waves. *Nautilus*'s nuclear power source gave it the almost endless on-station endurance required for this changing political landscape.

Debates about the application of nuclear power to surface vessels were already well under way by the time that *Nautilus* took to the seas. Developing a nuclear-powered carrier was perfectly feasible given the far greater internal space when compared to the submarine, although this argument could work both ways; the fact that aircraft carriers were so large meant that they did not have problems storing high volumes of conventional fuels. There were also all the usual budgetary arguments, as developing, installing and maintaining a nuclear reactor

RIGHT A close-up view of the island structure aboard the USS *John F. Kennedy* (CV-67) in 2004. The white domes at the top house SATCOM and Global Broadcast System (GBS) equipment. *(US Navy/Larry Kachelhofer, USN)*

aboard a carrier would further increase the cost of these already formidably expensive vessels.

Ultimately, however, once the nuclear-powered aircraft carrier was conceived mentally, its physical reality became almost inevitable if the US Navy was to retain its undeniable advantage over the world's oceans. By having a nuclear rather than conventional power source, an aircraft carrier could not only steam around the world almost indefinitely, but it could also do so at higher speeds (full-speed operations for conventional aircraft carriers are very fuel-hungry) and have greater power for onboard

ABOVE The first of the US Navy's nuclear-powered carriers, the USS *Enterprise* (CVN-65). Note the two bridle-catcher structures at the very front of the flight deck. *(US Navy photo by Photographer's Mate Airman Rob Gaston/ Released)*

BELOW The island of the USS *Enterprise* in 1967. Note the large white 'billboards' of the phased array radar system. *(Bill Larkins/CC BY-SA 2.0)*

A NOTE ON NOMENCLATURE

US Navy aircraft carriers are commissioned with various hull classification symbols to define either their role, size and/or form of propulsion. These are:

CV –   aircraft carrier
CVA –   attack aircraft carrier
CVB –   large aircraft carrier
CVL –   light aircraft carrier
CVN –   aircraft carrier (nuclear propulsion)
CVAN – attack aircraft carrier (nuclear propulsion)

equipment, particularly steam catapults, and the ever-expanding array of electrical equipment. Thus in 1958, the Navy received funding for the first nuclear-powered aircraft carrier, to be called the USS *Enterprise* (CVAN-65).

Enterprise was built between 1958 and 1961. It was commissioned on 25 November 1961 and in testimony to the integrity and relevance of its design it was not decommissioned until 3 February 2017, having served in conflicts ranging from the Vietnam War to Operation Iraqi Freedom. When viewed from the outside, the carrier immediately arrests with its sheer scale: it measured 1,123ft (343m) overall and had a beam of 133ft (40.6m), making it the largest warship in US naval history, a record it still holds to this day. The flight deck had an area of 1,079ft (329m) by 235ft 3in (71.8m). Displacement was 68,000 tons (61,689 tonnes). The size of its flight deck and internal space meant that it could handle the ship's complement of 5,828 personnel and a maximum air wing of 99 aircraft (although 60+ was more common). Onboard storage of aviation fuel was 50% greater than a *Kitty Hawk*-class carrier. There were other notable external changes from previous carriers. The island was small and square, but bristling with the evidence of modern surveillance and combat electronics, not least in the presence of large horizontal and vertical rectangular 'billboard' antennae that wrapped around the island. These were the outer faces of the Hughes SCANFAR system, the first phased array radar system to be deployed by the US Navy. The horizontal panels were the AN/SPS-32 air surveillance radar, with a range out to 400 miles (643km), while the vertical modules were the AN/SPS-33 target tracking system. SCANFAR provided a 360-degree surveillance and defensive arrangement, linked to three RIM-7 Sea Sparrow SAM systems as 'point defence'. Deep below decks, the step change within *Enterprise* was of course her powerplant. The ship had a total of eight Westinghouse A2W nuclear reactors, with a total output of 280,000shp (209,000kW), taking the vessel to a maximum speed of 33 knots (61km/h).

Enterprise was undoubtedly a mighty vessel, kept mighty through regular upgrades and modifications during the course of its service life; the ship that was decommissioned in 2017 was a very different vessel in terms of electronics and combat capability from that which entered service in the 1960s. But in a world of finite budgets, *Enterprise* placed a heavy demand upon the Pentagon's purse – it cost $451.3 million to build, more than $4 billion in US dollars at the time of writing. Moreover, the placement of the aircraft carriers on the strategic spectrum was changing significantly, not least because of the advent of nuclear-powered missile submarines armed with UGM-27 Polaris nuclear ballistic missiles; the first test launch had been on 20 July 1960 from the USS *George Washington* (SSBN-598). The missile submarines meant that the requirement for carriers to operate sizeable nuclear-capable bombers was reduced or removed. During the subsequent reappraisal, the carriers occupied a more tactical space, providing close-support operations plus a variety of other roles, such as anti-submarine warfare (ASW) and electronic warfare (EW). The breadth of combat roles necessitated a proliferation of personnel and equipment types on board, meaning that carriers could not be shrunk too much, but it was clear that a fresh type of carrier was required, especially as older generations were sailing towards decommissioning. It was from this reassessment of the carrier's role that the *Nimitz* class was born.

BELOW The USS *Enterprise* (CVAN-65) burns following a Zuni rocket explosion off the coast of Hawaii on 14 January 1969. Numerous 500lb (227kg) bombs subsequently exploded, killing 28 sailors and wounding 343 others. *(US Navy)*

LEFT **An artist's impression of the nuclear-powered aircraft carrier USS Nimitz (CVAN-68), as envisaged in 1968.** *(US Navy)*

The *Nimitz* class

While we rightly treat the *Nimitz* class as a single group, we must consider that the ten vessels which constitute the class have been constructed over a 38-year period (1968–2006). Thus the first ship to emerge, the USS *Nimitz* (CVN-68), has significant structural and technological differences to the last of the series, the USS *George H.W. Bush* (CVN-77), which was commissioned in 2009. Adding to the complexity of categorisation are the transformative effects of older vessels passing through Refueling and Complex Overhaul (RCOH) upgrades, which often result in substantial modifications to shipboard technologies and even structural features. To orientate ourselves to this evolving series, first we look at what defined the lead ship of the class, USS *Nimitz* herself, before providing an overview of the subclass categories. A detailed technical description of *Nimitz*-class carriers forms the meat of the rest of this book, but we should always be mindful that distinctions between individual ships and the constant evolution of technologies mean that exceptions and differences are present behind any general description.

The USS *Nimitz* is only marginally smaller than the *Enterprise*, but does full justice to the 'supercarrier' appellation. The core specifications are an overall length of 1,090ft (332.5m), a deep-load displacement of 91,500 tons (83,007 tonnes) and a complement of 5,950 personnel. The total air wing is around 87 aircraft (fixed and rotary wing). The flight deck was based heavily on that of the *John F. Kennedy*, although it had a slightly different angle (9 degrees) to port. An obvious visual difference of the original carrier's flight deck from that of the present day is that the 1970s carrier had two bridle catchers – projections from the end of the bow designed

THE *NIMITZ*-CLASS CARRIERS

Ship	Hull number	Laid down	Launched	Commissioned	RCOH
Nimitz	CVN-68	22 June 1968	13 May 1972	3 May 1975	1998–2001
Dwight D. Eisenhower	CVN-69	15 August 1970	11 October 1975	18 October 1977	2001–5
Carl Vinson	CVN-70	11 October 1975	15 March 1980	13 March 1982	2005–9
Theodore Roosevelt	CVN-71	31 October 1981	27 October 1984	25 October 1986	2009–13
Abraham Lincoln	CVN-72	3 November 1984	13 February 1968	11 November 1989	2013–17
George Washington	CVN-73	25 August 1986	21 July 1990	4 July 1992	2017–
John C. Stennis	CVN-74	13 March 1991	11 November 1993	9 December 1995	
Harry S. Truman	CVN-75	29 November 1993	7 September 1996	25 July 1998	
Ronald Reagan	CVN-76	12 February 1998	4 March 2001	12 July 2003	
George H.W. Bush	CVN-77	6 September 2003	9 October 2006	10 January 2009	

to catch the slinging bridles that were used to attach carrier-borne naval aircraft to the catapults. These were eventually removed in the early 1980s, when new generations of aircraft – ones that didn't require the bridle launch system – were embarked.

Other key changes over the lifetime of the vessel illustrate how an individual CVN evolves as the decades play out. Probably the biggest change has been in the frequent upgrading of the ship's electronic surveillance, communications, navigation and defensive suites. At the point of its commissioning, for example, the *Nimitz* had the SPS-10 surface radar and the SPS-43 2-D and SPS-48A 3-D air search radars. Today the *Nimitz* positively bristles with electronics, including the AN/SPS-48E 3-D and AN/SPS-49(V)5 2-D air search radars, AN/SPQ-9B target acquisition radar, AN/SPN-46 and AN/SPN-43C air traffic control radars, AN/SPN-41 landing aid radars, Mk 91 NSSM guidance systems, Mk 95 radars, AN/SLQ-32A(V)4 countermeasures suite and SLQ-25A Nixie torpedo countermeasures suite, plus a variety of satellite communications

USS *NIMITZ* – MAJOR PERIODS OF OVERHAUL

The following dates reflect major overhaul landmarks in the lifespan to date of the USS *Nimitz*, showing how systems are upgraded and developed over time. Note some key definitions:

■ **Post-Shakedown Availability (PSA)** – Maintenance and development to correct problems and deficiencies discovered during the shakedown cruise.

■ **Selected Restricted Availability (SRA)** – Regular period of maintenance and upgrade, including to major ship systems.

■ **Planned Incremental Availability (PIA)** – Planning and execution of depot-level maintenance, alterations and modifications to update and improve the ship's military and technical capabilities. Also **Extended Planned Incremental Availability (EPIA)** for longer periods of development.

■ **Complex Overhaul (CoH)** – Major depot maintenance period.

■ **Refueling and Complex Overhaul (RCOH)** – 3–4-year period of major maintenance, including refuelling of the nuclear powerplant.

- October 1975 to December 1975 – PSA
- May 1977 to July 1977 – SRA
- October 1978 to January 1979 – SRA
- October 1980 to January 1981 – SRA
- April 1982 to June 1982 – SRA (waist catapult bridle catcher removed)
- June 1983 to July 1984 – CoH (forward port sponson added; 3 × Mk 25 Basic Point Defense Missiles (BPDMs) replaced with 2 × Mk 29 launchers; 3 × Close-In Weapons System (CIWS) added; SPS-49 search radar replaces SPS-43)
- November 1985 to March 1986 – SRA (forward port sponson changed/enlarged)
- August 1987 to February 1988 – SRA
- August 1989 to March 1990 – SRA
- October 1991 to May 1992 – SRA
- December 1993 to January 1995 – SRA (port bow catapult bridle removed)
- June 1996 to January 1997 – SRA
- May 1998 to June 2001 – RCOH (starboard bow catapult bridle removed; top two levels of the island replaced; new antenna mast; new radar tower; RAM replaced CIWS at forward port sponson; RAM added to aft starboard sponson; 2 × CIWS at island/stern removed)
- February 2004 to August 2004 – PIA (catwalk grating replaced and flight deck resurfaced)
- March 2006 to September 2006 – PIA
- July 2008 to January 2009 – PIA
- November 2010 to March 2012 – PIA (2 × CIWS added to forward starboard sponson enlargement/new port stern sponson)
- January 2015 to October 2016 – PIA
- March 2018 to September 2019 – EPIA.

BELOW USS *Harry S. Truman* (CVN-75), left, transits the Atlantic behind the *Ticonderoga*-class guided-missile cruiser USS *Normandy* (CG-60), not pictured, during a drill on 18 July 2019. In the Persian Gulf in 2004–5, the carrier launched 2,577 combat sorties. *(US Navy photo by Mass Communication Specialist 2nd Class Michael H. Lehman/Released)*

(SATCOM) suites; the sensors, antennae and radomes for all these systems cluster thickly around the island.

Nimitz's air wing has also changed in composition over time. During the 1970s, the principal combat aircraft types aboard were the F-4 Phantom II, A-7 Corsair II and A-6 Intruder, with the F-4 soon replaced by the F-14 Tomcat; today the air wing is primarily F/A-18 Super Hornets, EA-18G Growlers and Seahawk helicopters.

Regarding the ship's integral air defence systems, at birth *Nimitz* relied upon the RIM-7 Sea Sparrow Missiles, launched from three eight-missile Mk 25 BPDMS units. These launcher units were later replaced in the 1980s by the Mk 29 Missile Launching System, while in the 1990s and early 2000s the ship began to receive the advanced RIM-116 Rolling

Airframe Missile (RAM) with the Mk 49 Guided Missile Launching System (GMLS). The SAM systems were supplemented by the fitting of Phalanx CIWS rotary cannon and Mk 38 25mm autocannon.

What has not changed in the *Nimitz* is its pulsing heart. All *Nimitz* class are fitted with two Westinghouse A4W reactors, producing a maximum power of 260,000shp (194,000kW), giving the ship virtually unlimited range between RCOHs. The ship can sail for 20–23 years before the reactor needs refuelling.

The extensive changes experienced by just the USS *Nimitz* are repeated, with many similarities and subtle variations, in the case of every ship in the class, although obviously the closer the carrier was built to current time, the fewer modifications have been made. (At

the time of writing, six of the ten *Nimitz* carriers have been into RCOH.)

Generally, we can divide the *Nimitz* carriers into three subclasses. The core *Nimitz* class refers to the first three of the carriers – *Nimitz*, *Dwight D. Eisenhower* and *Carl Vinson*, all commissioned between 1975 and 1982. The following five carriers – *Theodore Roosevelt*, *Abraham Lincoln*, *George Washington*, *John C. Stennis* and *Harry S. Truman* – belong to the *Theodore Roosevelt* subclass, which has minor structural modifications, such as improved ordnance magazine protection and upgraded flight deck protection. *Roosevelt* was also the first of the carriers to be constructed from a new modular building process, which reduced the building time of the carrier by 16 months compared to previous build methods. The final subclass is the *Ronald Reagan* subclass, which consists of USS *Ronald Reagan* and *George H.W. Bush*. Changes in this subclass include:

- A redesigned bulbous bow to increase speed, efficiency and stability.
- A redesigned island (20ft/6m longer and with one fewer deck) longer and more spacious Pri-Fly (Primary Flight Control – the control space overseeing the take-off and landing of aircraft).
- One aircraft weapons elevator relocated from the flight deck into the aft section of the island.
- Flight deck angle increased from 9.05 degrees to 9.15 degrees from the centreline.
- Integrated Communication Advanced Network (ICAN) installed throughout all areas of the ship.
- CIWS replaced with RAM.

(See the following chapters for more details about these modifications.)

ABOVE The USS *Ronald Reagan* (CVN-76), the ninth ship in the *Nimitz* class, sails through the Straits of Magellan, to San Diego, California. The carrier is home-ported at Yokosuka, Japan, as part of the United States Seventh Fleet. *(US Navy/ Photographer's Mate 3rd Class Elizabeth Thompson)*

RIGHT USS *George Washington* (CVN-73) moves out of dry dock at Newport News Shipbuilding after Refueling and Complex Overhaul (RCOH), which it entered in 2017. In addition to de-fuelling and refuelling its powerplant, the carrier's upgrades included: major structural updates to the island, mast and antenna tower; all aircraft launch and recovery equipment has been upgraded; the ship's hull has been repainted, including sea chests and freeboard; the propeller shafts have been updated and refurbished propellers installed. *(US Navy photo courtesy of Huntington Ingalls Industries by Ashley Cowan/Released)*

Both the *Ronald Reagan* and the *George H.W. Bush* are regarded as 'transition carriers', meaning that their design starts to lean towards their eventual replacement, the *Gerald R. Ford* series. *George H.W. Bush*, the very last of the *Nimitz* carriers, brought further enhancements, including a new radar tower, navigation and communication system upgrades, modernised launch and recovery equipment and an improved JP-5 fuel handling/storage system. After nearly half a century of service, the latest of the *Nimitz* carriers will take the class into service in the 2030s and beyond.

The future supercarriers

The *Nimitz*-class carriers are here to stay for some time yet, courtesy of the integrity of their original design and the outcomes of modernisation and upgrades. Yet during the early 2000s, it became clear that if the US Navy was to maintain its fleet of ten carriers, on the basis of at least three of those carriers forward deployed, then it would need steadily to introduce replacements for some of the older *Nimitz*-class vessels when they were eventually decommissioned. There was also a desire to see the next generation of carriers introduce cutting-edge technologies and processes, largely to reduce the total cost to the federal government over the lifespan of the carrier operation. These motivations resulted in what was initially called the CVN-21 programme, which in turn eventually produced the lead ship of an entirely new class, the *Gerald R. Ford*.

Entering service in 2017, the *Gerald R. Ford*

represents several major rethinks in carrier design. In fact, such is the level of revolution in automation and technology refinements that the new class will operate with 700 fewer crew than a *Nimitz*-class vessel. It aims to do so partly through the introduction of a new nuclear powerplant, the Bechtel A1B, which will require 30% less maintenance, thus the propulsion department will require 50% fewer personnel. There are also manpower savings in replacing the steam catapults with the new Electromagnetic Aircraft Launch System (EMALS) and introducing the Advanced Arresting Gear (AAG), two of the key flight deck features of the new class.

In addition to these critical changes, there are several other features that distinguish the *Gerald R. Ford* from its predecessors, all of which will be analysed in detail in later chapters:

- Improved deck design, with a smaller, redesigned island located further aft, resulting in an improved rate of aircraft sorties and operational efficiency (the aim is for 160 sorties per day for 30+ days), and a surge capability of 270 sorties a day.
- Higher-capacity ordnance elevators and improved, centralised ordnance storage to enhance the efficiency of weapon movement.
- The Mod 6 evolution of the Ship Self-Defense System (SSDS), which combines multiple sensors and defensive suites into an integrated platform, one that can operate autonomously or with a human in the loop.
- The fitting of the Dual Band Radar (DBR), which operates simultaneously over two frequency ranges (S-band and X-band), combining the capabilities of the X-band AN/SPY-3 Multifunction Radar and the S-band Volume Surveillance Radar (VSR) in a state-of-the-art defensive suite.
- The use of the RIM-162 Evolved Sea Sparrow Missile.

At the time of writing, the *Gerald R. Ford* is still ironing out numerous kinks in its systems; it remains to be seen how this process will affect the final configuration of the carrier and the subsequent examples in its class. Also, even as the carrier represents the current state of the art, further enhancements are being considered, such as the fitting of directed-

LEFT An F/A-18F Super Hornet assigned to Air Test and Evaluation Squadron (VX) 23 approaches the aircraft carrier USS *Gerald R. Ford* (CVN-78) for an arrested landing in July 2017. *(US Navy)*

energy weapons. In addition to *Gerald R. Ford* itself (which replaced the *Enterprise*/CVN-65), the next ship in the class, *John F. Kennedy* (CVN-79, replacing *Nimitz*) was laid down in 2015 and is intended for commission in 2020. To follow is a new *Enterprise* (CVN-80, to replace *Dwight D. Eisenhower*), to be commissioned in 2027, after which will follow two as-yet-unnamed carriers, CVN-81 and CVN-82, to replace *Carl Vinson* (2030) and *Theodore Roosevelt* (2034) respectively.

But while advanced technology is very much manning the wheel of future carrier development, one evident continuity is that the *Ford* class, just like the supercarriers that

preceded them, are big vessels: 1,106ft (337m) in length, 256ft (78ft) in beam on the flight deck and carrying more than 75 combat aircraft. It will take many more revolutions in engineering and technology before either the supercarrier becomes obsolete, or before it shrinks in size. Until then, the US supercarriers remain the most powerful warships ever to grace the seas.

BELOW USS *Theodore Roosevelt* (CVN-71) conducts a vertical replenishment (VERTREP) mission with the Military Sealift Command (MSC) ammunition ship USNS *Mount Baker* (T-AE 34). *Theodore Roosevelt* was the first of the *Nimitz*-class carriers to be built with modular construction processes. *(US Navy photo by Mass Communication Specialist 3rd Class Randall Damm/Released)*

Chapter Two

Structure, major systems and departments

US Navy supercarriers have been aptly described as 'floating cities'. Their scale for first-time visitors and new sailors alike is both disorientating and awe-inspiring, but over time they learn the logic of how the ship is organised and the functions of the major departments within it.

OPPOSITE A close-up view of the bows of the USS *Dwight D. Eisenhower* (CVN-69). Note how far the flight deck extends out either side in comparison to the hull at the waterline. *(Patrick Bunce)*

This chapter provides a means of familiarising ourselves with the essential structure and facilities of a US Navy supercarrier. To maintain some clarity, the *Nimitz* class will be our main vehicle of analysis, bringing in key distinctions and differences of the *Gerald R. Ford* class when appropriate or when the information is available. The sheer scale and complexity of a supercarrier means that this chapter cannot delve into every space and facility on the ships, although many of the major gaps here will be plugged in subsequent chapters. In any case, here we not only gain a detailed sense of supercarrier organisation, both physical and human, but also look at some of the major pieces of equipment, including the powerplant, that make these megaships function.

BELOW The front bow of the *Gerald R. Ford*-class carrier USS *John F. Kennedy*, as seen during construction in its dry dock area on 29 October 2019. *(US Navy photo by Mass Communication Specialist 3rd Class Adam Ferrero/Released)*

Physical overview

Hull stability

Looking at a supercarrier externally, we immediately notice some key features about its layout and design. From the outside, the carriers are dominated by two structural features – the broad expanse of flight deck and the island, located on the starboard side and of limited area footprint to maximise the space available for aircraft operations. What is striking is the difference between the beam of the flight deck and that at the waterline; on a *Nimitz*-class aircraft carrier, the former is 254ft (76.8m) overall – *ie* across the widest point of the flight deck – but 134ft (40.8m) for the latter measurement, giving the carrier a decidedly top-heavy appearance.

Despite the appearance, however, the ships are inherently stable, and have good seagoing qualities in even the heaviest seas. This is in part due to the wide and rounded design of the lower portions of the hull, supported by the

proper use of ballast and weight distribution. Much of the heaviest pieces of equipment – including both nuclear reactor compartments and main machine rooms – are allocated to the very bottom of the ship, as are some of the key storage areas, including some 3,000 tons (2,722 tonnes) of ordnance. Fluid storage is also concentrated within the lower half of the ship. Both drinking water and more than 3 million gallons of JP-5 aviation fuel are kept in vertical-profile tanks either side of the hull, and seawater ballast provides another stabilising factor. All the fluids on the ship, more than 5 million gallons (19 million litres) in total, constitute a movable ballast, and the compartmentalisation of the fluid storage spaces means that the weight distribution can be altered according to sea conditions, loading effects and to battle damage. There are five list-control tanks either side of the ship specifically for this purpose. The fluids also provide protective damage limitation should the hull be struck underwater by a torpedo or mine, the liquids absorbing some of the shockwaves of the explosion. The hull design includes a double-bottomed keel, the space between the plates providing, in effect, a stand-off space between the sea on the outside and the manned portions of the ship within.

The other stabilising factor for the supercarriers is simply sheer size. A *Nimitz*-class carrier has a length at the waterline of about 1,040ft (317m). This means that the length of the hull generally exceeds the length of any waveform, even in very severe weather, thus the ship cuts through even the largest waves with little problem.

Decks and internal structure

The inside of a *Nimitz*-class carrier has more than 2,000 individual compartments of every shape and size, from small individual administration rooms through to the vast hall-like space of the hangar deck. Simplifying the structure, the ship is divided by vertical frames and horizontal decks or levels. This structure includes 23 watertight transverse bulkheads and ten firewall bulkheads, which allow a seriously damaged part of the ship to be isolated, with flooding and fire contained.

Looking at the top-to-bottom deck structure,

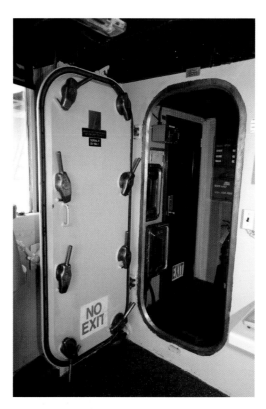

LEFT Just one of the many watertight doors set into CVN carrier bulkheads; the USS *Abraham Lincoln* lists 1,141 watertight closures in its structure. *(Patrick Bunce)*

we need to make a distinction between a deck and a level. Looking from the top down, just below the flight deck is the gallery deck then the hangar deck. (Both the flight deck and the hangar deck are studied in some detail in Chapter 3.) The hangar deck is two-thirds of the length of the carrier and three decks tall. It is level with the main deck fore and aft, and any deck above the main deck is classed as a level, described in ascending numbers (*eg* 01 Level, 02 Level), while decks below are referred to as decks, in descending order (*eg* 2nd Deck, 3rd Deck). Sources vary a little in their agreement of exactly how many decks and levels there are on a *Nimitz*-class carrier (some post-commission modifications have altered deck numbers), but there are about eight decks and 11 levels, with 8th Deck being the hold (which means that 7th Deck is the last deck with human occupation), and Levels 04–11 being the flight deck to the top of the island. The upright frames of the ship are also numbered, starting at the front of the ship and increasing in number as you move aft.

The island

The island's overall purpose is to act as a command and control centre both for piloting and navigating the ship and for performing

RIGHT One of the thousands of 'bull's-eye' plates aboard a CVN carrier, providing crew members with a means of logical orientation around the ship.
(Patrick Bunce)

To help the crew members navigate their way around the complex interior of a supercarrier, each compartment of the ship has an alphanumeric sequence displayed on its wall. This is known as a 'bull's-eye', and it not only indicates where the compartment is on the ship, but also indicates its function. The information is given in the following order: deck number, frame number, relation to the centreline of the ship (even numbers indicate you are to port, and odd numbers are to starboard) and compartment usage, with each element of the information separated by a hyphen.

An example of a bull's-eye given in naval manuals is: 3-75-4-M. It breaks down as follows:

3 = 03 Deck
75 = the compartment's forward boundary is on or immediately aft of ship's frame 75
4 = the fourth compartment outboard of the centreline to port
M = the compartment is used for ammunition storage

The codes for describing carrier compartment usage are:

A = supply and storage
B = guns
C = ship control
E = machinery
F = fuel
L = living quarters
M = ammunition
T = trunks and passages
V = void
W = water

aircraft launches and recoveries. The island also provides an elevated mounting for many of the ship's radars, sensors and communication systems and, as such, it is thickly clustered with domes, dishes, antennae and other high-tech features. It is a large structure, which on a *Nimitz*-class towers about 150ft (46m) tall, but just 20ft (6m) wide at the base, the profile kept deliberately narrow to avoid the island's footprint taking up too much space on the flight deck.

There are some differences in island design between the individual carriers. *Ronald Reagan* and *George H.W. Bush*, for example, feature a redesigned island that gives more space to the Primary Flight Control (Pri-Fly) facility (on the earlier carriers it is little bigger than a large domestic bedroom) and also has a composite mast containing most of the sensors. Some of the earlier carriers, specifically *Nimitz* and *Dwight D. Eisenhower*, had the top two levels of the island removed during their RCOH periods, the modification also allowing for the installation

of a new antenna mast. Looking ahead, the *Gerald R. Ford*'s island represents a significant redesign for the supercarriers. Incorporating new flat-panel array radar systems and Dual Band Radar (DBR), the island is actually reduced in length but 20ft (6m) taller than that of the *Nimitz* class. More dramatically, it is also positioned 140ft (42.6m) further aft and 3ft (1m) further outboard than the *Nimitz*-class islands.

Beneath the mainmast, the level (010) at the top of the island is Pri-Fly, occupying an elevated position with all-round views of the flight deck. Headed by the Air Boss, the Pri-Fly personnel have a command relationship to all aspects of aircraft launch, recovery and movement within a 5-mile (8km) radius of the ship. On the next level down is the navigation bridge, from where the ship is piloted and where navigation is conducted. The commanding officer (the captain) is often present on the bridge, from where he 'cons' (controls) the ship. Key personalities on the bridge are the helmsman, who steers the carrier under direction

LEFT An upward-looking view of the island of the USS *Dwight D. Eisenhower* (CVN-69). The Pri-Fly position is at the very top, surrounded by a concentrated array of deck lighting.

(Patrick Bunce)

ABOVE **A view inside the Flag Bridge of the USS** *Dwight D. Eisenhower* **(CVN-69); seen through the glass is the USS** *John C. Stennis* **(CVN-74). Both carriers were, at the time of the photograph (September 2019), docked in the Norfolk Naval Station, Virginia.** *(Patrick Bunce)*

from either the captain or his appointed Officer of the Deck; the lesser helmsman, responsible for passing power directions down to the engine room; and Quartermaster of the Watch, who oversees navigation.

The navigation bridge sits atop the next level down, which is the Flag Bridge. This is a relatively small space, tightly filled with electronic

BELOW **A telephone set inside the Flag Bridge provides communications straight to some of the key personnel involved with flight operations.** *(Patrick Bunce)*

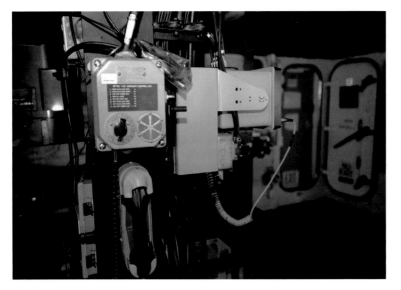

displays, for use by the admiral who is in charge of the entire CSG. The subsequent levels of the island contain spaces that help those above to make well-informed command decisions, such as the radar room and meteorological room. At the lowest level of the island is Flight Deck Control, where the physical execution of moving, launching and recovering the aircraft is performed, and from where the operational decisions made above are communicated outwards to the flight deck personnel.

The flight deck

The equipment and operations of the flight deck will be studied in detail in Chapter 3. Suffice to say here that the primary purpose of the flight deck is, of course, the safe launch and recovery of the carrier's aircraft. There are actually two active flight decks: the angled flight deck which is used for aircraft recovery and the straight flight deck used for launches, although launches can be made from the recovery deck also.

The supercarrier flight decks are made from a classified depth of high-strength low-alloy steel (HSLA), a metal offering greater impact strength and corrosion resistance than normal carbon steel. Most public access sources list the specific type of steel used in *Nimitz*-class carrier flight decks as HSLA-100 and HSLA-115. Atop this surface there is a thick coating of MS-375G, an abrasive heavy-duty, non-skid deck coating formulated with epoxy resins and designed both to give a firm grip between footwear/aircraft wheels and the deck, while also being incredibly hard-wearing in order to resist disintegration under repeated heavy impacts from both aircraft wheels and arrestor cables. The latter, as they stretch out under an aircraft arrest, whip the deck hard, and to reduce the effects of strikes there are impact pads installed in the deck surface at critical locations. The MS-375G coating, which is rippled to provide greater adhesion, nevertheless needs to be replaced in its entirety after a specified number of 'events' (launches and recoveries); it is provided in 1-gallon (3.8-litre) or 5-gallon (19-litre) kits. Note that the coating is also resistant to acidic and alkaline chemicals, solvents, grease, detergents, gasoline, jet fuels, hydraulic fluids and fire and jet blasts. The most significant pieces of major

ABOVE A close-up of a carrier flight deck plus one of the hundreds of padeye points for securing aircraft to the deck. Note the rippled effect of the non-slip surface. *(Patrick Bunce)*

RIGHT Flight deck illumination is prolific. During night landings, the lighting is triggered the moment a pilot makes an arrest, turning the flight deck into virtual daylight conditions. *(Patrick Bunce)*

equipment on the flight deck are the catapults, arresting gear and jet blast deflectors.

Gallery deck

The gallery deck is sandwiched between the flight deck and the hangar deck, and is the first of the carrier's main internal decks. This level of the ship is important for housing the Combat Direction Center (CDC, previously Combat Information Center/CIC), from where the carrier's defensive suites are controlled, and the Carrier Air Traffic Control Center (CATCC), which oversees and coordinates air operations outside the 5-mile (8km) operational radius of the CSG.

Other rooms on the gallery deck include a communications centre, both the captain's cabin and the flag cabin (centrally located, with the captain's cabin directly under the island),

RIGHT An F/A-18 Super Hornet with its wings folded on the flight deck of the USS *Gerald R. Ford* (CVN-78). Note the flat panel array radar structures on the island. *(US Navy)*

squadron ready rooms (aft and forward), where the pilots receive their operational briefings and don their flight gear), a refuelling station room and several workshops. The gallery deck also contains catapult machinery.

Hangar deck and surrounding levels

The hangar deck on a *Nimitz*-class carrier is divided into three hangar bays. The most apparent purpose of the hangar bay is that it is the place where the carrier's aircraft are stored, maintained and readied for transfer up to the flight deck during operations. The overall space required to accommodate these aircraft with a reasonable degree of convenience is huge – the hangar deck overall is three decks high and 110ft (34m) wide by 685ft (209m) long. Into that space the hangar bay personnel not only have to organise the placement and movement of more than 60 aircraft, but they also have to do the same with an endless array of parts and supplies, ranging from small boxes of screws up to entire aircraft engines. Four elevators (three on the *Gerald R. Ford* class) transport the aircraft and associated materials between the hangar deck and the flight deck.

At the very aft of the hangar deck is the jet engine shop, where the aviation mechanics can work on aircraft engines, including running them up to full power. (The jet engine shop is located at the rear of the ship so the engine thrust can be vented out to sea safely.) On the levels immediately adjacent to the hangar deck, we find many of the spaces devoted to aircraft maintenance and avionics, plus storage for spare parts, compressed gas bottles and other aircraft-related objects. Major pieces of equipment include the steam machinery for powering the catapult launchers.

Crew facilities

The fore and aft sections of the ship, below the main deck, feature a heavy concentration of the ship's crew quarters, plus the crew galleys and officer wardrooms. There are also recreational facilities, including appropriately named 'chill rooms' (places to watch TV and play games) and the ship's laundry facilities, the latter near the very rear of the ship. The laundry is spread over two decks, one room for washing the clothes and a dry area for airing and pressing.

The quality of berthings for the sailors has been a focal concern of the design of the *Gerald R. Ford* class. A feature – not entirely welcome – of the *Nimitz*-class carriers are the cavernous 180-man berthings, large and frequently noisy spaces not known for being conducive to rest and sound sleep. In response, and taking advantage of the reduced crew size, the designers of *Gerald R. Ford* have opted for 40-rack berths or even smaller berthings, which are significantly quieter. Each berthing tends to have three-rack beds, with each crew member having his or her own personal locker. Further thought has been put into the location of the berthing areas, which has resulted in not placing sleeping areas in close proximity with noisy spaces, such as mess decks. Each of the *Ford* berthings also now comes with its own block of showers, toilets and sinks; on the *Nimitz*-class carriers the crew might have to trek some distance through the ship to access these facilities.

The investment in crew well-being does not stop at the standard of the berthings. To keep the sailors and air crew fit, the *Ford* class features three purpose-built gyms, in contrast to the *Nimitz* class, where in most instances the gymnasiums were simply converted vacant spaces. In total the *Ford* gyms cover 3,085sq ft (2,579m^2) of floorspace and include the latest equipment types. Recognising that modern sailors tend to be heavy users of internet facilities, the ships also have many dedicated recreational lounges providing high-speed WiFi. TVs in the lounges also have WiFi-enabled on-demand functionality.

On a *Nimitz*-class carrier, the ship's air conditioning plant is located about a third of the way from the front of the ship, level with the hangar deck. CVN internet forums can feature some grumbling about the climatic living conditions experienced below deck, especially on hot deployments to the Middle East or tropical Pacific waters. The *Nimitz* carriers are interlaced with hot steam pipes, running off the reactors' steam generation system, but in

ABOVE A typical two-rack berthing aboard the USS *Dwight D. Eisenhower* (CVN-69), as would be used by junior or mid-rank officers. *(Patrick Bunce)*

the *Ford* class the nine air-conditioning plants are powered by electricity instead of steam. Publicity material also explains that almost every space around the ship will have proper ventilation through a flexible hose system that also ensures an even distribution of the air-conditioning effects.

One further interesting feature of the new *Ford* class is the provision of 19 'do-it-yourself' bays, spaces that are specifically designed to be repeatedly configured and reconfigured to different purposes, through using a flexible layout system

LEFT Passage between the decks on the carriers is accomplished either by conventional steps, as seen here, or via vertical ladders, the latter generally going down into engineering or ordnance spaces. *(Patrick Bunce)*

BELOW The captain's wardroom aboard the USS *Dwight D. Eisenhower* (CVN-69). *(Patrick Bunce)*

RIGHT One of the anchors of the USS *Dwight D. Eisenhower* (CVN-69), evidently weathered by its previous voyage. This anchor weighs 30 tons (27 tonnes). *(Patrick Bunce)*

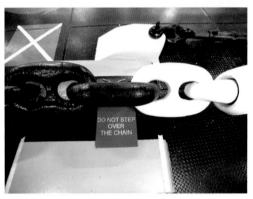

RIGHT Anchor links aboard the USS *Dwight D. Eisenhower* (CVN-69). The admonition on the red board is followed at all times, and is not just an instruction for visitors. *(Patrick Bunce)*

ABOVE In the foreground, one of the two anchor windlasses aboard the USS *Dwight D. Eisenhower* (CVN-69), the chain here emerging from the hawse pipe. *(Patrick Bunce)*

RIGHT The hawse pipe of a CVN anchor chain. *(Patrick Bunce)*

of consoles, lights and bulkheads. According to press reports, the 'flex-deck' system is also being retrofitted into some *Nimitz*-class carriers as they undergo major maintenance work.

Anchors and chains

Looking to the very front end of the ship, the fo'c'sle houses the supercarrier's anchor and anchor chain system. Bearing in mind the scale of the ships they have to hold, the dual anchors on the supercarriers are beasts indeed. On the *Nimitz* class, each of the two anchors weighs 30 tons (27 tonnes), but the anchor chain that supports it, measuring 1,082ft (329m), weighs 307.5 tons (279 tons). Each of the individual chain links weighs 365lb (166kg).

The anchor chain is separated into 12 'shots', each of 90ft (27m) in length, a shot defined as a section of chain between two detachable links. 'Swivel shot' sections prevent the chain from kinking when the carrier turns around the anchor. When the fo'c'sle crew drop anchor, typically they pay out five to seven times the depth of the water in anchor chain, and that way the chain sits on the bottom of the ocean and further acts as a stabilising force for the ship.

The anchor chain is stored in a lower chain locker, and the system is activated by powerful winches that draw the chain forwards or backwards to deploy or raise the anchors. Each of the chain links sits in an individual pocket on the windlass, ensuring that the chain doesn't slip during operation, an event that, given the weight of the chain system, would have catastrophic consequences. For the *Gerald R. Ford*, engineers have developed a far lighter system, with each of the two anchors weighing 16.5 tons (15 tonnes) and the individual links of the 1,440ft (439m) chain lightened to 136lb (62kg).

Lower decks

The lower half of the supercarriers is dominated by two large reactor compartments and associated equipment rooms, the propeller shaft alley and steering machinery and the ordnance magazines. (By placing them largely below the waterline these vital and sensitive spaces enjoy some protection from the surrounding sea.) On a *Nimitz*-class carrier, the major stores of ordnance are concentrated in two locations, one roughly amidships and the other almost equidistant between the rear magazine and the bows, with weapons elevators running the ordnance between magazines, ordnance assembly rooms and the flight deck. Separating the magazines is the forward reactor compartment and associated machinery room, with the aft reactor compartment and machinery room No. 2 positioned roughly in line with the front edge of the island (on the *Nimitz*-class carrier). We investigate ordnance handling in greater depth in Chapter 6, but within the bounds of public access materials, we can describe the basic operation of the nuclear powerplant.

Powerplant, propulsion and steering

The pulsing heart of any US *Nimitz*- and *Gerald R. Ford*-class carrier consists of two nuclear reactors situated deep within the bowels of the ship. The *Nimitz*-class carriers each have two Westinghouse A4W reactors, each providing 140,000shp (103,000kW), an immense amount of power. (Incidentally A = Aircraft Carrier; 4 = the type/version of reactor; W = Westinghouse, the manufacturer.) Things have been changed in the *Gerald R. Ford* class, which is receiving the new A1B reactor, manufactured by Bechtel. The reason behind the new powerplant type is that the *Ford* carriers, with their intensive emphasis upon automation and digitisation of processes, will require a lot more electrical output than the *Nimitz*-class vessels. The total thermal power of the A1B is in the region of 700MW, which is about 25% greater than that of the A4W. Calculated on this basis, the steam output from the A1B will produce enough steam to generate 168,000shp (125,000kW) of electricity, plus 350,000shp (250,000kW) to power the four propeller shafts. It is also calculated that the A1B will require 50% fewer personnel to operate compared to the Westinghouse reactors. Again, two of these powerplants will be installed upon each of the new *Ford* carriers.

The advantages of having a nuclear powerplant, compared to burning conventional fuels were outlined in Chapter 1, but the overarching benefit is the ability to steam around the world's oceans without the limitations of fuel supply. The Westinghouse A4W design, for example, can function at full capability for 20–23 years before it requires refuelling. The strategic opportunities made available by such an endurance are readily apparent.

Much information regarding US nuclear naval powerplants is strictly classified, and public access sources are largely confined to explaining general principles or secondary issues without giving away details of the specific technologies. Enough information is available, however, to give an insightful overview of how the powerplants operate and deliver such enduring force.

The US supercarriers are powered by pressurised water reactors (PWRs), a type of nuclear powerplant initially developed for the US Navy but which is today the most common of all nuclear energy production facilities, maritime or land-based, military and civilian. In crude description, the PWR develops and controls the nuclear fission process to generate heat, this heat being used to produce pressurised steam to power turbines that deliver various forms of energy to the ship.

The part of the system that generates the power is the reactor pressure vessel, which contains the reactor core, core shroud (more than 100 tons of lead cladding) and reactor coolant. The PWRs use highly enriched uranium fuel rods to create a nuclear fission reaction, which produces the immense heat. Pressurised water flows through the reactor vessel in a coolant loop; by keeping the water pressurised, the system prevents the water from turning into steam, at least for now. As this water passes through the reactor, it rapidly absorbs heat from the fuel rods. In the Westinghouse A1W and A2W reactors, the precursors of the A4W reactor fitted in the *Nimitz*-class carriers, the water temperature reached 525–545°F (274–285°C).

The superheated water, during its journey around the primary coolant loop, journeys onwards into a heat exchanger system, also called the steam generator. Here it passes through many hundreds of metal tubes (made from either Inconel, Alloy 600 or Alloy 690), which form a heat-transfer interface between the primary coolant loop and a secondary coolant loop. (Note that the water in both coolant loops

is driven around the system by large electrical pumps.) The water in the secondary coolant loop is kept at a pressure sufficiently low to allow it to boil, producing superheated, pressurised steam. The fact that the two coolant loops are kept fully independent of each other means that the steam product is not radioactive. The pressurised steam is now converted into useful work via two forms of turbine. Some steam is channelled into turbine generators, which create the ship's electricity supply, while other steam force is directed to the main propulsion turbines, which drive the ship's propellers. The steam then passes through a condenser, where it turns back into water and begins its journey once again through the coolant loop; both the primary and the secondary coolant loops are closed systems. One further point to note is that the system, unlike a diesel-powered vessel, does not require a supply of air or oxygen to function; indeed, it can be kept apart from the Earth's atmosphere altogether. For this reason, the design of the ship does not need to incorporate ventilation ducting into the reactor space, with the exception of the requirements of the reactor engineering team.

Maritime nuclear powerplants are reliable, stable (if managed properly) and powerful. Fitting one aboard a carrier, or other naval vessel, however, comes with a unique set of demands and requirements when compared to doing the same for land-based nuclear powerplants. For example, the naval nuclear powerplant has to be capable of rapid and frequent changes in power delivery, unlike a conventional civilian nuclear reactor that tends to produce power at a relatively constant rate hour upon hour, delivering that power for either use or storage within an electricity grid. There is also the unique environment in which the reactor has to perform, coping with the pitching and rolling of the ship. There are also obvious dangers that come from combat, and the risk of the reactor receiving major battle damage. The physical structures that protect the reactor from such damage are highly confidential, but we can confidently assume that the reactors aboard the carriers are likely to be the best-protected energy-production facilities in the world. Regardless of the threat of combat, however, just the proximity of the reactors to the

crew on board a carrier means that the safety and operating procedures must necessarily be of the highest standards. Furthermore, reactor design itself has to be modified for the compact space requirements and internal shape profile deep inside the hull of a supercarrier.

Both the *Nimitz*- and the *Gerald R. Ford*-class carriers have four propeller shafts, two port and two starboard. The fixed-pitch propellers are sizeable beasts: on the *Nimitz* class each of the bronze propellers measures 21ft (64m) across and weighs more than 30 tons (27 tonnes). Steering is performed by two rudders, each 29ft (8.8m) by 22ft (6.7m) and weighing 50 tons (45 tonnes).

The manoeuvrability imparted by these rudders, despite the great size of the ship, can be surprisingly impressive. Recent high-speed rudder tests by the *Abraham Lincoln*, *Harry S. Truman* and *Dwight D. Eisenhower* showed that the carriers could turn with such force that the ship was pushed into a 10–15-degree list, a very pronounced bank for vessels of such size. Should the direct control of the rudders fail (what is known as a 'steering casualty'), usually from a failure in the hydraulic fluid system, the aft steering division of the ship can take direct control of the rudders to prevent the ship becoming dead in the water. There are two aft steering rooms, mirrored on either side of the ship, each responsible for an individual rudder. Fuel-powered pumps (two per rudder) in aft steering can be fired up, and these power rams that will in turn move the rudders. The main focus of aft steering is to bring the rudder back

to midship, then once it is back to midship the crew will lock it in place and attempt to make a repair. The actual steering commands come down to the aft steering personnel verbally from the bridge. Should mechanical means further fail, then aft steering can actually manually manipulate the rudders from the Ram Room, turning the rudders via hand cranks and massive screw-thread shafts.

Departments

Having analysed the core physical structure of the carrier, subsequent chapters explore both the key operational systems that make the aircraft carrier do what it does best – launch and recover aircraft – but also the ship as a human system. A US supercarrier is, above all, a vast work of human engineering, the whole functioning as a single unit through the most intricate but surprisingly robust system of communications and roles. Before we embark on that analysis, however, it is worth breaking down the major departments of a typical carrier, to orientate ourselves to the ship's major functions. Here we present them in alphabetical order. (Much of the information below relates to a public domain departmental breakdown of the USS *George H.W. Bush*, CVN-77; there may be subtle variations in the organisation and terminology used on other US supercarriers, although the overall principles hold good.)

Administration Department

The Administration Department consists of around 45 people organised into six divisions, a relatively small number considering that they are responsible for the administrative maintenance of all 3,500 or so naval personnel on board the carrier. Specific responsibilities include areas such as pay and allowances, crew information and memos, separations and re-enlistments, education and career advice. The Administrative Department also runs the shipboard drug and alcohol awareness programmes.

Aircraft Intermediate Maintenance Department

The Aircraft Intermediate Maintenance Department (AIMD) is responsible for providing maintenance for both the embarked carrier air wing, but also for the aircraft of the CSG ships and independent units operating in collaboration with the CSG.

Air Department

The Air Department is responsible for the launch and recovery of aircraft from the flight deck, and thus its smooth functioning is crucial to the overall mission capability of any US supercarrier. Specific duties of the Air Department include operating the launch catapults, arresting gear and visual landing aid systems; safely moving the aircraft around the flight deck and hangar bay; maintaining aircraft fuelling systems; and providing firefighting capabilities in the flight deck and hangar bay.

Combat Systems Department

The Combat Systems Department (CSD) operates and maintains the warship's defensive communications and monitoring systems, plus the digital infrastructure on which the carrier's command and control systems depends. A US Navy document explaining the CSD aboard the USS *George H.W. Bush* clarifies these responsibilities as

the maintenance and operational reliability for air search, air traffic control, surface navigation radars, the ship's internal and external telephone and radio communications, Global Positioning System and navigational sensor, control and display systems, a variety of secure and non-secure network software and hardware that provide e-mail, Web and other services. It also is in charge of inbound and outbound network security, command and control systems and weapons systems, which enables the ship and the carrier strike group's war fighters. (https://www.public.navy.mil/airfor/cvn77/ Pages/Departments.aspx)

Command Religious Ministries Department (CRMD)

The CRMD is responsible for religious ministry programmes and counselling services aboard the carriers, not only providing religious services for both Catholic and Protestant traditions, but also facilitating the free expression of other forms of faith. Various other pastoral duties of

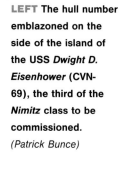

LEFT The hull number emblazoned on the side of the island of the USS *Dwight D. Eisenhower* (CVN-69), the third of the *Nimitz* class to be commissioned. *(Patrick Bunce)*

the CRMD include implementing community relation projects (COMRELs), school volunteer projects, plus acting as a point of liaison between the aircraft carrier and the Red Cross and the Fleet and Family Service Center. (The latter provides a broad spectrum of programmes designed to support the well-being of the entire naval community, with regional centres dotted throughout theatres of operation and stateside.)

BELOW An Aviation Boatswain's Mate (Fuel) 3rd Class lugs a fuelling hose across the flight deck during flight operations aboard the USS *Harry S. Truman* (CVN-75) in the Persian Gulf in 2008. *(US Navy photo by Mass Communication Specialist 3rd Class Ricardo J. Reyes/ Released)*

Deck Department

The primary duty of the Deck Department personnel, ranked Boatswain's Mates, is to maintain and operate the carrier's anchors, which are housed in the ship's fo'c'sle. Beyond this duty they are also responsible for the life rafts (about 127 50-man boats), the Underway Replenishment (UNREP) stations, mooring lines, the condition of the ship's exterior hull and the functioning of various critical mechanical devices, including cranes, booms and davits.

Dental Department

The Dental Department provides oral health care to all naval and air wing personnel aboard the carrier, with the services delivered by about 18 personnel, including five dental officers. On the *George H.W. Bush*, the department typically treats more than 60 patients every day, delivering everything from routine dental hygiene through to oral surgery. The carrier has extensive facilities, including 'six dental operatories, a surgical suite and a fully equipped dental laboratory'. During instances of mass casualty emergencies or the call to general quarters, the dental team will also serve as a support to other shipboard medical teams.

Engineering Department

One of the most technically skilled departments for the carrier, the Engineering Department operates and maintains the ship's endless array of electrical and mechanical machinery,

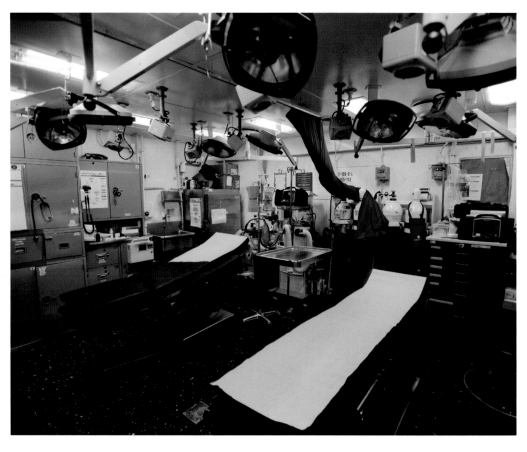

with the exception of the onboard nuclear reactor. With more than 300 personnel from all major engineering disciplines, the department engineers include professional firefighters, expert machinists, welders, electricians, diesel mechanics and mechanical technicians. As well as working aboard the carrier, the engineers will also assist in meeting engineering challenges among other CSG vessels.

Health Services Department/ Medical Department

This department delivers primary medical services to all the sailors and aviators on the carrier, and can handle casualties from other ships in the CSG. Medical facilities include operating theatres, intensive care units, X-ray facilities, the laboratory and a medical ward with more than 50 beds. In addition to looking after the crew's physical needs, including vaccinations, physiotherapy and occupational health, the Medical Department also provides psychiatric/psychological expertise.

Intelligence Department

The Intelligence Department handles the round-the-clock influx of intelligence information flowing into the warship from internal divisions, EW capabilities and external agencies, distributing this information to relevant departments and personnel on board, such as the Combat Direction Center (CDC), the captain and the CSG commander. Departmental divisions can include the Carrier Intelligence Center (CVIC), the Ship Signal Exploitation Space (SSES) and the EW Module.

Legal Department

The Legal Department's primary role is to promote order and discipline throughout the ship, but it also provides a legal advisory service for the ship's chain of command, ensuring that all actions are taken within a proper legal and ethical framework. The department also offers legal counselling to individual crew members.

Media Department

The Media Department is kept busy as the warship's public affairs wing, handling not only mission information presented to the world's media, but also the distribution of important stories, briefings and events internally among the ship's crew, via printed publications, social media and video and audio broadcasts. The department includes professional photographers, video producers and graphic designers and is responsible for all the ship's design services.

Navigation Department

The Navigation Department has the fundamental responsibility for navigating the huge carrier safely through the world's coastal and deep-blue waters. The tools for doing so are a mixture of high-tech digital systems – shipborne radar plus Global Positioning System (GPS) and networked satellite information – with a backup competence in traditional methods of maritime navigation, including paper navigation charts, compasses, sextants and even astronavigation.

BELOW The island of the USS *Dwight D. Eisenhower* (CVN-69). The new antenna mast was fitted during the ship's RCOH between May 2001 and March 2005. *(Patrick Bunce)*

ABOVE **A view through the aft window of Primary Flight Control (Pri-Fly), focusing on the Visual Landing Aids position in the foreground.**
(Patrick Bunce)

Operations Department

Operations is a sizeable department (roughly 300 personnel) that focuses on the ship's warfighting mission, planning exercises and operations for the ship, carrier air wing and the CSG, and also monitoring and controlling tactical air engagements and operating the onboard defensive weapons suite. In addition, the department monitors and evaluates atmospheric and oceanographic information, factoring that information into operational planning, training and exercises.

Reactor Department

The Reactor Department consists of more than 400 personnel, dedicated to the efficient and safe running of the carrier's nuclear powerplants. On their shoulders rests the responsibility not only for the ship's propulsion but also for catapult launches and electrical power generation, all of which require

pressurised steam (as we have seen earlier in this chapter). The Reactor Department also produce and distribute the ship's fresh water supply, as well as delivering the steam used in heating, laundry and the galley.

Safety Department

This department oversees and educates the ship's company on all matters relating to occupational and operational safety, ensuring that the crew works in a healthy and safe environment and that safety procedures are optimised and properly distributed.

Supply Department

The Supply Department of nearly 400 personnel is in charge of logistical and supply services. It provides the crew with almost every personal and operational requirement, including major essentials such as food and fuel, managing not only the storage, monitoring and distribution of the stocks but also arranging and facilitating resupply operations either at sea or in port. The department also implements Morale, Welfare and Recreation (MWR) activities, to keep the ship's crew entertained during long periods out at sea.

Training Department

The Training Department designs and implements shipboard training programmes to ensure that the crew is properly skilled and ready for combat operations and their general duties. Each new crew member to the ship will undergo an indoctrination training programme in the first few weeks aboard.

Weapons Department

The Weapons Department has the sensitive role of storing, assembling (particularly fitting fuses and fins to mob/missile bodies) and handling all conventional weapons and explosive devices, from small arms through to aircraft ordnance. The department consists of more than 300 personnel in five divisions.

The interrelationship between all of the carrier departments is symbiotic. A problem in one department will quickly have a knock-on effect in others – thus the ship's captain will strive for perfection on every deck. How the systems function together will increasingly be the focus of our analysis in subsequent chapters.

ABOVE An Aviation Ordnanceman uses an ammunition skid to move BLU-111 GP 500lb bombs to an aircraft on the flight deck of USS *Abraham Lincoln* (CVN-72), during operations in the Persian Gulf in June 2008. *(US Navy photo by Mass Communication Specialist 2nd Class James R. Evans/Released)*

BELOW One of the many ordnance elevators aboard the USS *Dwight D. Eisenhower* (CVN-69), indicating its maximum working load of 10,500lb (4,772kg). *(Patrick Bunce)*

Chapter Three

Flight deck, hangar deck and key flight personnel

Although a US supercarrier, when set alongside most other vessels, is enormous in comparative terms, every square foot is packed with purpose. Nowhere is this more apparent on the flight deck and hangar deck, which have to hold and operate a carrier air wing (CVW) of up to 90 aircraft.

OPPOSITE A US Navy Petty Officer 3rd Class signals for sailors to set up the aircraft barricade during a drill aboard USS *George Washington* (CVN-73). *(US Navy photo by Petty Officer 3rd Class Jacob D. Moore/Released)*

The flight deck of a modern supercarrier is an astonishing military space. Just viewed in terms of its physical area, it is unfailingly impressive – a *Nimitz*-class carrier flight deck covers 4½ acres (1.8 hectares) and measures 1,092ft (332.8m) long by 250ft 8in (76.4m) at its widest part. The *Gerald R. Ford* class has inched up the flight deck real estate even more – it is 1,106ft (337m) in length and 256ft (78m) in width, with a smaller (but taller) carrier island footprint in addition (see Chapter 2). As fact-hunters are keen to point out, it would be possible to play three NFL games on the flight deck simultaneously.

But such stats are misleading. As an empty space, the flight deck is enormous, but as an operational space it is packed and tight, such that the tolerances between people and jets are measured in mere single-digit feet. At its maximum capacity, a *Nimitz*-class carrier flight deck can have 20 aircraft present, stacked up either waiting to take off or having just landed. Around these jets will swarm a small army of flight deck personnel, refuelling and rearming the aircraft according to pre-set mission parameters, performing emergency maintenance and resetting catapult and arrestor gear systems for the next event. In these circumstances, a large expanse of flight deck can suddenly appear very small indeed, with tiny margins of error in terms of safety.

In this chapter we explain the physical space of both the flight deck and the hangar deck in terms of layout and equipment. We also explore the flight deck as a human system, looking at the specific roles of flight deck personnel and how they integrate and communicate to bring order from potential chaos. Within this human picture we define the activities and roles of Pri-Fly and Flight Deck Control (FDC), introduced in the previous chapter. Armed with this knowledge we go into Chapter 4, which explains in detail how flight operations are conducted, with a clear understanding of the dramatis personae and the equipment behind the carrier's air operations.

ABOVE Overlooking the flight deck, Aerographer's Mate Airman Taylor Kane uses an anemometer to measure windspeed and direction aboard the aircraft carrier USS *George H.W. Bush* (CVN-77). *(US Navy photo by Mass Communication Specialist 3rd Class Margaret Keith/Released)*

LEFT These US Navy illustrations show the essential layout and equipment positions of a CVN flight deck. *(US Navy)*

Flight deck layout

Taking the bird's eye view of a *Nimitz*-class carrier, the flight deck as a whole is occupied by the two marked flight strips: 1) the angled deck, turned to 9 degrees port and running between the stern for about three-quarters of the length of the ship; this deck is used principally for flight recovery; 2) the forward flight deck that runs straight out over the ship's bow, and is the main deck for launching aircraft. As explained in the introduction, the placement of these two decks means that the carrier can both launch and recover aircraft simultaneously.

The flight deck is divided up into several key areas, each given its own distinctive nickname and purpose. The following table (right) lists some of the most important.

The flight deck is also punctuated by the four giant elevators that raise the aircraft from the hangar deck below. There are three elevators on the starboard side, numbered 1, 2 and 3 from forward to aft, with No. 3 located aft of the island. Almost opposite elevator No. 3 on the port side is elevator No. 4.

Name	Location	Purpose
Junkyard	Aft of the island	Parking area for fire engines, aircraft tractors and cranes
Hummer Hole	Area just inboard of the island	Used for parking of E-2C and C-2 aircraft
The Street	The space between catapult No. 1 and No. 2	–
The Rows	Areas to right of catapult No. 1 and left of catapult No. 2	Parking areas for F/A-18s during recovery operations
The Finger	Aft of elevator No. 4	Parking area for a single aircraft
The Ramp	Beginning of the flight deck at the stern of the carrier	–
The Bomb Farm	Small area between the island and the starboard side of the ship	Used for storing ordnance ready for loading
The Crotch	The location where the angled flight deck ends and the port bow begins	–
The Six Pack	Centre of flight deck, along the 'foul line'	Major parking area for aircraft
The Corral	Area in front of the island up to elevator No. 1	Working area

Steam catapults

The *Nimitz*-class carriers have four catapults on the flight deck, two port catapults running out over the angled flight deck (catapults No. 3 and 4), and two forward catapults (catapults No. 1 and 2) launching out over the bows. The catapults are of the steam-powered type, either the C-13-1 (on the USS *Nimitz*, USS *Dwight D. Eisenhower*, USS *Carl Vinson* and USS *Theodore Roosevelt*) or C-13-2 (on the USS *Abraham Lincoln*, USS *George Washington*, USS *John C. Stennis* and USS *Harry S. Truman*). The principal specification differences between the two types can be summarised as follows:

	C-13-1	C-13-2
Power stroke	309ft 8¾in	306ft 9in
Track length	324ft 10in	324ft 10in
Weight of shuttle and pistons	6,350lb	6,350lb
Cylinder bore	18in	21in
Power stroke displacement	1,148cu ft	1,527cu ft

Source: http://navyaviation.tpub.com/14001/ css/Chapter-4-Steam-Catapults-139.htm

LEFT The shuttle track of a steam catapult aboard the USS *Dwight D. Eisenhower* (CVN-69).

(Patrick Bunce)

The basic mechanics of the steam catapult involves drawing steam from the ship's reactor system and moving it to the catapult dry-steam receivers or wet-steam accumulator, where it is kept under the pressure required to launch the aircraft. A critical point to note in this regard is that each individual aircraft has its own pressure setting; furthermore, the pressure setting for each aircraft can vary according to the aircraft's take-off weight, a figure affected by factors such as fuel levels and ordnance load. As we will see, if the catapult power isn't adjusted precisely to the aircraft's weight, bad things can happen.

The launch pressure is controlled by varying the amount of steam released from the steam receivers/accumulator into the launching engine cylinders (each catapult has two such cylinders) via the capacity selector valve (CSV) assembly, which controls the launch valve opening rate. When the steam rushes into the cylinders, the pistons inside are driven forward with immense power – both the C-13-1 and C-13-2 can deliver 80,000lb (36,363kg) of force at 140 knots (259km/h). The pistons are attached to a shuttle, which in turn connects to the front landing gear of the aircraft, thereby providing the means of launch. As the pistons and the shuttle near the end of their power stroke, a tapered spear at the front of the piston pushes into a set of water-filled cylinders, the pressure build-up of the water progressively arresting the piston until a complete stop. At this stage, the pistons and shuttle can be

retracted back to their original position. This action is performed by a grab mechanism, attached to a retraction engine, being advanced forward along the catapult trough and connected to the shuttle assembly. The retraction engine is then reversed and the catapult is returned to the battery position.

The pistons connect to the shuttle via a small metal lug on the tip of each piston; these lugs actually protrude through a gap along the top of each cylinder, with rubber flanges sealing the gaps against pressure leaks. The shuttle makes a positive connection with the aircraft via a towbar mounted on the forward landing gear.

The *Gerald R. Ford* class has made an important technological leap forward in catapult technology through its adoption of the new EMALS. This system will offer across-the-board advantages in comparison to steam catapults – as long as it functions properly, of course. In one of the early assessment papers for EMALS, published in the late 1990s, authors of the Naval Air Warfare Center explained both the disadvantages of the steam catapult system and comparative advantages of EMALS:

The U.S. Navy is presently pursuing electromagnetic launch technology to replace the existing steam catapults on current and future aircraft carriers. The steam catapults are large, heavy, and operate without feedback control. They impart large transient loads to the airframe and are difficult and

BELOW A US Navy manual diagram shows the position and names of flight deck markings aboard a CVN.
(US Navy)

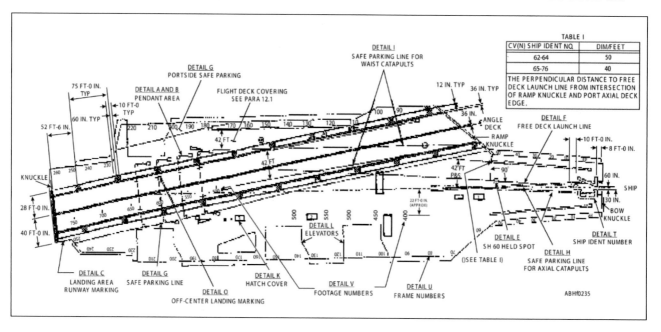

time consuming to maintain. The steam catapult is also approaching its operational limit with the present complement of naval aircraft. The inexorable trend towards heavier, faster aircraft will soon result in launch energy requirements that exceed the capability of the steam catapult. An electromagnetic launch system offers higher launch energy capability, as well as substantial improvements in areas other than performance. These include reduced weight, volume, and maintenance; and increased controllability, availability, reliability, and efficiency.

(Doyle et al., n.d., 1)

Touching on the mention of 'reliability', one additional problem with the steam catapult is that occasional erratic bursts of tow force can result in damage to airframes, plus the efficiency of the system is quite surprisingly low (about 4–6%). EMALS, by contrast, has a 90% power conversion efficiency.

EMALS uses a linear induction motor (LIM) to generate magnetic fields that propel a shuttle along a track to launch the aircraft, in much the same manner as the new Electromagnetic Rail Guns (ERGs) use magnetic force to fire ordnance. The energy generated during each 45-second recharge period is immense: during the 2–3 seconds of launch, up to 484MJ are released, taking a 100,000lb (45,454kg) aircraft to 130 knots (240km/h) over a 300ft (91m) launch distance. Because the power required could not be supplied on demand by the ship's own onboard power sources, the energy is stored ready using four kinetic disk alternators.

The first EMALS launch took place in 2010, and since then the technology has been more thoroughly tested and refined. Theoretically, it is hoped that a perfectly functioning EMALS will result in a 25–33% greater sortie generation rate than the traditional steam catapult. Continuing tests, though, exposed high failure rates, in the region of one failure in every 240 launches (although these figures relate to 2013 data). Concerns regarding EMALS were being expressed by the Department of Defense (DoD) in 2018, however, and even US President Donald Trump levelled criticisms at the mechanism. Given the relative youth of the system, however, it is likely that performance

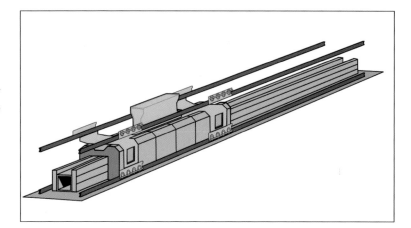

issues will gradually be resolved to satisfy operational standards.

Jet blast deflectors

While the US supercarriers' catapults are capable of taking aircraft to launch speed, the carriers assist their launch through two means: 1) the ship sailing into the wind, thereby increasing the windspeed and lift naturally; and 2) the aircraft spooling up to full power before being released under catapult force. The latter requires, in the case of the jets, taking the

ABOVE An artwork showing the linear induction motor used in the Electromagnetic Aircraft Launch System (EMALS), the new system of aircraft launch fitted aboard the *Gerald R. Ford* class of carriers. *(Tosaka/CC BY-SA 3.0)*

BELOW A view of the jet blast deflectors from the underside. This JBD is aboard the USS *Gerald R. Ford* (CVN-78), so is of the newer heatproof tile type, rather than active seawater cooling. *(US Navy photo by Mass Communication Specialist 1st Class Jonathan Pankau/Released)*

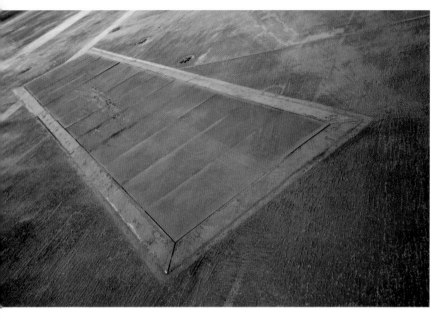

ABOVE One of the
impact pads on
the flight deck of a
CVN; the arresting
cables strike these
pads during recovery
operations, and the
damage of that action
is evident here.
(Patrick Bunce)

engines up to full power, the afterburners lit
from the stationary aircraft. The exhaust thus
generated is obviously fearsomely dangerous,
as even at minimum it will reach a temperature
of 2,300°F (1,260°C) and a velocity of 1,800ft/
sec (549m/sec). The jet blast deflectors (JBDs)
are structures designed to deflect this thrust
up and away from the crew around the aircraft
(although standard safety procedures should
mean that no one is standing directly in line
with the jet blast on launch). They also protect
surrounding aircraft on the flight deck.

Each catapult system on the supercarriers
has its own JBD. They are basically flat, thermally
protected deck panels that lie flush with the
deck when aircraft are rolling forward to their
take-off position, but which are hydraulically
raised to a 45-degree angle behind the aircraft
ready for take-off. While the upper surface
of the JBD is the no-stick deck surface, the
2016 patent for 'Cooled jet blast deflectors for
aircraft carrier decks' (US657113B1) explains
that 'The underside surface of each deflector
panel is formed from a thermal insulating
material to provide thermal protection from
heating by impinging jet exhaust plumes, and
is subsequently cooled by blasts of fluid or air
beneath the deck when the deflector panel is in
its lowered retracted position' (US Secretary of
the Navy, 2002). The cooling is provided by the
pumping of seawater through the JBD structure,
via the fire-suppression water system. This rapid
cooling effect is critical, as the superheated JBD
will damage aircraft tyres if an aircraft rolls over it
in an uncooled state.

Some *Nimitz*-class carriers, starting with
the USS *George H.W. Bush*, have adopted an
alternative to the water-cooled JBDs. Although
the water system is effective, it nevertheless
increases the complexity and maintenance
requirements of the JBDs. Also, even the most
efficient cooling system cannot prevent the
heavy damage inflicted on the JBDs' upper
surfaces, which need regular replacement. The
George H.W. Bush therefore adopted JBDs
without active cooling, instead having metal
panels coated with heat dissipating ceramic
tiles, in the same manner as the protective
tiles applied to the outer surface of the Space
Shuttle. The chief advantage of these tiles is
that they can withstand greater temperatures
than the metal versions, plus they are far more
easily maintained, as the ship can store spare
tiles and replace them quickly as necessary.

Arresting gear

Arresting gear refers to the mechanism
applied to bring landing aircraft to a stop
within the length of the carrier deck. This is no
mean feat mechanically. A jet aircraft landing on
a conventional land runway will usually require
between 5,000 and 8,000ft (1,524 and 2,438m)

RIGHT A necessary
note of caution painted
on the side of the
island of USS *Dwight D.
Eisenhower* (CVN-69).
'PKP' and 'CO2' refer
to the location of fire-
suppression systems.
(Patrick Bunce)

to come to a complete stop; a carrier aircraft has to do the same within about 350ft (107m) of its wheels touching the deck.

The *Nimitz* carriers have the Mk 7 Mod 3 arresting gear installed. An official US Navy source describes the overall function of the arresting gear as follows:

Aircraft arrestments aboard carriers are classified as either a normal arrestment or an emergency arrestment. Simply stated, arrestment is accomplished in the following manner: the arresting hook of the incoming aircraft engages a wire rope cable, called a deck pendant, that spans the flight deck in the landing area. The force of the forward motion of the aircraft is transferred to purchase cables that are reeved around a movable crosshead of sheaves and a fixed sheave assembly of the arresting engine. The movable crosshead is moved toward the fixed sheave assembly as the aircraft pulls the purchase cables off the arresting engine, forcing a ram into the cylinder holding pressurized hydraulic fluid (ethylene glycol). This fluid is forced out of the cylinder through a control valve that meters the flow to an accumulator until the aircraft is brought to a smooth, controlled arrested landing.

(US Navy, 2010, 3-1)

Expanding this explanation a little, the US supercarriers have a total of four arresting cables, or cross-deck pendants. They are arranged in parallel lines, Nos 1–4 from aft forward, in the rear third of the angled recovery deck. The simple reason that there are four cables is that it gives the pilot effectively four chances to snag a cable on the approach, although all carrier pilots aim for the third wire as standard, this reducing the risk of landing short. The pendants have to be inordinately strong to cope with the arresting process.

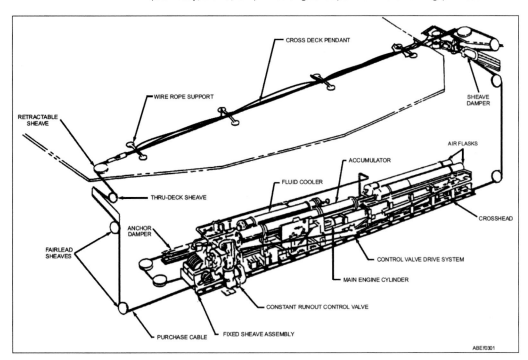

LEFT The mechanical layout of the Mk 7 arresting gear. *(US Navy)*

of the multiple wires that form the cable having a minimum breaking strength of 205,000lb (93,181kg), or the sisal-core cross-deck pendant in 1⅜in (34.9mm) diameter with an oiled-hemp core. Both the polyester-core and the hemp-core versions perform the same functions, providing a flexible and cushioning centre to help protect the wires from overloading under tension. To ensure that the pendants engage with the trailing arrestor hook on the aircraft, they are raised above the deck surface on wire supports, which consist of pre-shaped leaf springs that maintain a cross-deck pendant height of 2–5½in (50–140mm). The height is regulated by adjusting the wire support's contour height.

Barricade webbing assembly

There are emergency situations in which an aircraft has to be recovered without the benefit of the standard arrestor gear. These usually occur when the aircraft has a failure of arrestor hook, or the aircraft landing gear is damaged in such a way that it cannot

ABOVE Here we see the deformation of a cross-deck pendant (three-wire) by the nose gear of an F/A-18 Hornet as it lands and passes over the wire at 135 knots (250km/h) aboard USS _Harry S. Truman_ (CVN-75). _(Pinch/e2a2j/US Navy)_

Not only do they contend with the weight and speed of the aircraft, but also normal procedure dictates that upon aircraft contact with the carrier deck, at about 85% power, the pilot throttles to full power to ensure that if he misses all the cables he has sufficient force simply to lift off again from the deck (this sort of aircraft is known as a 'bolter').

The pendants themselves are either 1⁷⁄₁₆in (36.5mm) diameter polyester-core wires, each

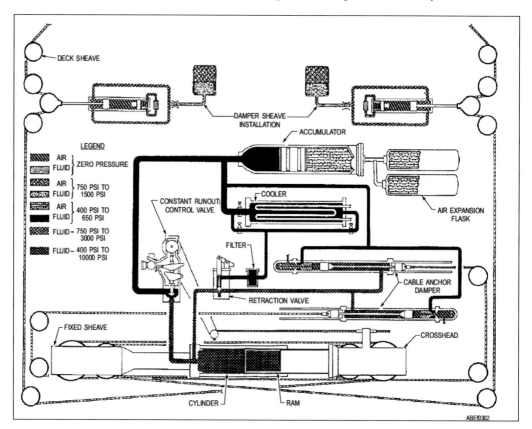

RIGHT This diagram shows the fluid flow around the Mk 7 Mod 3 arresting gear during an arrestment operation. _(US Navy)_

ADVANCED ARRESTING GEAR

As with its catapults, the *Gerald R. Ford* class of carriers has also broken away from the *Nimitz*-class technologies in its arresting gear. It is being fitted with the Advanced Arresting Gear (AAG), developed by General Atomics. Publicly accessible details about the system are, at the time of writing, limited, but in overview it arrests the aircraft using rotary engines with simple energy-absorbing water turbines (or twisters) coupled to a large induction motor to provide finer control of the arresting forces. This last point is crucial. With the future of carrier aviation opening up to a greater spectrum of aircraft types, including light UAVs, there is a requirement for more finesse and range in the arrestor settings, and the AAG is intended to provide this.

perform the standard landing manoeuvre. The Barricade Webbing Assembly is much as its name describes – it is essentially a heavy-duty webbing net that is strung across the flight deck and raised between powered barricade stanchions, the top of the barricade at a height of 20ft (65.6m) from the deck. The net is also attached to arresting engines, to provide mechanical inertia. If all goes to plan, the jet will fly into the barricade for a very dramatic and abrupt arrest.

The EC/C2 barricade assembly, used for jet arrests, consists of nylon or polyurethane semi-coated vertical engaging straps, suspended vertically between upper and lower load straps. The engaging straps are spaced regularly, allowing the aircraft's nose to pass through them, after which the straps contact the

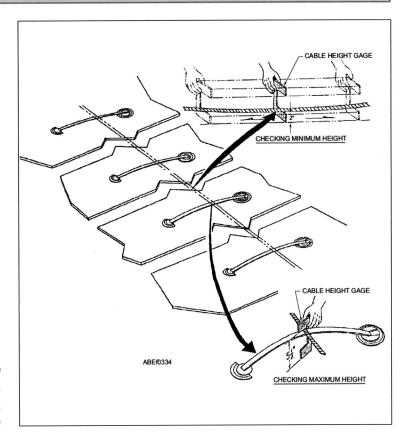

CABLE HEIGHT GAGE

CHECKING MINIMUM HEIGHT

CABLE HEIGHT GAGE

ABEf0334

CHECKING MAXIMUM HEIGHT

RIGHT The procedure for checking the height of the cross-deck pendants. The height should be 2in (51mm) minimum and 5½in (139mm) maximum.
(US Navy)

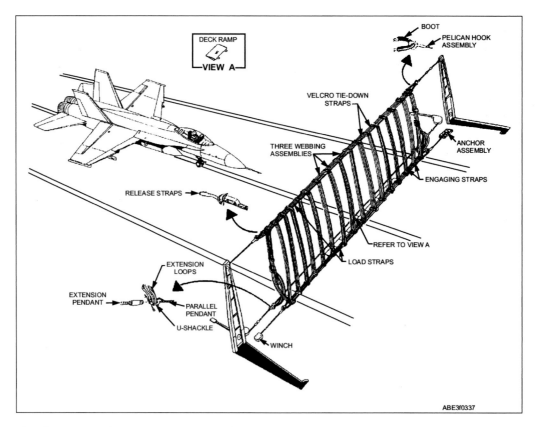

ABE3f0337

aircraft's wings and wrap around the aircraft, bringing it to a halt. The E-C/E-2 barricade is somewhat different in that it has a 40ft (12.1m) opening in the centre of the webbing, which allows the props of the E-2/C-2 aircraft to pass through without getting tangled up during the arrestment. The systems also feature multiple-release assemblies, forming a breakable connection between the upper and lower load straps of the barricade and the tensioning pendants of the barricade stanchions. The US Navy explanation of these systems is:

The multiple-release assembly consists of a number of release straps attached to loops at the ends of the load straps. They are then attached to the tensioning pendants by a pelican hook assembly. During an emergency arrestment, the force of the aircraft engaging the barricade breaks the multiple-release straps, releasing the barricade from the tensioning pendants allowing it to fall over the aircraft. The energy of the engagement is then transferred from the barricade through the purchase cable to the arresting engine.

(US Navy, 2010, 3-37–3-38)

Note that because of the impact damage inflicted on a barricade after a landing, it has to be discarded after a single use. Three barricades are usually kept in the barricade storage room on the hangar deck, but the small number is usually sufficient – barricade landings are extremely rare.

Flight handling personnel

The Air Department of a supercarrier is one of the largest of the ship's departments, and its 600 or so personnel are responsible for the 'safe and efficient launch and recovery of aircraft'. The department is divided into five divisions, here explained by the US Navy's Public Affairs office:

V-1 Division is tasked with the security and movement of aircraft on the flight deck. Included in this is the Crash and Salvage crew who are the flight deck's fire department and rescue team. The V-1 Division handles, directs, moves aircraft on flight deck. It also operates aircraft handling/servicing equipment and mans the crash/salvage team.

V-2 Division maintains and operates the four steam catapults and associated machinery, Visual Landing Aids (VLA) and arresting gear.

V-3 Division is responsible for the security and movement of aircraft in the ship's three hangar bays. V-3 Division handles, directs, moves aircraft on the hangar deck. It operates aircraft elevators, hangar bay doors and assigned firefighting equipment.

V-4 Division operates the aircraft fueling system, providing fuel services to air-wing aircraft. V-4 Division is responsible for fuel storage and transfer equipment, fuel purity, and fueling of all aircraft.

V-5 Division operates the ship's aircraft control tower, commonly known as 'Pri-Fly (Primary Flight Control)', as well as running the department office where the paperwork never seems to end. Pri-Fly is manned by the Air Officer (Air Boss), Assistant Air Officer (Mini Boss) and assistant subordinates. It is responsible for aircraft on deck and for visual control of all aircraft operating in the carrier's control zone.

(https://www.public.navy.mil/AIRFOR/cvn73/ Pages/Air-Department.aspx)

Looking specifically at the personnel who crowd the flight deck, the role of each is partly demarcated by the colour of the jersey, explained later in this chapter, plus patterns

on the helmet. This colour-coded scheme is important for both communications and safety – it is imperative that each person understands the complex interrelationship of the roles, and performs them without deviation (within reason) from the standardised procedures laid down in Navy manuals.

LEFT An Aviation Boatswain's Mate (Handler) 3rd Class aboard the USS *Harry S. Truman* (CVN-75) taxies an aircraft during flight operations, using the illuminated signal wands. *(US Navy photo by Mass Communication Specialist 3rd Class Ricardo J. Reyes/ Released)*

BELOW A 'Shooter' signals the launch of a McDonnell Douglas T-45C Goshawk from Training Wing 1 (TW-1) from the flight deck of USS *John C. Stennis* (CVN-74). *(US Navy photo by Mass Communication Specialist 2nd Class Ron Reeves)*

The flight deck of an aircraft carrier is often described as 'the most dangerous place on earth'. It is worth unpacking some of the thinking behind this statement. The most aggressive dangers are those presented by the jet exhaust, which can either horribly burn a crew member or literally blow him overboard. At full power, a jet engine can also drag a fully grown human into the air intake, such is the inrush of air. Turning engine props and helicopter rotary blades are similar dangers, the blurring circumference of the blades all too easy to miss in the sensory overload of the flight deck. (All flight deck crew wear double hearing protection – foam ear inserts plus conventional padded ear defenders – so auditory warning signs are distinctly muted.) Of course, another danger presented by aircraft is that of simply being run over by one during movement around the flight deck or, with far worse consequences, being hit by one during launch or recovery. Beyond the threats of aircraft under power, an operational carrier flight deck is also choked with fuel lines and fused ordnance, all of which can result in explosive or inflammable catastrophe if mishandled. Furthermore, these objects, plus the numerous chocks, chains, towbars and arresting wires that snake across the deck, present a multitude of trip and impact hazards. As one NATOPS (Naval Air Training and Operating Procedures Standardization Program) manual notes: 'More than one crew member has received stitches after walking into a missile fin.' Added to all these hazards is the possibility of being run over by some of the mechanised Ground Support Equipment (GSE), such as aircraft tugs. Medical personnel aboard the USS *Dwight D. Eisenhower* told the author that the most common type of injury aboard the ship was head lacerations; from flight deck to keel, an aircraft carrier has few surfaces that are not made from unyielding metal.

Added to the mechanical and material dangers we can also add those of the natural environment. A carrier flight deck is mercilessly exposed to the elements, which can include near-hurricane-force winds, quite capable of blowing someone overboard, driving rain and oppressive levels of heat and direct sunlight. During recent operations in the Persian Gulf, it was not uncommon for flight deck temperatures to exceed 122°F (50°C), resulting in many cases of dehydration and heat exhaustion.

Yellow Jerseys

Aircraft Handling Officer (ACHO)

The ACHO, also known simply as the 'Handler', takes the lead supervisory role for the handling of embarked aircraft on the carrier, assisting the Air Boss in conducting flight operations. The ACHO is also in charge of the Air Department Training Team (ADTT).

Flight Deck Officer

The Flight Deck Officer is responsible for all aspects of safe and efficient operations on the carrier flight deck, including the training of personnel, the good condition of any support equipment and the physical condition of the flight deck itself.

Catapult Officer

The Catapult Officer is more commonly known as the 'Shooter'. It is his responsibility to ensure that all aircraft are launched safely and efficiently, and his chain of command runs directly from the Air Boss, via the Handler. The Shooter's role is critical, as not only does he monitor the condition of all launch equipment, but he also reviews and assesses crew launch performance. For this reason, the Shooter is a naval aviator or naval flight officer, an individual who can bring his knowledge of naval aviation to launch procedures. The Shooter gives the final hand signal to the pilot that he is free to take off, and he will also ensure that catapult weight settings are correct for successful launch.

Aircraft Crash and Salvage Officer (Air Bos'n)

The Air Bos'n oversees Crash-and-Salvage crews and fire parties that stand at readiness on the flight deck during operations. He also

THE ICCS/BUBBLE

Note that when performing his duties, the Catapult Officer is located in the Integrated Catapult Control Station (ICCS), known as the 'bubble'. The bubble is a control booth in which the Shooters can safely observe the deck around them through toughened glass panels, and in which are located all the necessary comms and catapult controls to effect a launch. The ICCS is retractable: it can be lowered until perfectly flush with the flight deck when not in use. Two ICCS are located on the flight deck of a *Nimitz*-class carrier: one between catapults No. 1 and No. 2 and a second on the port side of the carrier, left of catapult No. 4. Although the ICCS are the preferred location for the catapult officers, they can also use open-air 'remote stations' located just off the sides of the flight deck.

BELOW A top view of the Integrated Catapult Control System (ICCS), or the 'bubble', in its lowered position. *(Patrick Bunce)*

implements general firefighting and safety training among Air Department personnel who serve on the flight deck.

Arresting Gear Officer (AGO)

The AGO, or 'The Hook', is responsible for the operation of all recovery equipment and related procedures, including applying the correct settings to the arrestor gear. Another role of the AGO is to monitor the landing deck area for any obstructions, human or material. If there are any such obstructions, the AGO declares a 'foul deck'; if all is well, the deck is given a 'clear' status and the aircraft is free to land.

Plane Directors

The Plane Directors provide visual directions to cockpit crews, instructing them where to move on the flight deck. The instructions are conveyed by hand signals; during night-time conditions the directors utilise a set of illuminated yellow wands to ensure visibility. Note that when not employed on the flight deck the Plane Directors, who are typically enlisted aviation boatswain's mates, will work in the hangar area.

LEFT The retractable sheave assembly of the Mk 7 arresting gear; the actual cross-deck pendant has been removed during maintenance. *(Patrick Bunce)*

LEFT A pair of Aviation Boatswain's Mates (Equipment) raise the jet blast deflectors on the flight deck of USS *Gerald R. Ford* (CVN-78). *(US Navy photo by Mass Communication Specialist 1st Class Jonathan Pankau/ Released)*

ABOVE Jersey colours, combined with helmet colours and other markings, denote the function of crew on the flight deck. (Patrick Bunce)

using radio communications and light signals to ensure that all the aircraft have the correct glidepath angle, altitude and line-up to perform a safe landing. Because the LSO must have a fundamental understanding of naval aviation, he is also a qualified and experienced pilot.

Squadron Plane Inspectors

Known appropriately enough as the 'Troubleshooters', these personnel conduct safety and airworthiness inspections of the aircraft on the flight deck.

Medical

The medical crew stand by to deliver immediate medical assistance to any crew member injured on the flight deck.

Blue Jerseys
Aircraft Handling Crew and Chock Crewmen

Rushing quickly between the aircraft on the flight deck, these personnel are responsible for aircraft handling equipment, including tractors and aircraft-starting units, and for securing the aircraft at the deck with wheel chocks and chains.

Elevator Operators (EOs)

The EOs take charge of operating the carrier's four elevators, moving the aircraft between the flight deck and the hangar deck.

Red Jerseys
Crash and Salvage

Waiting at the ready in special firefighting vehicles (see feature box), the Crash-and-Salvage crews will perform rescue and firefighting duties at the scene of any incident.

Ordnance Officer

The Ordnance Officer takes charge of the safe handling and loading of any aircraft ordnance on the flight deck. This responsibility not only means fitting fused ordnance to the aircraft before missions, but also unloading unexpended ordnance from returning aircraft.

CAG Arm and De-arm Team

This team perform arming and de-arming roles on the ordnance that arrives at the flight deck from the ship's magazines.

BELOW 'Blueshirts' tractor drivers, responsible for towing, chocking and chaining aircraft. Note that they each have an NWC- 4 Universal Wheel Chock. *(US Navy photo by Mass Communication Specialist 2nd Class (SW) Jennifer S. Kimball/ Released)*

White Jerseys
Safety Officer and Crew

The safety personnel closely monitor the performance of all procedures on the flight deck to ensure that these correspond with all recognised safely protocols.

Landing Signal Officer (LSO)

Notable by the absence of helmet (which might interfere with the LSO's visual acquisition of incoming aircraft), and known affectionately as 'Paddles', the LSO communicates directly with aircraft during the recovery phase operations,

P-25 FIRE FIGHTING VEHICLE AND AFFF

The principal emergency response vehicle aboard an aircraft carrier is the P-25 Fire Fighting Vehicle, manufactured by Entwistle. This compact, low-profile vehicle is ideal for moving around the confined deck space with high manoeuvrability. For firefighting, it has an onboard 750-gallon (2,839-litre) water tank plus a 50-gallon (189-litre) tank of Aqueous Film-Forming Foam (AFFF) concentrate, which it can control through a variable foam portioning system. AFFF is a chemical developed from the 1960s, purposely designed to extinguish and secure flammable hydrocarbon fuel fires. One of the virtues of AFFF is that it forms an aqueous film on the surface, preventing the evaporation of the AFFF that could eventually result in the reignition of the fuel. AFFF is also designed to reseal holes made in its film by falling debris. AFFF systems are integral throughout US supercarriers, with numerous stations and hoses at the ready. (On the deck, AFFF hose stations are indicated by an 18in (457mm) wide green strip marked with the white letters 'AFFF'.) A recent report about the potential toxicity of the substance, however, may result in its eventual replacement.

ABOVE Sailors on USS *Gerald R. Ford* (CVN-78) check the Aqueous Film-Forming Foam (AFFF) system during an operational test on the ship's flight deck. *(US Navy photo by Mass Communication Specialist 3rd Class Zachary Melvin/ Released)*

Explosive Ordnance Disposal (EOD)

The EOD operators must dispose, disarm or neutralise any defective or dangerous ordnance.

Ordnance Handlers

Known humorously as 'BB stackers', the Ordnance Handlers are responsible for moving ordnance around the flight deck and also for loading and unloading it on to the aircraft themselves.

RIGHT Equipment stored in one of the Repair Lockers aboard the USS *Dwight D. Eisenhower* (CVN-69). The Repair Lockers are stations for emergency response to fires and other critical incidents. *(Patrick Bunce)*

Purple Jerseys
Aviation Fuel Crews

The carrier flight deck and the hangar deck feature multiple fuelling stations, and the fuel crews are responsible for both refuelling and defuelling the aircraft. They also supply automotive gasoline to any deck or hangar vehicles, plus lubricating oil to the catapults and fuel to the jet engine test cell. On account of the colour of their jerseys, the fuel crews are known as 'Grapes'.

Green Jerseys
(Catapult Crew)
Catapult Safety Observer

The Catapult Safety Officer ensures that all individuals involved in the catapult launch of an aircraft follow the correct launch procedures and safety protocols.

Topside Safety Petty Officer (TSPO)

The TSPO checks that holdbacks and repeatable-release assemblies are properly installed, and that the aircraft launch bar is seated in the shuttle spreader, or, for bridle aircraft, that the bridle is engaged with the spreader and the aircraft's tow fittings. TSPOs are the last to exit from beneath the aircraft prior to launch.

Holdback Personnel

The Holdback Personnel install aircraft holdbacks, repeatable-release assemblies and tension rings and bars. They also verify the position of the aircraft over the catapult prior to launch.

Centerdeck Operator

The Centerdeck Operator performs a crucial communication role, relaying to the Launching Officer information regarding the aircraft type, gross weight, side number and capacity selection valve settings, to ensure that the catapult is properly configured for the specific aircraft ready to launch.

Jet Blast Deflector (JBD) Operator

The JBD operator raises and lowers the jet blast deflectors prior to and after each aircraft launch.

Weight Board Operator

The Weight Board Operator confirms the gross weight of each aircraft with the air crew just prior to launch and passes this information to the Shooter, who applies the correct weight settings to the catapult. The operator will display the weight information to the pilot using a special weight board and the pilot will, using hand signals, indicate whether this displayed weight is too low, too high or correct.

Green Jerseys
(Arresting Gear Crew)
Topside Petty Officer (TPO)

The TPO supervises the arresting gear crew, responsible for both the correct performance of arresting gear operations and for maintaining the equipment.

Deck-Edge Operator

The Deck-Edge Operator retracts the arresting gear after the recovery of each aircraft.

Hook Runners

Following the successful landing of an aircraft on deck, the Hook Runners ensure that the cross-deck pendant and purchase cable have been disengaged from the aircraft tail hook. Once this is done, they give the signal to the Deck-Edge Operator to retract the arresting gear.

Deck Checkers

The Deck Checkers perform a series of checks to ensure that the cross-deck pendant is in the correct position for aircraft recovery, that there are no personnel in the landing area and that the landing area is also free of Foreign Object Damage (FOD). The latter is especially important, because any foreign objects on the flight deck can turn into lethal missiles when propelled by jet thrust, or can destroy an aircraft engine if ingested through the intake. When the flight deck is non-operational, squadron, air wing and ship's company Air Department personnel perform a detailed check of the flight deck surface, forming a line across the width of the flight deck, then walking slowly from bow to stern, inspecting the surface carefully.

Aircraft Maintenance Crew

The Aircraft Maintenance Crew are squadron personnel responsible for the maintenance and serviceability of squadron aircraft.

Helicopter Landing Signal Enlistedman (LSE)

The Helicopter LSE provides hand signal directions to the cockpit crew of helicopters during take-off and landing.

Photographers

The onboard photographers capture still images and video footage, which is then utilised either for training and analysis purposes or providing to the media.

Brown Jerseys
Plane Captains

The Plane Captains service the aircraft before and after each flight, ensuring that the aircraft are in a proper condition to continue operations.

ABOVE Landing Signal Officers (LSOs) guide pilots during their final approach on the flight deck aboard USS *Harry S. Truman* (CVN-75). They are both holding a 'pickle switch', used to control features of the Optical Landing System (OLS). *(US Navy photo by Photographer's Mate 3rd Class Christopher B. Stoltz/Released)*

involves knowing about the personnel in Pri-Fly, several levels above the flight deck, and the operators in Flight Deck Control (FDC).

Primary Flight Control

The Primary Flight Control, or Pri-Fly, is a compact space up on Level 10 of the carrier island. There are multiple people confined in this space, each occupying a key role in that most central of carrier duties – ensuring the safe take-off and return of the aircraft within a 5-mile (8km) radius. During operations, Pri-Fly positively thrums with noise, voices and activity. One of the key elements of this space is a 'checks and balances' approach to communications. Information streaming into Pri-Fly, and flowing outwards, is continually shared and cross-referenced by people in multiple positions, thereby reducing the risk of major errors, which might be all too easy to make under the extreme pressures of the Pri-Fly space.

Taking the Pri-Fly of a typical *Nimitz*-class carrier, and working in a clockwise direction from the left (aft) position, the duties of the operators are as follows:

Visual Landing Aids – Here the operators control various flight deck lighting systems and other features that assist a pilot in landing the aircraft. They include a laser at deck level, invisible to those up on the Pri-Fly; as the pilots approach, they see the laser, which illuminates the arrestor wires and helps them to make an effective approach and to catch the wire properly.

BELOW The Air Boss position inside Pri-Fly of the USS *Dwight D. Eisenhower* (CVN-69). An Air Boss is ultimately responsible for the launch, recovery, movement (on both flight deck and hangar deck) and refuelling of the aircraft. *(Patrick Bunce)*

The list of flight deck crew here is not exhaustive. Other individuals include the Supply VERTREP Coordinator, responsible for monitoring and controlling helicopter-borne resupply operations, plus a variety of tractor drivers and engineering personnel. Yet however many people are on the flight deck, constant all-round awareness and diligent observation of communication protocols are key to preventing this busiest of operational spaces descending into chaos and lethality.

In addition to the personnel above, understanding how a flight deck works also

Gear Personnel – They are in charge of adjusting the weight settings of the arresting-gear wires. This is a critical job, with huge safety implications. Set the tension too high, and the aircraft could be stopped far too quickly, slamming it down on the deck with damaging consequences. Too low a tension, and the aircraft could fail to stop in time on the deck, or could lose landing control. Each individual aircraft has a specific weight, and that weight itself fluctuates with factors such as the amount of fuel the aircraft has burned during its operations, or weight changes due to the amount of ordnance either retained or deployed. All this information is relayed to Pri-Fly by the pilots on their approach.

AIR BOSS

The weight setting is therefore imperative to ensure the safety of the aircraft.

Aft Spotter – They are the eyes and ears to the Air Boss. They keep track of all the aircraft aft of the ship. They check factors such as the approaching aircraft's arrestor hook and landing gear are down and what type of aircraft it is, relaying this information to the Gear Personnel and to the Air Boss, so that there is overlapping information and communication, to reduce the possibility of mistakes. The Aft Spotter watches all the arresting wires to make sure that they are all set properly; they also observe that nobody is actually standing in the landing area or the catwalks around the edge of the landing area. The return of aircraft to the carrier is arranged in the manner of an oval-shaped 'racetrack' around the ship. When an aircraft is spotted about 2–3 miles astern of the carrier, to starboard, this position is called the 'Initial'. As the aircraft flies around the carrier in a loop to establish its final landing pattern, there are eight other designated positions around the racetrack. This way the carrier flight control staff are able to stack up multiple aircraft on the racetrack, with identifiable positions – all this information is relayed to Air Boss and Mini Boss so that they

BELOW Sailors perform a pre-operation inspection on a catapult on the flight deck of carrier USS *John C. Stennis* (CVN-74). *(US Navy photo by Mass Communication Specialist 3rd Class Mitchell Banks/ Released)*

have full situational awareness of all the aircraft in the sky at that time.

Air Boss and Mini Boss – Air Boss (officially 'Air Officer') and his assistant the Mini Boss (Air Officer Assistant) perform multiple coordination and command roles within Pri-Fly, and exercise ultimate control over the air operations around the ship. They largely perform the same roles,

although the Mini Boss focuses his attention forward of the ship, while the Air Boss directs it aft, although they will routinely swap sides to refresh their attention and focus. They receive multiple streams of communications at any one time, from ceiling-mounted speakers, desk-mounted speakers and their own personal headsets; this way they can hear all communications from the pilots, Flight Deck Control and the flight deck. (In essence, the rest of the personnel on Pri-Fly are responsible for collecting all relevant information about the aircraft and relaying it through to the Air Boss and Mini Boss.) They track the condition of both the pilots and the aircraft; if there is a problem with an aircraft, the Boss/Mini will place this aircraft in an advance position in the pattern so that it can land first. Similarly, if the aircraft poses the risk of causing a deck accident, it will be placed in the stack last, so that should it crash-land, by that time all other aircraft will be safely down. The Boss/Mini can also have a say over order of aircraft take-offs, although that responsibility is usually taken by the Aircraft Handler down on the flight deck.

Forward Spotter – This person performs the same duties as the Aft Spotter, but concentrating on the forward portion of the landing racetrack. Forward Spotters will also track which aircraft are about to launch, ensuring that the decks are clear of personnel.

ADMACS Operator – This operator uses the Aviation Data Management and Control System (ADMACS) to record everything that the aircraft does upon launch and recovery. This includes technical issues and pilot performance; everything is logged on the system whenever an aircraft enters the remit of Pri-Fly.

Tower Supervisor – An enlisted crew member whose job it is to oversee all other enlisted personnel in Pri-Fly. He will ensure that everyone is doing his or her job correctly and will assist

ADMACS

ADMACS is described by the Navy as:

a tactical, real-time data management system that connects the air department, ship divisions and embarked staff who manage aircraft launch and recovery operations aboard ships. ADMACS communicates real-time aviation and command-related data across the system's local area network and the Consolidated Afloat Network and Enterprise Services (CANES) network. Important data, such as the position and location of aircraft on flight and hangar decks, is then electronically displayed in the flight deck control room. ADMACS also displays the status of Aircraft Launch and Recovery Equipment (ALRE), fuel, weapons and other aviation and ship-related information. (https://www.navair.navy.mil/lakehurst/product/aviation-data-management-and-control-system-admacs)

ADMACS is designed specifically to reduce the workload of air operations through automation, and is essentially a computerised version of the 'Ouija Board' tabletop analogue models of the flight and hangar decks, although during interviews with the author, personnel noted that they still relied heavily upon the tactical 3D board. In 2020, all carriers will be equipped with the ADMACS Block II Phase I standard.

BELOW An upward view of the tower of USS *Dwight D. Eisenhower* (CVN-69) illustrates the angled windows at every level, which ensure a good view of the flight deck. *(Patrick Bunce)*

as necessary. As the Pri-Fly space gets very loud and crowded during operations, the Tower Supervisor will often help to pass information between positions, say if the Aft Spotter can't get the attention of the Air Boss, the Tower Supervisor can relay that information. The Tower Supervisor also answers internal phone calls from other parts of the ship, and communicates the messages to Air Boss and Mini Boss.

Flight Deck Control

The personnel who man FDC take charge of the physical movement of aircraft aboard the ship. As any aircraft lands on deck, the Aircraft Handling Officer (AHO, the individual in control of the FDC operations, aka the 'Handler' or 'Mangler') and his staff establish where the aircraft will physically go on the expanse of the flight deck or down below to the hangar bay. They also put in place practical movement orders to determine if the aircraft will participate in the next event and make it ready to launch. All the decisions made in the FDC are communicated with aircraft directors on the flight deck.

Apart from the AHO, the FDC personnel, or deck handlers, perform several other functions to ensure the safe and efficient movement of the aircraft, and their readiness to perform whatever duties are required of them. Maintenance

personnel inform the handler of the physical status of each aircraft, such as whether it is ready for launch or if there are problems that necessitate switching it out for another aircraft. Weapons personnel ensure that each aircraft receives the ordnance specifically designated for the mission, while the 'fuelies' control the aircraft refuelling. It should be noted that refuelling of aircraft aboard the carriers is only performed on deck, and never in the hangar bay; a deck fuel fire can be far more easily controlled than a blaze below decks.

Ouija Board

Within the FDC, the piece of equipment that most immediately arrests attention is known as the 'Ouija Board'. Set horizontally at waist height, the Ouija Board is a $\frac{1}{16}$-scale plastic representation of both the flight deck and the hangar deck beneath it (the latter is set as a second 'shelf' below). Every key feature of the flight deck is shown on the model – lights, catapults, flight deck markings and so on – and there are also flat models of each aircraft type, which are moved around the board by the Elevator Operators (EOs), faithfully representing in real-time the movement and position of every aircraft outside and below. (Moving an aircraft off the deck outline to a white space beyond indicates that that aircraft is airborne.) To designate the status and present/future procedures of each

aircraft, various small objects – nuts, bolts, wingnuts, coloured tacks and pins, etc. – are placed atop the aircraft models.

The system used varies from carrier to carrier. On the *Dwight D. Eisenhower*, for example, green pins represent the 'first go' aircraft (the aircraft that 'shoot' first off the flight deck), while the yellow pins indicate 'second go' aircraft (the next to launch); as the aircraft go back and forth, they cycle between green and yellow pins. White pins indicate that the aircraft needs to go down to the hangar bay. A child's jack atop the aircraft plate means, with a straightforward linguistic connection, that the aircraft needs to go up on jacks for maintenance, such as changing a nosewheel tyre. A nut tells the personnel that the aircraft needs a low-power turn; a larger nut indicates a high-power turn.

The Ouija Board is undoubtedly a relic of a previous age, having now been in service for more than 70 years. Despite this, and the advent of the high-tech alternatives discussed here, the manual Ouija Board remains popular; even in the *Gerald R. Ford* class, which has thoroughly automated the procedures of on- and below-deck aircraft control, a Ouija Board is still present. The principal value of the board is that it provides an accurate system of aircraft management even in the case of major electrical failure; quite simply, it requires

no power supply to operate. Furthermore, the Ouija Board, through its 3D composition and horizontal presentation, enables the FDC crew to have a concrete visualisation of the flight deck activity and a sense of physical orientation to the deck space and hangar bay activity. On the negative side, the Ouija Board is vulnerable to being knocked and its pieces scattered, plus it is hard to share the data from the table quickly with other departments.

Consequently, the FDC does have digital versions of the Ouija Board present. At the time of writing, chief among these is the ADMACS Flight Deck Management System (FDMS). This presents a screen-based version of the Ouija Board, operated with mouse and keyboard. As with the Ouija Board, it presents critical information, such as the status of ALRE, fuel, maintenance requirements and ordnance, and does so through automated processes.

Recognising the ergonomic and conceptual benefits of a horizontal table, however, since 2016 the TechSolutions company, sponsored by the Office of Naval Research (ONR), has been developing the Deployable Ship Integration Multitouch System (DSIMS). This computerised system presents the same view as the Ouija Board, but allows touch-screen drag-and-drop functionality, with all-built-in automated communications to allow the direct transfer of movement decisions up and down the

ABOVE A view of the Ouija Board system from the Aircraft Handling Officer's position aboard USS *Dwight D. Eisenhower* **(CVN-69).**
(Patrick Bunce)

An AHO aboard *Dwight D. Eisenhower* explains something of what it is like to operate the Ouija Board:

This way everyone on the flight deck understands [the situation]. They come in here and look at the Ouija Board and they know exactly what's launching next and what they have to move. Essentially it's like playing chess. I have limited space on the flight deck, so we have to play chess with the moving pieces. From the outside they [the flight deck personnel] are predicting and planning for two events ahead, in terms of where they are going to put aircraft. They are resetting the deck for two events ahead.

We have four elevators – Nos. 1, 2, 3 and 4 – and usually during the cycle [of flight operations] I try not to bring anything up. Usually in the morning I try to ensure that whatever I need on the flight deck is up on the flight deck. There will be some instances as we move along where I need to bring more aircraft out of the hangar bay to make the flight schedule.

Hangar deck

In addition to the practical and mechanical tasks that are performed in the hangar bays, the spaces are also used for various other

ABOVE Some of the many minor pieces added to the Ouija Board on the hangar deck of USS *Dwight D. Eisenhower* (CVN-69), to denote various aircraft states. *(Author)*

command chain. At the time of writing, open access sources suggest that the DSIMS has been fitted, likely in the *Gerald R. Ford* class, but the author is unable to confirm exact details of the installation. Regardless of whether the ADMACS or DSIMS is used, talking to FDC personnel aboard the *Dwight D. Eisenhower* it was clear that the situation was not one of 'either/or' – both the manual and digital systems were used to complement one another.

Returning to the conventional Ouija Board operation, the EOs who operate it are in contact with another area upstairs in the island called 'Spin'. From Spin the personnel have a complete view of the entire flight deck, and

RIGHT The tailhook of a KA-6D Intruder aircraft of Attack Squadron 34 (VA-34) approaches the arresting cable on the USS *Dwight D. Eisenhower* (CVN-69) during the FLEET EX '90 exercise. *(NARA, JO3 Oscar Sosa, USN)*

purposes, including ceremonies, briefings and physical exercise. The chief activity within the hangar bay, however, is aircraft maintenance. This duty is primarily performed by the AIMD noted in Chapter 2. This department is divided into four divisions, here explained in a US Navy web document for USS *George Washington*:

IM-1 The Staff Division, consists of a production staff to manage 57 Maintenance Work Centers in the processing of hundreds of repairable items on a daily basis.

IM-2 The General Maintenance Division, performs repairs on aircraft engines, propeller assemblies, hydraulic components, metal and composite aircraft structures, aviation life support systems and personal survival equipment.

IM-3 The Avionics/Armament Division, performs repairs on assigned test benches/sets and aircraft electrical and electronic components to support aircraft communication and navigation equipment, computers, radars and electronic countermeasures systems. IM-3 also provides intermediate support for weapons systems such as bomb racks, missile launchers and aircraft guns.

IM-4 The Support Equipment Division, aids flight and hangar deck operations by inspecting, repairing and servicing ground support equipment for work on and around aircraft. AIMD doubles its assigned manpower during each at-sea operating period upon the arrival of sea duty detachments of technicians (SEAOPDETS), from shore-based Fleet Readiness Centers.

(https://www.public.navy.mil/airfor/ cvn73/Pages/AIRCRAFT-INTERMEDIATE- MAINTENANCE-DEPARTMENT-(AIMD).aspx)

The level of maintenance required by the aircraft dictates its placement around the hangar bay. When aircraft are 'spotted' (placed) around the

BELOW The Hyster 60 is one of the smaller types of forklift trucks used on US CVNs since the early 2000s. *(Patrick Bunce)*

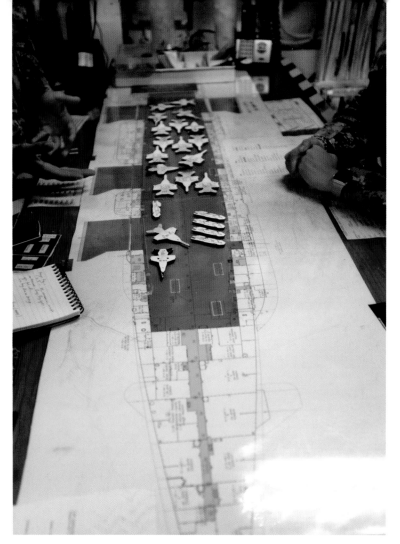

hangar bay, some are going to be below the flight deck for longer than others, and these tend to be placed in 'deep bury spots', with other aircraft on a faster turnaround blocking them in.

The individuals who take charge of spotting the aircraft perform a crucial role in the ship's operational capability. Inefficiency in placing or moving aircraft in the hangar bay can mean critical delays in moving operational assets up to the flight deck.

The hangar bay might not have the self-evident dangers of the flight deck, but the presence of large quantities of aviation fuel (large numbers of aircraft auxiliary fuel tanks are often stored overhead in a forward section of the hangar bay) and possibly ordnance, plus the confines and time pressures of the working space, make the dangers very real. Each hangar bay has a Conflag Station, a control and communications hub for responding to a sudden emergency. A Conflag Station is manned at all times if aircraft are present in the hangar bay. Not only can operators there communicate a fire emergency from the Conflag Station to all relevant emergency responders, but they can also open or close

ABOVE The hangar deck Ouija Board serves the same function as the similar apparatus in FDC, visualising the movement of aircraft around, to and from the hangar deck. *(Patrick Bunce)*

BELOW A strap system on the ceiling of the hangar deck is used for suspending empty aircraft auxiliary fuel tanks. *(Patrick Bunce)*

BELOW Navy Petty Officer 3rd Class Brittney Vice dismantles a pressure-reducing valve for inspection aboard the aircraft carrier USS *Harry S. Truman* at Norfolk Naval Station, Virginia, 2019. *(US Navy photo by Navy Petty Officer 3rd Class Sam Jenkins/Released)*

76ft- (23m) wide division fire doors, to isolate an individual bay. They can also initiate the AFFF sprinkler fire-suppression system fitted throughout the bay. One important point, however, is to ensure that the AFFF is never activated unnecessarily. The aircraft in the hangar bay often sit with their cockpit canopies open, and the AFFF chemicals, and the saltwater used as the main constituent of the system, are highly damaging for sensitive digital cockpit instrumentation. When the ship returns to sea after a long period in port, however, the hangar bay crew test every single sprinkler system to ensure its functionality. On the USS *Dwight D. Eisenhower*, hangar bays No. 1 and 3 have two AFFF stations, and hangar bay No. 2 has five stations. There are also extensive CO_2 and PKP (a potassium bicarbonate-based dry-chemical fire suppression agent) systems around the hangar bay.

During the author's visit to the USS *Dwight D. Eisenhower*, two 'yellowshirts' explained the daily routines that govern life on the deck:

We have meetings every day at 0645 and at 1845, before turnovers, so we pass any information down to the next shift [there are two shifts aboard the carrier, day and night] [Above that] The chain of command will pass down information – first to the Leading Chief Petty Officer (LCPO), then the Leading Petty Officer (LPO), then the Deck PO, and finally to the Bay POs. The Bay POs are in charge of each hangar bay, and they are supposed to know everything about what goes on there – which aircraft are in maintenance, where people are, what needs to get done. Normally the Deck PO coordinates with flight control to define where each aircraft will be going. Then they make a plan of how we are going to run it. For example, first we'll drop Elevator No. 1 from the flight deck to the hangar bay level, bring in the assorted aircraft we'll need, then move on to another elevator. . . .

As with the flight deck, the hangar bays also contain a Ouija Board, identical in format to that in the FDC, with a similar system of nuts, bolts, pins and assorted small objects to denote the aircraft. It is used to plot the movement of the

CARRIER AIRCRAFT MAINTENANCE PLANNING

A detailed outline of the command-and-control procedure for aircraft maintenance, as performed by the AIMD, is outlined in the *CVN Flight/Hangar Deck NATOPS Manual* (NAVAIR 00-80T-120).

10.3.2 Aircraft Maintenance Aircraft movements for a given operating schedule are normally planned well in advance of a flight deck evolution. In planning aircraft movements, spots, etc., the Aircraft Handling Officer (ACHO) shall know approximately how long it will take to repair various common discrepancies on a particular aircraft and what type of spot is required. All this requires a timely and constant exchange of information among the Aircraft Handling Officer, CARAIRWING maintenance representative, and squadron maintenance personnel. It is essential for the ACHO to have knowledge of aircraft maintenance and/or to have access to personnel who can advise him of aircraft maintenance requirements.

1. The ACHO shall familiarize himself with the status of all aircraft onboard, keeping current by quick exchange of information with the CARAIRWING maintenance representatives and the squadron maintenance representatives. Using the maintenance spot request sheets [. . .] the ACHO can integrate required maintenance with operations.

2. In order to function most efficiently under all circumstances, the following are applicable:

   a. Flight Deck Control shall be the nerve center for all planned/ unplanned maintenance within the air wing. The squadrons shall keep Flight Deck Control (FDC) informed and aware of all maintenance associated problems as they occur, via the CARAIRWING representative. Herein, an accurate and timely status of each aircraft shall be maintained on the status board by maintenance representatives of each squadron, along with configuration and controlling discrepancies.

   b. Whenever the status of an aircraft changes, the maintenance representative of the squadron concerned shall immediately report this information to the ACHO, via the air wing maintenance representative. Representatives shall be prepared to furnish such information as the ACHO may require for proper planning upon request. Failure to keep FDC informed of aircraft status changes, maintenance requirements, etc., will have a deleterious impact on the squadrons' ability to conduct maintenance, launch alert aircraft, or perform other deck-related functions. The ACHO shall know as soon as a squadron maintenance representative does.

3. All maintenance requests, requests for specific aircraft sortie assignments, and aircraft status changes shall be routed from the designated squadron maintenance chief through the Air Wing representative for consideration by the Aircraft Handling Officer.

4. All maintenance requests shall be submitted to the Air Wing representative prior to the last two recoveries of the day or night flight operations.

LEFT An Aviation Electrician's Mate 2nd Class cleans a searchlight from an MH-60R Seahawk helicopter attached to the 'Griffins' of Helicopter Maritime Strike Squadron (HSM) 79 in the hangar bay of USS *Abraham Lincoln* (CVN-72). *(US Navy photo by Mass Communication Specialist 3rd Class Jeremiah Bartelt/Released)*

BELOW The hangar bay is also used for ceremonial occasions. Here sailors attend a chief-pinning ceremony aboard the USS *Dwight D. Eisenhower* (CVN-69). *(US Navy photo by Mass Communication Specialist 3rd Class Kaleb J. Sarten/Released)*

aircraft around the hangar deck and bays and between the flight deck. An ADMACS provides a digital version.

Aircraft handling equipment

With more than 70 aircraft on board a US supercarrier, movement of the CVW assets is naturally a matter of mechanical muscle. To move the aircraft efficiently, there is a variety of Ground Support Equipment (GSE) used on board, in the form of tow tractors and spotting dollies, manned by an Aviation Boatswain's Mate Handler (ABH).

Tow tractors

Tow tractors are the primary means of shifting aircraft around the deck spaces when they do not have their engines running. Each tractor connects to the aircraft via a drawbar, and the weight of drawbar pull depends not only on the type of tractor used, but also on the condition of the surface over which the vehicle is operating. For example, on a perfectly dry surface a tractor with an 8,000lb (3,636kg) drawbar pull can draw a tow aircraft weighing 80,000lb (36,363kg), or ten times the drawbar pull. On a wet and fuel-soaked flight deck, however, the wheel traction is severely reduced, so the drawbar pull is significantly diminished. An experienced tractor operator will be able to judge the effect of the conditions on the movement.

The major types of tractor found on a US supercarrier are as follows:

A/S32A-32 Towing Tractor (SD-2 Spotting Dolly) – The A/S32A-32 is known as both a towing tractor and a spotting dolly. Its low profile (it is just 30in/762mm high) means that it can move confidently beneath the wings of aircraft on crowded decks, while its three-wheel configuration allows a very high degree of manoeuvrability. The vehicle can even spin on its own axis, and can attach itself to the front wheel of an aircraft, then turn that aircraft

through 360 degrees while the centre of the landing gear remains stationary. Maximum speed is 2mph (3.2km/h) when pulling a load and 5mph (8km/h) unloaded; the drawbar pull of the vehicle is 14,000lb (6,363kg). The vehicle is powered by JP-5 jet fuel.

A/S32A-31A Aircraft Tow Tractor – Another aircraft-towing tractor, the A/S 32A-31A is a six-wheeled vehicle with dual rear-drive and front-wheel steering and a three-speed automatic transmission. The wheel layout means that the A/S32A-31A does not have the singular manoeuvrability of the A/S32A-32, having a turning radius of 132in (3.35m; the turning radius of the A/S32A-32 is 0in). One of the key

BELOW An Aviation Boatswain's Mate (Equipment) moves supplies around the hangar bay of USS *Dwight D. Eisenhower* (CVN-69) using a pallet truck. *(US Navy photo by Mass Communication Specialist 3rd Class Kaleb J. Sarten/ Released)*

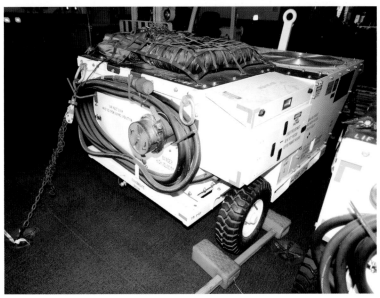

RIGHT A rear view of an MSU-200NAV Air Start Unit; note the use of the aircraft chock to secure its wheels. *(Patrick Bunce)*

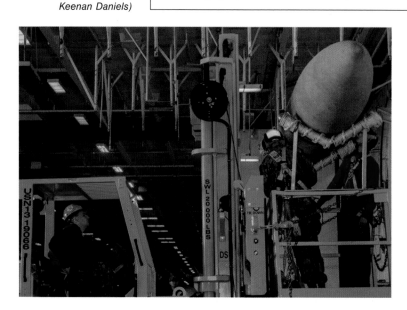

RIGHT An annotated US Navy diagram showing A/S32A-32 Aircraft Towing Tractor. *(US Navy)*

BELOW Sailors use a forklift truck to store a fuel cell in the hangar bay roof slings aboard the USS *Nimitz* (CVN-68). *(US Navy photo by Mass Communication Specialist Seaman Keenan Daniels)*

ABHf0209

1. Seat	12. Blank	24. Spotlight
2. Blank	13. Fuel fill	25. Emergency arm spread control buttons
3. Control handle	14. Tie-down and lift ring	26. Emergency arm control valves
4. Lifting arm control box	15. Headlight	27. Slave receptacle
5. Instrument and engine control access panel	16. Parking brake	28. Blank
6. Hydraulic oil fill	17. Horn Button	29. Lifting arms control panel
7. Blank	18. Blank	30. Blank
8. Engine compartment access panel	19. Caster	31. Lifting arms
9. Axle pin holder	20. Emergency stop switch	32. Chassis
10. Blank	21. Main tires	33. Lifting hydraulic cylinder
11. Emergency stop switch	22. Right-hand lifting arm control panel	34. Spread hydraulic cylinders
	23. Light switch	

functional attributes of the A/S32A-31A is that it has mounting provision for the MSU-200NAV Air Start Unit (MSU) on the rear of the tractor. This unit, powered by fuel from the vehicle's own 85-gallon (322-litre) internal tank, is designed to deliver aircraft main engine start (MES) and to supply onboard Environmental Control Systems (ECS) with compressed air. The drawbar pull is 8,500lb (3,863kg).

A/S32A-45 Mid-Range Tow Tractor

(MRTT) – Offering a drawbar pull of 10,000lb (4,545kg), the A/S32A-45 has an enclosed two-seat cab (the driver sits on the left of the vehicle), giving it a height of 46in (1.19m). It is powered by a four-cylinder diesel engine, with rear-wheel drive and a three-speed automatic transmission. It is one of the faster of the towing trucks, capable of 15mph (24km/h) forward and 7mph (11km/h) in reverse (no load).

A/S37A-3 Shipboard Mobile Electric Power Plant (MEPP) – The MEPP is a four-wheeled, diesel-powered vehicle fitted with 115-volt alternating current (VAC), three-phase, 400-Hertz (Hz) or 28 VDC electrical power for aircraft aboard ship. All controls for the power delivery are located to the right of the driver's seat, which is located on the left side of the vehicle.

Specialist equipment

Apart from the towing/spotting vehicles, several other pieces of aircraft handling equipment deserve a mention (they are specifically highlighted in the training manuals):

NWC-4 Universal Wheel Chock – Used for almost all shipboard aircraft, the NWC-4 is made from polyurethane and features two moulded-tread blocks (one fixed, at the end of the bar, and one movable) to give contact with the aircraft wheels, fitting landing gear up to about 45in (1.14m) in diameter. The US Navy manual clearly describes the advantages of the system:

The molded tread increases traction and also displaces liquids on the deck by a squeegee-type action. The polyurethane end blocks are sufficiently rigid to prevent

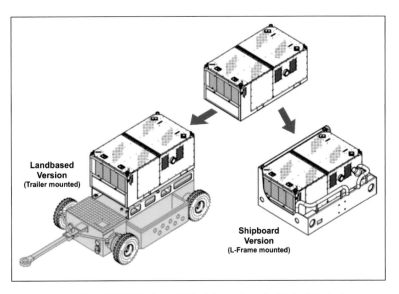

ABOVE The MSU-200NAV Air Start Unit. It is equipped with built-in test equipment (BITE) and full authority digital engine control (FADEC) system. *(US Navy)*

crushing, but will still deform enough to permit the aircraft tire loads to be readily transferred through the end block to the flight deck. The polyurethane end blocks not only provide vastly superior traction, but they require no painting, will not corrode, are self-extinguishing in fire, and are environmentally and chemically resistant to deterioration.

(US Navy, 2001, 2-25)

TD-1B Aircraft Tie-down Chain Assembly – The TD-1B assembly is a quick-release tie-down chain assembly used to secure aircraft to

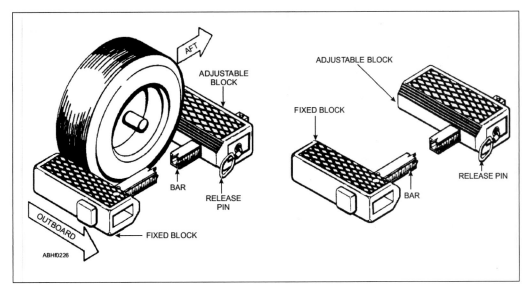

LEFT The NWC-4 Shipboard Aircraft Wheel Chock. The polyurethane end blocks are largely immune to the adverse conditions aboard a carrier at sea. *(US Navy)*

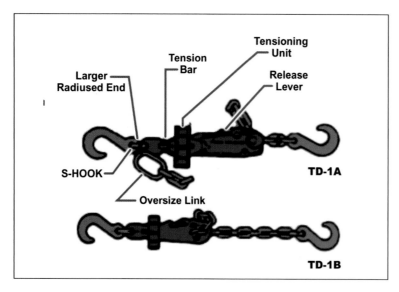

ABOVE **The TD-1A and TD-1B Aircraft Tie-downs. These pieces of equipment have now been in use for well over a decade at the time of writing.** (US Navy)

the deck. (Scattered across the flight deck and hangar decks, embedded flush into the surface, are hundreds of tie-down points, consisting of two cross-steel bars set over a depression.) With S-hooks at both ends, the TD-1B features a tensioning system to quickly ratchet the tie-down until it is taut, with a safe working load of 10,000lb (4,545kg), but also a release lever to disconnect the fitting quickly when needed.

High-power Tie-down Assembly – Also called the Aero Full-power Tie-down Assembly, this chain linkage system is mainly used when an aircraft has to perform a full-power turn-up of its engines (meaning that it has engaged full afterburners) but stay secured to the deck for maintenance and monitoring purposes. (There are special open areas at the back of the carrier where the aircraft can open up the taps and safely vent the exhaust overboard.) Weighing 102lb (46kg) and with no lengthening/shortening feature (which would potentially weaken its break strength, although two tie-downs can be linked by a dummy link), each of these tie-downs can take a working load of 30,000lb (13,636kg). Note that the tie-down has to be fitted to special high-strength deck fittings during engine run-up.

ALBAR Universal Aircraft Towbar – The ALBAR provides a towing interface between the nose of the aircraft and the towing/spotting vehicle. The acronym stands for Adjustable Length Towbar, and it is provided in four lengths: Model 8 ALBAR (9ft/2.7m long), Model 15 ALBAR (15ft/4.5m long), Model 20 ALBAR (20ft/6m long) and Model 24 ALBAR (25ft/7.6m long). Each of these models is designed for use with different aircraft types:

The 8 ALBAR is designed for shipboard movement and spotting of H-46 helicopters on LHAs, LHDs, and LPDs. The 15 ALBAR

LEFT **An Aviation Machinist's Mate Airman carries several tie-down chains across the flight deck of the USS *Harry S. Truman* (CVN-75), during Operation Iraqi Freedom in 2007.** (US Navy photo by Mass Communication Specialist Seaman Justin Lee Losack/Released)

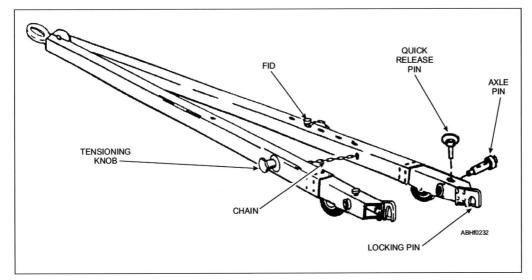

LEFT The ALBAR Universal Aircraft Towbar, designated 'universal' because a single type of towbar can be fitted to all carrier-based aircraft. *(US Navy)*

is the standard towbar for moving most land-based and shipboard-based aircraft weighing up to 90,000 pounds. Its configuration is virtually identical to the existing model ALBAR towbar, but it can be easily expanded to make the 20 and 24 ALBARs. The 20 ALBAR was designed to handle the CH-53E helicopter when it is equipped with an in-flight refueling probe, the AV-8B, and the F/A-18 ashore. Because of the lower height of the shipboard A/S32A-31A tow tractors, the F/A-18 can be safely towed aboard CVNs with the 15 ALBAR. The 24 ALBAR was expressly designed to handle the SH-60B helicopter. This extra length is needed to reach into the tailwheel for towing this aircraft. The ALBAR concept offers many advantages, including that spare parts, except leg extensions, are identical. The 20 and 24 ALBARs can be broken down for shipment in a standard 15-foot towbar container. Bent towbar tubes on the 20 and 24 ALBAR (caused by 'jack-knifing' the tractor) can be easily repaired with replacement extensions, or the damaged extension can be removed, leaving a usable 15 ALBAR.

(US Navy, 2001, 2-28–2-29)

Elevators

The primary mechanical interface between the flight deck and the hangar deck are the large aircraft elevators (four on the *Nimitz*-class carriers, three on the *Gerald R. Ford* class. (The positions of these elevators are noted in Chapter 2.) The elevators are made from welded steel or aluminium, and on the *Nimitz*-class vessels each measures 52ft (15.2m) wide and 70ft (21.3m) long inboard and 85ft (25.9m) long outboard, with a total area of 3,880sq ft (360m^2). Each elevator is capable of lifting 47 tons (42.6 tonnes), meaning that it can take two fully loaded F-18s or F-14s at any one time.

Operation of the elevators is shared between V-1 (flight deck), V-3 (hangar deck) and A Division (machinery room). Each individual elevator is manned by a qualified director and operator on the flight deck, the same on the hangar deck, and one qualified operator in the pump room.

Mechanically, the elevators are raised and lowered by hydraulics, with a manually operated gear system. When it is moving, the elevator platform slides within guide rails bolted to the ship's structure, one on the aft side and one on the forward side of the platform, with two sets of double guide rollers and one face roller on the forward and aft sides of the platform.

When not in use, the elevator platforms are raised to the flight deck level, secured in place by horizontal locking bars. During operations, by contrast, the elevators might be in a frequent rapid movement. The Navy manual *Aviation Boatswain's Mate H* (2001) explains the cycles of elevator operation, plus some of the control and safety features built into the system.

With all pumps in use and the elevator loaded to capacity, the duty cycle is about 60 seconds. This includes 15 seconds at the top and 15 seconds at the bottom stations for loading and unloading. When the elevator is operating on the cycle specified, should there be a loss of electric power at any point in the cycle, the residual capacity of the pressure tanks is sufficient to permit returning the loaded platform to the flight deck. It should also be possible to raise the loaded elevator at any time within 30

minutes of loss of power, in spite of normal system leakage. There are two control stations for each of the deck edge elevators. One control station is located on the hangar deck and one in the gallery walkway on the flight deck. The control station is bolted to the hangar deck where the operator has an unobstructed view of the deck edge elevator opening on that deck. This station contains a master switch; horn button; horn cutout switch; power available light (white); control energized light (green); on certain ships, a hand wheel for manual operation; and a gearbox assembly.

(US Navy, 2001, 2-21)

BELOW **Utilising one of the enormous aircraft elevators, sailors conduct a mass casualty drill in the hangar bay of the aircraft carrier USS *Theodore Roosevelt* (CVN-71).** *(US Navy photo by Mass Communication Specialist 3rd Class Terence Deleon Guerrero/Released)*

Framing each elevator are deck-edge elevator doors. These close off the hangar deck opening to the aircraft elevators, preventing topside weather, smoke, fire or other maladies from working their way down below deck. They are also light-tight, so the hangar deck can remain illuminated even when the ship is under black-out security conditions topside. It takes 60 seconds for the doors to open or close.

The hangar deck and the flight deck of a supercarrier are utterly business-like spaces, full of noise, heat, light and energy. It is during operations that these spaces have to choreograph and coordinate the launch and recovery of aircraft, and how that is done is the subject of our next chapter.

ABOVE Navy ordnance personnel move BLU-110/111/117A/B bombs (identified by the three yellow bands around the nose) on the hangar deck using a forklift. The bombs are in their factory-shipped state, so they have likely just arrived by UNREP or dockside replenishment.
(US Navy)

LEFT A US Navy F/A-18C Hornet assigned to Strike Fighter Squadron One Four Seven (VFA-147) catches the arresting gear wire, while landing on board the USS *Nimitz* (CVN-68) during Operation Southern Watch, Persian Gulf.
(NARA, PH3 Christopher Mobley, USN)

Chapter Four

Flight operations

Given the sheer complexity and danger of carrier flight operations, it is impressive that they are carried out with such fluency and competence on a regular basis. Captain (USN) Charles 'Pete' Conrad, a naval aviator and a NASA astronaut (he was the third man to walk on the moon), once remarked that 'In looking back over everything that I've done in the Navy and in the Space Program, I think that absolutely nothing matched night carrier aviation. I still think that separates the men from the boys. It's more difficult than any of the other things I did, including landing on the moon.'

OPPOSITE **An F/A-18F Super Hornet from Strike Fighter Squadron (VFA) 103 prepares to make an arrested landing on the flight deck of USS *Abraham Lincoln* (CVN-72).** *(US Navy photo by Mass Communication Specialist 3rd Class Jeremiah Bartelt/Released)*

In this chapter, we explore in some depth how carrier air operations are conducted, from the development of an initial Air Plan to the moment an aircraft returns from a sortie, lands on the carrier and turns off its engines. The whole effort has an almost orchestral harmony to it, albeit one conducted with metal, fuel, ordnance and computers, but it remains an extraordinary testimony to technical and human engineering.

The Carrier Air Wing

The structure and aircraft types of the Carrier Air Wing (CVW) have changed fairly fluidly and frequently since the advent of the *Nimitz*-class carriers in the 1970s, dependent upon the contemporary strategic and tactical outlooks and the naval aircraft available. Looking at the composition prevailing at the time of writing, a *Nimitz*-class CVW approximates to the following:

- 4 × Strike Fighting (VFA) squadrons – Each squadron is composed of 12 F/A-18E/F Super Hornets or 10 × F/A-18C Hornets. (More about individual aircraft types is explained later in this chapter.) Note that some air wings have individual US Marine Corps Fighter Attack (VMFA) squadrons. Looking to the future, both the US Navy and the US Marine Corps will replace F/A-18 aircraft with the F-35C Lightning II.

- 1 × Electronic Attack (VAQ) squadron – 5 × EA-18G Growlers.
- 1 × Carrier Airborne Early Warning (VAW) squadron – 4 × E-2C Hawkeyes or 5 × E-2D Advanced Hawkeyes.
- 1 × Helicopter Sea Combat (HSC) squadron – 8 × MH-60 Seahawks.
- 1 × Helicopter Maritime Strike (HSM) squadron – 11 × MH-60R Seahawks (3–5 of which are frequently based on other ships in the CSG).
- 1 × Fleet Logistics Support (VRC) squadron detachment – 2 × C-2A Greyhounds.

The CVW is heavily weighted towards fighter/strike capability, in keeping with the carrier's primary roles of close air support, suppression and interdiction, but with a spectrum of other assets to cover various EW, maritime and logistical roles. It is worth briefly defining each of the aircraft types above to fully understand the operational power of a supercarrier.

Boeing F/A-18 Hornet/Super Hornet

The Boeing F/A-18 Hornet family represents near state-of-the-art in naval aviation. (Note that the F/A-18 was originally designed and built by McDonnell Douglas with Northrop, but Boeing took over production and development in 1997.) In basic operational profile it is a twin-engine,

supersonic, all-weather, carrier-capable, multi-role combat jet. The first variant – the F/A-18A – went into US Navy and Marine Corps carrier service from 1983, quickly proving itself in action with its exceptional manoeuvrability, top speed of Mach 1.8 (1,190mph/1,915km/h) and useful ordnance load. The F/A-18C is a single-seat variant that emerged from a block upgrade in 1987, featuring improved radar, avionics and weapons systems, the latter including the AIM-120 AMRAAM air-to-air missile and AGM-65 Maverick and AGM-84 Harpoon air-to-surface missiles.

The big evolutionary leap in the F/A-18's design came with the F/A-18E and F/A-18F Super Hornet variants, which first took flight in November 1995. The motivation behind the Super Hornet was the requirement to improve the aircraft's combat radius and the payload capacity, which lagged significantly behind the earlier F-14 Tomcat in these areas. In many senses, the Super Hornet is a new aircraft altogether, rather than a subtle variant of the original. It is a full 20% larger and has a 7,000lb (3,200kg) extra empty weight. It can carry 33%

more fuel than its predecessors, resulting in a 41% increase in mission range and a 50% greater endurance. It has the capacity for carrying 17,750lb (8,050kg) of external fuel and ordnance, as opposed to the 13,700lb (6,200kg) of the F/A-18C/D. The enlarged airframe also made more space for advanced avionics and weapon systems. Two versions of the Super Hornet are utilised on US carriers: the F/A-18E single-seater and the F/A-18F two-seater.

EA-18G Growler

The EA-18G Growler is a specialised offshoot of the F/A-18F Super Hornet two-seater, the Growler serving as an electronic warfare aircraft and replacing (from 2009) the Northrop Grumman EA-6B Prowlers that previously undertook this carrier-based role. In performance characteristics, the Growler

has little to distinguish it from the other Super Hornets – necessarily so, as Growlers will typically accompany the other aircraft throughout a mission, deploying an array of jamming and target-detection technologies in support, specific devices including AN/ALQ-99 jamming pods and also, from 2021, the Next Generation Jammer (NGJ). The NGJ will be a significant addition, remedying some of the reliability issues with the AN/ALQ-99, plus its tendency to interfere with the aircraft's own active electronically scanned array (AESA) radar system, while also offering cyber-attack capabilities.

E-2C Hawkeye/E-2D Advanced Hawkeye

Recognisable from its twin turboprops and its large overhead-mounted radome, the Hawkeye is an all-weather, carrier-capable tactical airborne early warning (AEW) aircraft that entered service (as the E-2A) in the 1960s. The much-improved E-2C variant first flew in 1971 and became operational two years later.

The E-2C carries a highly sophisticated array of long-range radar systems and identification

BELOW Laser-guided bombs line the flight deck of the USS *John F. Kennedy* (CV-67) in preparation for air strikes against Iraq during Operation Desert Storm. The A-6E Intruder aircraft in the background is armed with laser-guided bombs. *(US Navy photo)*

friend or foe (IFF) technology, the data from which are analysed by powerful onboard digital computer signal processing and its human crew (the aircraft has a five-man crew). In terms of its operational contribution to a CSG, the Hawkeye delivers a tactically useful spectrum of surveillance and command-and-control functions, including:

- Long-range detection and monitoring of aircraft, ships and land vehicles.
- Battlespace command and control, including directing fighters during aerial engagements and strike aircraft during ground-attack sorties.
- Providing air traffic control services to military aircraft.
- Control of search-and-rescue missions.
- Relay of radio messages (air to air and ship to ship).

The E-2D Advanced Hawkeye is essentially the same aircraft, but with improved T56-A-427A engines and packaged with a new avionics suite of additional technological reach. Among the improvements is the Lockheed Martin-built APY-9 UHF-band radar, which when using the Link-16 and Cooperative Engagement Capability (CEC) data-links, can provide an off-board fire-control system for the Boeing F/A-18 and for Aegis warships firing Raytheon Standard SM-6 surface-to-air missiles. A Tactical Targeting Network Technologies (TTNT) data-link connects into the Naval Integrated Fire Control-Counter Air (NIFC-CA) system; one of its key benefits is that aircraft will be able to launch missiles at targets without even having their own radars active.

MH-60 Seahawk

The MH-60 Seahawk is the key rotary-wing asset aboard the supercarriers, a twin-turboshaft multi-mission helicopter and essentially a maritime version of the US Army's UH-60 Black Hawk. In Navy use, the Seahawk comes under several model designations, including SH-60B, SH-60F, HH-60H, MH-60R and MH-60S. The differences between the models are of varying degrees of significance and subtlety, defined by the technologies that dictate mission focus and flying performance. The primary versions

deployed aboard modern US carriers, however, are the SH-60B and MH-60R. Both of these are packed with the sensors, radar and armament to perform anti-ship and anti-submarine warfare. The SH-60B, for example, includes a towed Magnetic Anomaly Detector (MAD), forward-looking infrared (FLIR) turret, APS-124 search radar, ALQ-142 ESM system, anti-submarine torpedoes (Mk 46, Mk 50 or Mk 54 Lightweight Torpedo) and AGM-114 Hellfire missiles. The MH-60R is fundamentally an improved SH-60B, with more advanced combat data systems, including the AN/APS-147 multi-mode radar/IFF interrogator and advanced airborne fleet data-link plus a fully integrated glass cockpit with increased use of digital monitors rather than analogue controls.

In addition to their anti-ship and anti-submarine roles, the carrier helicopters can be called upon to perform a multitude of other tasks, including search-and-rescue, insertion of naval special warfare team, medical evacuation (MEDEVAC) and vertical replenishment (VERTREP).

C-2A Greyhound and V-22 Osprey

The C-2A Greyhound is actually a derivative of the E-2 Hawkeye, with the latter's twin-turboprop high-wing design, but minus the large radome and other electronic warfare components. Physical modifications are a widened fuselage

ABOVE An MH-60S Seahawk helicopter assigned to Helicopter Sea Combat Squadron (HSC) 7 performs a night take-off from USS Dwight D. Eisenhower (CVN-69), the personnel of Pri-Fly observing top right. *(US Navy photo by Mass Communication Specialist 3rd Class Kaleb J. Sarten/ Released)*

and a rear loading ramp. Another notable feature is the way the aircraft is fitted with four vertical stabilisers, three of which are fitted with rudders. The reason behind this configuration is that if the aircraft had been fitted with a single stabiliser to give directional control, that feature would have been higher than an aircraft carrier could accommodate below decks.

The primary role of the Greyhound since the 1960s is what is known as Carrier Onboard Delivery (COD), more specifically the ferrying of personnel, supplies and high-priority cargo between land and the aircraft carrier at sea. It is a role that it performs with aplomb. Not only does the Greyhound have the flying characteristics ideal for carrier operations, but it can also carry up to 10,000lb (4,500kg) of cargo, 26 passengers or 12 litter patients over ranges of 1,300nm (1,496 miles/2,407km). However, in February 2015 the Navy confirmed that the C-2A would eventually be replaced in the COD role by the Bell Boeing V-22 Osprey, which with its ground-breaking tiltrotor design, delivers the V/STOL characteristics of a helicopter combined with the long-range cruise performance of a standard turboprop aircraft. The range of the Osprey is actually below that of C-2A (about 879nm/1,011 miles/1,627km) but the new aircraft has double the internal cargo carrying capacity at 20,000lb (9,070kg), or it can carry 15,000lb (6,800kg) cargo as an underslung external load. The first deployments of V-22s to carriers are occurring at the time of writing, but the full transition will not be completed until the mid- to late 2020s.

Lockheed Martin F-35C Lightning II

Some controversy hangs over the F-35 Lightning at the time of writing, with critics pointing to the fact that one of the largest and most expensive military programmes in US history is still dogged by technical and performance issues. The F-35 is what is referred to as a 'fifth-generation' multi-role combat aircraft, designed for both ground-attack and air-superiority missions. With stealth characteristics built into its material construction and planform, high performance and manoeuvrability and the most advanced networked avionics, the F-35 has been produced in three versions. The F-35A operates using

conventional take-off and landing (CTOL); the F-35B has a short take-off and vertical landing (STOVL) capability; while the F-35C is designed specifically for catapult-assisted take-off but arrested recovery (CATOBAR), and thus is the version intended for carrier service.

Carrier operations demand aircraft with slightly different flying characteristics compared to land-based aviation, and the F-35C has slightly larger wings and control surfaces than the F-35A, partly in compensation for the folding wingtip sections. The landing gear is also strengthened. After a long and troubled programme of development, the first F-35C carrier landing took place on 3 November 2014 aboard the USS *Nimitz*, and

CARRIER UAVS

While land-based military aviation gravitates ever more quickly towards the development and deployment of combat Unmanned Aerial Vehicles (UAVs), the US Navy has been a little more cautious in its approach to UAVs on carriers. In 2010/11, the US Navy launched the Unmanned Carrier-Launched Airborne Surveillance and Strike (UCLASS) programme, intended to define and develop a naval UAV, primarily for stealth strike missions but also with the possibility of providing air-to-air support for piloted fighters during air-superiority engagements. Development contracts were awarded to Boeing, General Atomics, Lockheed and Northrop Grumman in August 2014, and prototypes emerged. Two Northrop Grumman X-47B UAVs – Salty Dog 501 and Salty Dog 502 – demonstrated that UAVs could safely land on and take off from carriers, but in 2015 the Navy shut down the Unmanned Combat Air System Demonstrator (UCAS-D) programme, deciding that the focus should be on unmanned aerial refuelling vehicles as a proof of concept, before the step was taken towards combat UAVs. At the time of writing, attention is directed to the Boeing MQ-25A Stingray as the Carrier-Based Aerial-Refueling System (CBARS). The Stingray is a tailless drone powered by a Rolls-Royce AE 3007N turbofan. The aircraft will be capable, eventually, of transporting 15,000lb (6,800kg) of aviation fuel (currently it is often other

Hornets that perform the air-to-air refuelling role), extending the combat radius of 4–6 Hornets by 700nm (810 miles/1,300km). The MQ-25s are being slowly introduced into carrier service, partly with the intention of seeing how successfully they integrate into overall carrier aviation before UAV combat carrier aircraft are considered more fully.

BELOW The future of carrier aviation? An X-47B Unmanned Combat Aerial Vehicle (UCAV) demonstrator flies near the USS *George H.W. Bush* (CVN-77). *(US Navy photo by Erik Hildebrandt/Released)*

since early 2018 operational testing has been conducted aboard the USS *Abraham Lincoln*. Squadron-size operational deployments to US carriers are intended to begin in 2020, with the long-term aim of replacing the Hornet and Super Hornet squadrons.

Flight operation planning

A carrier operation begins with the development and propagation of an Air Plan, which is essentially a detailed outline of every aspect of the intended sorties. Several elements and bodies feed into the production of the Air Plan. Taking the chain of command back to source, the context for the Air Plan is typically an Air Tasking Order (ATO) produced by the theatre Air Operations Center (AOC) under the direction of the Joint Force Air Component Commander (JFACC). The ATO specifies the sorties required for a 24-hour period, defining the sorties by mission, aircraft type, targets, call signs and various other required information. When it arrives with the carrier, the ATO will be sent to the Operations Department, where the flight operations will be scheduled by two divisions within the department: Air Operations and Strike Operations.

Using the ATO, the personnel of Strike Operations will map out the Air Plan, which digs into the practical requirements for the forthcoming sortie. Air Plan elements include:

a. *Event numbers*
b. *Launch times*
c. *Recovery times*
d. *Mission*
e. *Number and model of aircraft, including spares*
f. *Total sorties*
g. *Sunrise, sunset, moonrise, moonset, moon phase*
h. *Date*
i. *Fuel*
j. *Alert aircraft*
k. *Logistics aircraft*
l. *Tactical frequencies*
m. *Ordnance loading*
n. *Daily Air Plan Cartoon*
o. *Notes as required. Notes shall include the following:*
   i. *EMCON/Zip Lip conditions*
   ii. *Ready deck schedule*
   iii. *Any other hazards/restrictions to flight or other pertinent information.*
(US Navy, 2014, 2-2)

Once Strike Operations has prepared the Air Plan, it then goes to the Operations Officer, via the Air Operations Officer, for approval and signature. If it is approved, it is then submitted to the squadrons and the various other agencies on board the ship responsible for making the operation a reality. Under normal conditions, the Air Plan is typically distributed the evening before the operations, although under high-tempo combat conditions the advance warning might be a matter of mere hours.

Events, cycles and weather criteria

Before delving into the practical implementation of the Air Plan, it is worth clarifying some fundamental governing principles of carrier operations. The CVW organises its missions on the basis of Cyclic Operations, which are defined as 'the continuous process of launching and recovering aircraft'. Cyclic Operations also help break down the carrier's operational efforts into understandable packages called 'cycles'. Each cycle consists of a specific number of aircraft being launched and recovered as a group, with each of these cycles typically having a duration of about 1 hour 30 minutes, although this duration can be significantly affected by the requirements of the ATO and the limitations of fuel provision, or, conversely, the availability of air-to-air tanker refuelling. Cycles are also known as 'events'.

A very useful explanation of the nature of carrier cycles/events comes from the 2014 US Naval Air Training Command publication *Flight Training Instruction: CV Procedures (UMFO) T-45C*:

Each cycle, or event, is usually made up of 12–20 aircraft. These events are sequentially numbered and correspond to the respective cycle in the 24-hour fly day. Event 1 corresponds to the first cycle, Event 2 to the second cycle, and so on. Prior to flight operations, the aircraft on the flight deck are arranged ('spotted') so that Event 1 aircraft can easily be taxied to the catapults once they have been started and inspected. Once the Event 1 aircraft are launched, which generally takes about 15 minutes, Event 2 aircraft are readied for the next cyclic launch. The launching of aircraft makes room on the flight deck to land aircraft. Once Event 2 aircraft are launched, Event 1 aircraft are recovered, fueled, re-armed, re-spotted and readied to be used for Event 3. Event 3 aircraft are launched, followed by the recovery of Event 2 aircraft (and so on throughout the fly day/night). After the last launch of the night, all of the aircraft are generally stored up on the bow in order to keep the landing area clear until the last aircraft lands. They are then re-spotted about the flight deck and secured until the next morning's first launch.
(US Navy, 2014, 2-3)

The challenge of carrier air operations is therefore to synchronise and control this ballet of aircraft, within the confines of schedules and safety parameters that can be measured in matters of minutes if not, at crucial moments, in seconds.

Another key factor governing carrier air operations is the weather. Windspeeds are not so much of a problem for carrier aircraft, to a degree. Indeed a strong headwind is a positive advantage by increasing the airspeed over the wings, adding natural lift to supplement the speed generated by the catapult launch and the jets' own thrust. As part of the carrier's launch procedure, it will turn directly into the wind for launches, supplementing the headwind with the speed of the carrier itself (up to 30 knots), although navigational and operational requirements will typically limit the amount of time a carrier can remain sailing onwards in one direction, and there may be a break in events while the carrier turns about and sails back to its starting point. (For this reason, meteorological reports are a key ingredient of the carrier's tactical options.)

Strong winds do affect air operations, however, when they produce heavy seas, which in turn results in the pitch and roll of the flight deck. The extent of this movement can be severe enough to override the capabilities of some of the carrier's major landing instruments, such as the Improved Fresnel Lens Optical Landing System (IFLOLS – see page 101). Excessive crosswinds can also have a dangerous impact upon aircraft recovery operations. If, for example, the recovery crosswinds are greater than 7 knots, 'rates of descent 3 to 6 feet per second in excess of those experienced during normal operations can be expected, even with corrective pilot technique' (US Navy, 2007a, 8-2). Because of the US supercarriers' stabilisation systems, the carrier aircraft can continue to operate in severe weather conditions, although the greatest of the challenges during these conditions is aircraft recovery, where the deck constantly presents itself at different angles to the line of approach.

Prior to the launch of the first event,

the ship's meteorological personnel begin feeding regular weather reports, predicting visibility as much as possible and refreshing the forecasts every 30 minutes. A key tool in the meteorologists' arsenal is the Hazardous Weather Detection and Display Capability (HWDDC) system, which underwent installation on *Nimitz*-class carriers from 2007. The HWDDC is a weather radar processor and web-display server that takes real-time weather radar data and imagery from the SPS-48E radar system and converts it to accurate and understandable weather measurements, displayed as a straightforward web page. In addition, the carrier weather experts rely on satellite feeds, but also on traditional weather-reading instruments (anemometers, wet-and-dry bulb thermometers, aneroid mechanical barometers, etc) that have graced ships for centuries.

Of greatest importance for carrier operations is visibility conditions. Poor visibility has many tactical implications, ranging from navigational problems to interference with precision-guided munitions (PGMs), but for the CVW and flight control and flight deck personnel the most pressing of the issues is how visibility affects aircraft launch and recovery.

In naval aviation, the visibility conditions are defined according to one of three 'Cases':

a. *Case I departures and recoveries are utilized during daytime operations (day ops) when weather conditions are VMC. Case I weather requires the ceiling to be no lower than 3,000 feet and not less than 5 NM visibility.*

b. Case II operations are utilized during day ops when it is anticipated the aircraft may enter IMC. Case II weather requires the lowest ceiling to be 1,000 feet or above and 5 NM visibility. Case II is normally called for when an overcast layer is present.
c. Case III weather is any ceiling below 1,000 feet or a visibility less than 5 NM. All night operations are conducted under Case III. For the purpose of determining Case III operations, night is defined as 30 minutes prior to sunset until 30 minutes after sunrise.

(US Navy, 2014, 2-4)

The weather conditions rarely result in a cancellation of flight operations, unless they are truly extreme, but they do have an important effect upon operational planning and the procedures used by flight deck personnel and those involved with air traffic control, as we will see later.

Catapult launch

About 60–90 minutes before flight operations commence, all air crew and related operational personnel attend a pre-flight briefing, a short meeting that provides key mission information, such as 'current and forecasted weather, the ship's current and forecasted position, significant operations in the area, recent intelligence analysis, SAR (or Combat Search and Rescue (CSAR)) specifics, divert airfield information and current operating conditions in the region' (US Navy, 2014, 2-4). Then the strike lead will brief on the specifics of the mission itself, providing details on targets, timings and the necessary coordination between multiple aircraft.

Once the mission parameters are understood by all, the air crew consults with the aircraft maintenance control to ensure that all is ready with the aircraft. Particularly important is that they study the Aircraft Discrepancy Book (ADB), which records the aircraft's weight, including the weight of fuel and stores. All these weights need to be correct so that the proper catapult launch settings can be made; verified weight information is sent to the FDC via a Weight Sheet (or Weight Chit) or through computerised means.

With this procedure completed, the air crew now suit-up for operations, and head up to the

BELOW An F/A-18F Super Hornet of Strike Fighter Squadron 103 on the flight deck of USS *Dwight D. Eisenhower* (CVN-69) during operations in the Arabian Sea in December 2006. *(US Navy photo by Petty Officer 3rd Class Jason Johnston/Released)*

ABOVE Aviation Boatswain's Mate (Equipment) Airman Ryan Martin, right, shows Aviation Boatswain's Mate (Equipment) Airman Nicoles Schulmeister how to signal properly with a weight board during flight operations aboard USS *Nimitz* (CVN-68). *(US Navy photo by Mass Communication Specialist 3rd Class Jake Berenguer)*

NATOPS RECOMMENDED PRE-FLIGHT CARRIER AVIATION CHECKS

Once at the aircraft, conduct a normal preflight in accordance with NATOPS. Begin the preflight by checking the area around the aircraft for FOD, leaking or pooling fluid (oil, hydraulic fluid, fuel, etc.) and the general condition of the aircraft. Take note of any intake/exhaust covers on the aircraft. Make sure tie down chains are not rubbing against any brake lines or hydraulic lines. Observe whether a tow bar is connected and that the nosewheel is centered. Check the landing gear struts, tire pressure and integrity, launch bar, and holdback. Inspect the tailhook and ensure the hook point is greased. If the tail of the aircraft is over water, do not attempt to preflight that portion of the aircraft. The plane captains will check your tailhook during the hook check after taxiing clear of the edge. During the preflight, remain vigilant of jet exhaust and other hazards.

After manning up, conduct normal cockpit inspection and checks, ensuring both ANTI-SKID switches are set to OFF. Check that the cockpit panels, gauges and instruments are secure. Loose gauges or instruments can be dangerous during a catapult launch. All crews must be strapped in and ready to start no later than 30 minutes prior to scheduled launch. The Air Boss will make a 'start engines' call over the flight deck announcing system (5 MC), and the start signal will be given by the yellowshirts. At that time, and not before, crews will run through the normal start sequence adhering to any plane captain signals.

(US Navy, 2014, 2-5)

flight deck in full flight gear typically no later than 45 minutes before launch. There they conduct their pre-flight checks (see feature box).

Once the aircraft has started, the chocks and chains are removed and the aircraft taxies up to the catapult, where a green jersey member of the flight deck crew will display the aircraft's loaded weight on a weight board; the pilot checks the figure against the weight chit, indicating if they match (thumbs up in daylight, or circling flashlight at night) or making adjustments if they do not.

Catapult procedures

Following directions from the taxi director, the pilot positions the aircraft correctly for the launch. A series of hand signals provide the directions. Note that if the hand signals are performed above the waist, they are intended for the air crew, whereas below the waist they are meant for the flight deck crew. The signals are as follows:

BELOW Greenshirts rush forward to retrieve a holdback bar following the launch of an F/A-18E Super Hornet assigned to Strike Fighter Squadron (VFA) 195 aboard USS *Ronald Reagan* (CVN-76). *(US Navy photo by Mass Communication Specialist 2nd Class Tyra M. Campbell/Released)*

a. **Extend launch bar**: Director rests right elbow in left palm at waist level with right hand held up vertically and then brings right hand down to horizontal position.

b. **Disengage nosewheel steering**: Director points right index finger to his nose and presents a lateral wave with open palm of the left hand at shoulder height.

c. **Taxi ahead**: Director extends arms forward at shoulder level with hands up at eye level, palms facing backward and makes beckoning arm motion, speed of arm movement indicates desired speed.

d. **Slight turn left/right**: Director will nod head in direction of turn while giving taxi ahead signal.

e. **Brakes on (when in holdback)**: Director extends arms above head with open palms toward aircraft and then closes fists.

f. **Tension**: Director extends arms slightly overhead with fists closed and then opened with palms forward (indication to release brakes); then hand toward bow is swept down to a 45-degree position toward deck, while other hand is swept up 45 degrees toward sky. Pilot releases brakes, heels to deck, stays at idle awaiting runup signal.

g. **Retract launch bar**: Director rests right elbow in left palm with right arm extended horizontally at waist level and then raised to vertical.

h. **Engine runup**: Catapult Officer/Catapult Safety Petty Officer (CSPO) makes circular motion with index and middle finger at head level. Pilot advances throttle to MRT and executes Control Check 'wipeout' and engine instrument check. [MRT is 100% thrust in the 'normal engine' state, *ie* without afterburner; with afterburner is Combat-Rated Thrust (CRT).]

i. **Acknowledge salute**: Catapult Officer/CSPO returns salute.

j. **Launch signal**: Catapult Officer/CSPO squats, touches the deck and returns the hand to horizontal in the direction of the launch.

k. **Hang fire**: Catapult Officer/CSPO extends right-hand index finger overhead and points horizontally at left palm extended vertically.

l. **Suspend**: Catapult Officer/CSPO raises arms above head with wrists crossed (indicating the launch is to be suspended).

m. **Throttle back**: Catapult Officer/CSPO extends arm in front of body at waist level and thumb extended up, then grasps thumb with other hand and rocks as if pulling throttle back.

(US Navy, 2014, 2-7)

A. AIRCRAFT POSITIONING

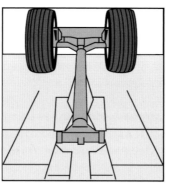

B. AIRCRAFT ENGAGEMENT

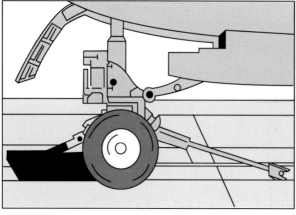

C. AIRCRAFT HOOKUP

Eventually the catapult director will signal the pilot to extend the launch bar, at the same time disengaging the nosewheel steering (NWS). If the alignment is correct, the launch bar will engage with the shuttle, and the aircraft will stop moving as the holdback engages the catapult buffer. The pilot now applies the brakes, but when he receives the 'take tension' signal from the catapult director, he releases the brakes, causing the aircraft to squat. The catapult director now gives the 'run-up' signal, and the pilot runs the engine up to 95%, at this point placing the launch bar switch to 'RETRACT'. Now the pilot takes the engine run-up to maximum power, at which point he gives a right-handed salute to the Catapult Officer/CSPO, to indicate that he is ready for launch. The officer will make some final checks, ensuring that the flight deck is clear of individuals and obstructions, then he bends down and touches the deck to signal the launch. The catapult is now fired, with launch

ABOVE Sanding and lubricating a catapult track on the flight deck of USS *Abraham Lincoln* (CVN-72), to ensure the catapult's smooth running. *(US Navy photo by Mass Communication Specialist Seaman Mohamed Labanieh/ Released)*

LEFT A topside petty officer for the waist catapult checks that the holdback bar is in place prior to launch. *(US Navy photo by Mass Communication Specialist Seaman Kyle D. Gahlau/Released)*

ABOVE A Grumman C-2A Greyhound prepares for launch from catapult No. 3 aboard the aircraft carrier USS *Carl Vinson* (CVN-70) during flight deck certification off Virginia in July 2009. Note that the C-2 is equipped with the eight-blade Navy Propeller 2000 (NP-2000). *(US Navy photo by Mass Communication Specialist 2nd Class John Shepherd/Released)*

speed reached in about two seconds; as a general rule, the aircraft should achieve 120 KIAS (knots indicated air speed) by the time it reaches the edge of the deck.

Departure procedure

Depending on the weather conditions outlined above, the flightpath taken by the aircraft as they leave the carrier changes accordingly.

Case I – The aircraft leaves the catapult and establishes a positive rate of climb, the pilot makes a clearing turn, climbs to 500ft and sets on a parallel base recovery course (BRC), which means the course on which the ship is currently sailing. This departure is flown at 500ft (152m) and 300 KIAS until the aircraft reaches 7 DME at which point the aircraft climbs on

visual meteorological conditions on course. DME stands for Distance-Measuring Equipment, which is equipment (airborne and ground) used to measure the slant range distance of an aircraft from the DME navigation aid, in nautical miles.

Case II – The Case II launch proceeds in much the same way as in Case I, with the aircraft performing the clearing turn and going to 500ft (152m) at 300 KIAS on parallel BRC. At 7 DME the pilot turns to intercept the 10 DME arc, continuing the turn until the aircraft moves on to a departure radial. At this point the 500ft limitation is lifted if the pilot can continue to climb in visual conditions.

Case III – A Case III departure is one that launches into the most severe weather conditions or into darkness. To ensure that safe distance is maintained between aircraft, 30 seconds is imposed between launches. When launched, each aircraft climbs straight ahead at a speed of 300 knots (555km/h), crossing 5nm (9.2km) at 1,500 AGL (Above Ground Level, different from altitude, which is calculated as above sea level) or above. At 7nm (13km), the aircraft turns to intercept the 10nm (18.5km) arc, continues climbing and joins the departure radial.

LEFT Shooters aboard USS *Abraham Lincoln* (CVN-72) make the final gesture indicating that the F/A-18E Super Hornet can now launch. *(US Navy photo by Mass Communication Specialist 3rd Class Jeremiah Bartelt/Released)*

Aircraft recovery – systems

As the opening of this chapter explains, landing aircraft on a carrier is one of the most hazardous and demanding activities in all the armed forces. Only a combination of very intensive training of air crew (including the repeated monitoring of pilot performance), the coordinated efficiency of the flight deck personnel, plus the use of advanced landing technologies, prevents disaster happening on a regular basis. In the remainder of this chapter, therefore, we will look in detail at the process by which aircraft are recovered safely to the flight deck. Before explaining how this process is designed and enacted, however, we first need to familiarise ourselves with the key pieces of technology used to bring aircraft down safely on to a very small piece of solid ground in the middle of endless ocean.

TACAN

TACAN stands for Tactical Air Navigation system, and it is fitted to all air-capable US Navy ships (it is also a common land-based system). Often referred to as 'father', TACAN is polar-coordinate a type radio air-navigation system that provides a TACAN-equipped aircraft with the following information:

■ Distance information.
■ Bearing information, specifically in reference to magnetic north of the location of the TACAN surface facility in relation to the aircraft's position.
■ An identification signal composed of a two- or three-character Morse code signal to identify the TACAN surface facility being used.

Inside the aircraft, the pilot can observe TACAN displays, which give the distance of the aircraft (in nautical miles) from the surface beacon and

the direction of flight, in degrees-of-bearing, to the geographic location of the surface beacon. Pilots can therefore use the bearing and distance from a beacon, and use it to fix their geographic position.

IFLOLS

A little background history is best for understanding IFLOLS. In the early days of carrier aviation, the pilot landed on a carrier flight deck largely guided by his own visual judgement, aided by a Landing Signal Officer (LSO) waving coloured flags, paddles or other indicators to provide a degree of correction from the flight deck. This system worked reasonably in the prop era, when aircraft landing speeds were relatively low, but fared less well in the subsequent jet age. As aircraft landing speeds

ABOVE Crash-and-Salvage team members attach the sling of a carrier vessel crash crane to an F/A-18 Hornet in order to remove the aircraft from the landing area of the flight deck during a drill aboard the USS *George Washington* (CVN-73). *(US Navy photo by Photographer's Mate 3rd Class Michael D. Blackwell II/Released)*

RIGHT Interior Communications Electrician 3rd Class Christopher Perez controls the Improved Fresnel Lens Optical Landing System (IFLOLS) from Pri-Fly aboard USS *Dwight D. Eisenhower* (CVN-69). *(US Navy photo by Mass Communication Specialist Seaman Apprentice Dartez Williams/Released)*

became ever quicker, the distance at which they had to acquire visual landing guidance extended well beyond that which a human with a flag in each hand could provide. It was clear that technological assistance was now required.

Britain's Royal Navy arrived at the first solution to what is known as an Optical Landing System (OLS), with the Deck Landing Mirror Sight (DLMS). Developed by Commander (E) H.C.N. Goodhart RN in the late 1940s and early 1950s, the DLMS was based on the idea of placing a large mirror on angled-deck aircraft carriers, in which the pilot could physically see his approach relative to an ideal glidepath. Due to the sheer size of the mirror required, this idea was impractical. Goodhart resolved the issue by instead using a small gyroscopically stabilised concave mirror on the port side of the carrier, framed either side by lines of green-coloured datum lights. Into the mirror itself was shone an orange source light, which the pilot could acquire visually several hundred yards away from the ship. To achieve and maintain the correct landing glidepath, the pilot had to keep the orange light – or the 'meatball' as the US Navy adopters soon called it – level with the datum lights. If the meatball was above the datum lights, he was too high, and too low if the meatball was below the datum lights.

Although the DLMS did not do away with the requirement for an LSO, it did significantly improve the accuracy of carrier deck landings. In the hands of the US Navy, the DLMS was soon improved, in the form of the Fresnel Lens

Optical Landing System, or FLOLS. As the title of this system suggests, FLOLS replaced the single optical mirror with a Fresnel lens, a lens formed from a series of annular steps rather than a single sheet of glass, resulting in intensive magnification of light sources. First developed in the 18th century, the Fresnel lens took its name from French physicist and engineer Augustin-Jean Fresnel, who applied the system with great effect to lighthouses, a technology still in use today.

FLOLS worked on the same principle as the DLMS, but offered greater precision through projecting five vertical source lights, and improved the clarity and range of visual acquisition.

The Mk 6 Mod 3 FLOLS came into service in the early 1970s and remained on US carriers until the late 1990s, when it was replaced by the Improved Fresnel Lens Optical Landing System (IFLOLS). The functional principles behind both FLOLS and IFLOLS are essentially the same, therefore we will describe the latter system in detail. The chief differences to note are that IFLOLS has a total of 12 vertical source lights, as opposed to the FLOLS' seven, providing even greater precision in glideslope information, with the vertical coverage increased to 1.7 degrees, as compared to the 1.5 degrees of FLOLS. It also uses a fibre-optic source light projected through the Fresnel lens, with a visual acquisition range of 1.5nm (2.8km), compared to 0.75nm (1.4km) in FLOLS.

In more detailed description, IFLOLS features a lens assembly – a box containing 12 vertical cells through which fibre-optic light is projected. The upper ten of the lights are amber in colour, while the bottom two lights are red. The glidepath adopted by the pilot determines which of the source lights is visible, the light seen being the 'meatball', or simply 'ball'. The position of the ball is relative to the horizontal banks of green datum lights, ten each side of the source lights, on the exact midpoint. As with previous OLS types, the position of the ball in relation to the datum lights tells the pilot whether he is too high or too low on the approach. If the pilot can see the red lights at the bottom of the source light strip, he is dangerously low.

If the pilot uses IFLOLS optimally, it will take him on a 3.5-degree glideslope to intercept

BELOW **The IFLOLS lighting configuration.** *(US Navy)*

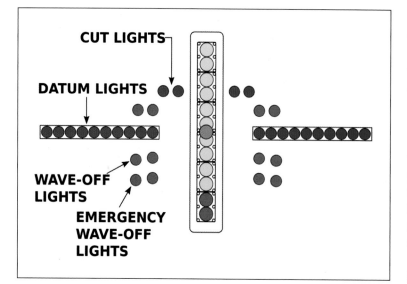

the No. 3 wire. To ensure that the information remains stable despite sea conditions, IFLOLS has three stabilisation modes:

- **Line stabilisation** – compensates for the ship's pitch and roll.
- **Inertial stabilisation** – compensates for pitch and roll, but also for the heave (up and down motion) of the flight deck.
- **Point stabilisation** – fixes the glideslope at a point about 2,500ft (762m) aft the lens.

There are some other lights on the IFLOLS display that give the pilot important information. Four green 'cut lights' are mounted horizontally and centred astride the upper half of the source lights. These lights are used by the LSO during what are known as 'Zip Lip' (no radio communications) or similar Emissions-Controlled (EMCON) landings. The NATOPS manual explains:

As the aircraft approaches the groove, the LSO will momentarily illuminate the cut lights to indicate a 'Roger ball' call. Subsequent illumination of the cut lights indicates a call to add power. Zip Lip is normally used during day Case I fleet operations to minimize radio transmissions.

EMCON is a condition where all electronic emissions are minimized.

(US Navy, 2014, 1-12)

There are also panels of red 'wave-off lights', seven either side. The purpose of these lights, which are also controlled by the LSO, is to tell the aircraft to perform an immediate wave-off (*ie* abort the landing and fly past the carrier). This is a compulsory instruction, usually given when the deck is 'foul', meaning that there are people or other obstructions in the landing area.

MEATBALL MOTHERHOOD

The following rules for 'meatball motherhood' – in other words, how to make the correct approach in relation to IFOLS – are provided in official US carrier manuals:

a. Attempt to fly the 'cresting' ball, because slightly above glideslope (high) is better than below (low).
b. Never lead a low or slow.
c. Always lead a high or fast.
d. If low and slow, correct low then slow.
e. If high and fast, correct fast then high.
f. Fly the ball all the way to touchdown.
g. Never re-center a high ball in close, but stop a rising ball.

Automatic Carrier Landing System (ACLS)

The ACLS is specifically the AN/SPN-46(V)3 Precision Approach Landing System (PALS) manufactured by Textron Systems. It displays 'needles' that indicate aircraft position in relation to glideslope and final bearing. The system incorporates a ring laser gyro stabilisation unit to stabilise the system across a variety of sea states, and uses two DBR antennae and transmitters to provide accurate glideslope and azimuth information to two aircraft in a 'leapfrog' pattern (as one aircraft lands, the ACLS acquires another aircraft).

The ACLS is a highly sophisticated system;

in its most advanced setting what is referred to as the 'look ma, no hands' approach to landing on an aircraft carrier. It offers four basic modes for approach:

Mode I – an automatic approach in which the aircraft flight controls are coupled with the ACLS. Command and error signals are sent to the aircraft, and the aircraft's onboard systems translates them into control actions, providing a hands-off approach and landing (essentially an auto-pilot landing).

Mode I Alpha – an automatic, hands-off approach up to the visual acquisition of the IFLOLS, at which point the pilot takes over and flies the recovery himself.

Mode II – similar to an ILS approach. Error signals are transmitted to the aircraft, which displays the needles on a crosshair display.

Mode III – Carrier-Controlled Approach (CCA), akin to a Ground-Controlled Approach (GCA). The controller provides azimuth and glideslope information to the pilot.

The ACLS is currently intended to serve aboard US aircraft carriers until 2025, by which time it will be replaced by the next-generation JPALS (see feature box).

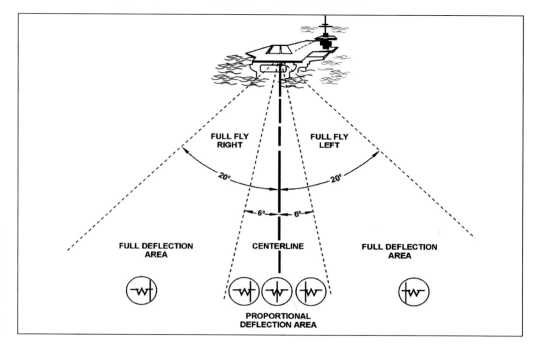

RIGHT A diagram showing correction to the final bearing using an ICLS, ACLS or other Carrier-Controlled Approach (CCA).

(US Navy)

JPALS

A next-generation landing system to be installed on US aircraft carriers is the Joint Precision Approach and Landing System (JPALS), manufactured by Raytheon and approved for production by the Naval Air Systems Command (NAVAIR) on 25 March 2019. It is designed to be installed in all three variants of the Lockheed Martin F-35 Lightning II plus the MQ-25A Stingray in-flight refuelling UAV, although Raytheon states that it has facility to fit the technology aboard any aircraft with a GPS, an inertial navigation system, a reprogrammable radio and appropriate levels of digitisation, an umbrella that includes the Super Hornets, the Osprey and the Hawkeye. The corresponding shipboard system will ultimately be fitted to all 11 serving US Navy carriers.

As officially described, the JPALS is a differential, GPS-based precision landing system to guide aircraft on to carrier or assault vessel decks, providing a form of 'tunnel' on the pilot's heads-up display, down which he flies the aircraft to a consistent landing point every time. Specifically, Raytheon states that the system will take the aircraft to a landing spot just 8 × 8in (20 × 20cm) on the deck, even in adverse weather and Sea State 5 conditions, the integrity of the connection protected by anti-jamming and encryption technology. JPALS has a long reach – a pilot making an approach for landing will first connect to the system at 200nm (370km) distance, at which point they will start to receive range and bearing information. At 60nm (111km), the aircraft is then automatically logged into a JPALS landing queue, entering two-way data-link communication. From 10nm (18.5km), the pilot then begins to receive precision landing data, provided by visual instructions, and he follows this data until the point of touchdown. What is critically different about JPALS is that it relies purely upon automatic digital communication; there are no radio transmissions between a pilot and air traffic control. As such, JPALS takes its place within a family of innovation that promises greater automation in the carrier operations of the future.

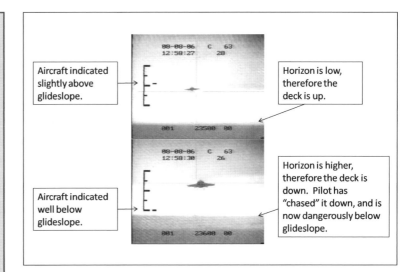

Aircraft indicated slightly above glideslope.

Horizon is low, therefore the deck is up.

Aircraft indicated well below glideslope.

Horizon is higher, therefore the deck is down. Pilot has "chased" it down, and is now dangerously below glideslope.

Instrument Carrier Landing System (ICLS)

The ICLS uses the AN/SPN-41 transmitters to give the pilot an alternative source of instrument approach information. The system has two transmitters, one for azimuth located at the stern of the ship, and one for elevation situated above the flight deck, aft of the island. Aboard the aircraft, the ICLS receiver shows the angular information via a crosshair indicator, with the vertical needle of the display corresponding to azimuth and the horizontal needle corresponding to elevation, or glideslope. NATOPS provides further important clarifications: 'Because the ICLS is a one-way transmission from the ship to the aircraft receiver, it is susceptible to pitching deck conditions. In order to differentiate between ICLS and Automated Carrier Landing System (ACLS) approaches, the ICLS is referred to as "bull's-eye"' (US Navy, 2014, 1-10). So, while the ICLS can provide a useful guidance information 20 miles (32km) out from the carrier, just prior to landing the pilot will switch to a visual landing aid system, such as IFLOLS.

Manually Operated Visual Landing Aid System (MOVLAS)

Should IFLOLS fail for any technical reason, such as equipment malfunction or the limits of the stabilisation system being exceeded, MOVLAS is available as a backup shipboard landing aid system (it is also used for pilot/LSO training). MOVLAS has a similar lighting system as IFLOLS, designed to provide glidepath

ABOVE The view of the MOVLAS Repeater on the Integrated Launch and Recovery Television Surveillance System (ILARTS). *(US Navy)*

information, with the key difference that the LSO directly controls the position of the ball via a hand controller. A MOVLAS repeater is also located on the LSO platform, so that the LSO can monitor the glideslope that is being presented to the pilot.

MOVLAS can be operated in three modes:

Mode I – in this instance the light box is installed on the port side directly in front of the IFLOLS lens, with MOVLAS presenting the meatball information but using the datum, wave-off, and cut lights of IFLOLS.

Mode II – in this setup, MOVLAS is completely independent of IFLOLS, located 75–100ft (23–30.4m) aft of the inoperable IFLOLS system. As well as the meatball presentation, here MOVLAS also uses its reference datum, wave-off and cut lights.

Mode III – this installation is similar to Mode II, but is located on the starboard side of the flight deck, aft of the island structure.

Long-Range Laser Lineup System

The Long-Range Laser Lineup System is a visual aid to the pilot to assist with proper lineup during the approach to the carrier. It uses a system of

eye-safe, low-intensity, colour-coded laser beams projected out to a distance of 10 miles (16km) at night. The colour and flash tempo of the lasers as perceived by the pilot indicate whether he is on the centreline to touchdown or he needs to correct a degree of error. On the centreline, with just 0.5 degrees of variation, he will see a steady yellow light. As he goes off course, the lights will change as follows:

Error to starboard:
Steady green – 0.75 degrees
Slow green flash – 4.0 degrees
Fast green flash – 6.0 degrees

Error to port:
Steady red – 0.75 degrees
Slow red flash – 4.0 degrees
Fast red flash – 6.0 degrees.

Drop-Line Center Line Extension

Not an electronically active guidance feature, the Drop-Line Center Line Extension is a vertically aligned sequence of lights at the stern of the ship, these extending down from the centreline on the landing deck. On the approach to the ship, if the glidepath is correct, the pilot will see the deck centreline and the dropline properly aligned; if the glidepath needs adjustment, the dropline will either be port or starboard of the deck centreline.

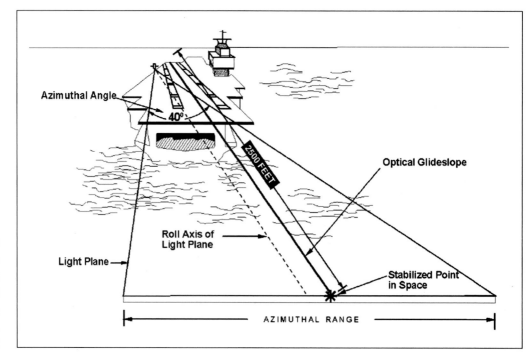

RIGHT A diagram entitled 'Characteristics of point-stabilized plane' shows the ideal glidepath into a carrier for optimal recovery.
(US Navy)

The features described above are the major landing systems the pilot and the flight controllers will use during aircraft recovery, but there are others (without being exhaustive) that deserve a brief mention. The Virtual Imaging Systems for Approach and Landing (VISUAL) is an electro-optical sensor and display system that shows both ship personnel and approaching pilots enhanced images of the aircraft and ship, respectively, in low visibility and night conditions. It integrates an Electro-Optical Tracking System, LSO Workstation and Fixed Glidepath Sensor, which together not only provide visual acquisition of the aircraft but also display key information regarding approach and landing. Related to visual presentation of landings, all take-offs and recoveries are filmed and recorded, from multiple positions. The Integrated Launch and Recovery Television Surveillance System (ILARTS) delivers a CCTV display of carrier flight operations, displaying the images in real time to TV monitors in key flight locations around the ship, including the LSO HUD (head-up display), the flag bridge, the navigation bridge, the Combat Information Center (CIC), the squadron ready rooms, the flight-deck and aviation maintenance control centers and Pri-Fly Control. Sewing all the information sources together is the Integrated Shipboard Information System (ISIS), a data management system used by the CATCC and Pri-Fly to collate, distribute and display core flight information between all relevant parties.

CATCC

Much like any regular airport or military air base, a carrier requires sophisticated air traffic control, and this is delivered via the Carrier Air Traffic Control Center (CATCC). The CATCC, located below deck in a small, busy, digitally illuminated room, has three major functions:

a. Tracking the status of all carrier flight operations.
b. Control of all airborne aircraft within the Carrier Control Area (CCA) not under the control of the tower (Air Boss). The CCA includes all airspace within 50nm (92.6km) of the carrier.
c. Providing departure and approach radar control of aircraft at night and in IMC.

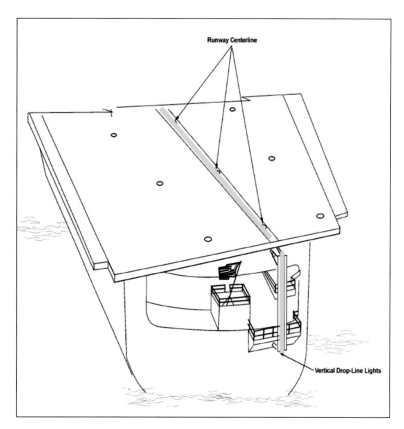

ABOVE The Drop-Line Center Line Extension lights at the rear of the carrier help the pilot to make a precise alignment with the centreline of the recovery flight deck. *(US Navy)*

BELOW The Air Boss position in Pri-Fly. *(Patrick Bunce)*

ABOVE Two Air Traffic Controlmen track aircraft and communicate with pilots during flight operations in the CATCC aboard USS *Harry S. Truman* (CVN-75). *(US Navy photo by Mass Communication Specialist Seaman Donovan M. Jarrett/ Released)*

The CATCC divides itself into three key branches: Air Ops, the ATO (within Air Ops) and CCA.

Air Ops

The Air Ops branch is responsible for ensuring that accurate and timely information and critical flight operations data is distributed to all relevant personnel throughout the ship. The branch includes the following personnel, with details given here on their principal duties (note that in every case the list is far from exhaustive), as provided in NAVEDTRA 14342A, *Air Traffic Controller (AC)* (US Navy, 2011):

Air Operations Officer
- Review Air Plan for fuel and logistics requirements.
- Supervise and coordinate the execution of the Air Plan.

- During flight operations, remain informed of the status of an aircraft operating under CATCC control, and ensure that all pertinent information is provided to other carrier work centers and personnel including Commanding Officer, Bridge, Pri-Fly, Strike Operations, COC, Handler, LSO, etc.
- Ensure that all operational information (excluding intelligence information) required for the aircraft missions are provided to pilots prior to and during flight operations.
- Ensure that all pertinent flight information is provided to inbound and outbound flights between the carrier and shore facilities.
- Conduct air wing and squadron briefings as required to evaluate flight operations.

Air Operations Watch Officer
- Ensure that CATCC is manned 1.5 hours prior to scheduled flight operations and that the checklist specified in CV NATOPS is accomplished.
- Ensure Prelaunch Briefing information is timely and efficiently distributed 2.5 hours prior.
- Provide the Bridge, Pri-Fly, Strike Operations, Aircraft Carrier Intelligence Center (CVIC), Operations Officer, CCA, Carrier Air Group (CAG), battle group representative, air wing operations, and squadron ready rooms with all pertinent information about flight operations, including any changes to the Air Plan.
- Remain informed of the status of all helicopters operating with the carrier.
- Manage fuel assets, and monitor tanking station assignments and tanking procedures.

RIGHT With arrestor hook and landing gear down, an F/A-18E Super Hornet from Strike Fighter Squadron (VFA) 103 makes a recovery approach to the flight deck of USS *Abraham Lincoln* (CVN-72). *(US Navy photo by Mass Communication Specialist Seaman Apprentice Stephanie Contreras/Released)*

- Ensure that accurate divert/bingo fuel and foul-deck endurance information is recorded for each aircraft model. ['Bingo' fuel means that the aircraft has just enough fuel to reach its landing point, as long as any other manoeuvres cease immediately.]

ATO

- Act as the point of contact for transfers of passengers, mail and cargo.
- Prepare messages pertaining to ATO functions.
- Establish and utilize a priority system for manifesting personnel for flight aboard CODs/VODs in accordance with OPNAVINST 4630.25.
- Be familiar with load capacity/restrictions, survival equipment carried, and emergency egress procedures for all aircraft types used for logistics purposes.
- Ensure proper personnel, equipment, and materials are positioned to facilitate rapid loading and unloading of COD/VOD aircraft to minimize on-deck time and to lessen the impact on scheduled flight operations.

Air Operations Supervisor

- Ensure assigned personnel are properly trained and qualified for the following tasks: Air Ops Plotter, Status Board Keeper, Land/Launch Recorder.
- Ensure Air Ops is properly manned and ready for flight operations.
- Ensure status boards are accurate and complete.
- Ensure all Air Ops personnel know and

understand communication and patch panel procedures.
- Ensure all CATCC systems/equipment are being operated per Emission Control (EMCON) restrictions.
- Ensure the Master Air Plan is maintained and that changes and revisions are disseminated to all relevant work centers and personnel including CDC, Pri-Fly, Strike Operations, squadron ready rooms, CCA, CVIC, Flight Deck Control (FDC), Bridge, battle group representative, and air wing operations.
- Ensure pre-launch information is accurate and complete.

Air Ops Plotter

- Obtain the ship's position every hour during non-flight operations and every 30 minutes during flight operations. Correlate the position with the Direct Altitude and Identity Readout (DAIR) and Ship's Inertial Navigation System (SINS) position.
- Determine the range and bearing to divert/bingo fields and nearest land, and update the status boards in Air Ops and CCA.
- Depict ship's position in relation to airways, hot areas, etc. on appropriate charts.
- Record weather at ship and bingo fields on status boards in Air Ops and CCA.

Status Board Keeper

- Check the communications equipment for proper operation with Pri-Fly, CDC, FDC, squadron ready rooms, and CCA.
- Exchange information as required with Pri-Fly, CDC, FDC, squadron ready rooms, and CCA.

ABOVE The T-45C Goshawk is the primary carrier aviation training aircraft. This one, assigned to Training Air Wing (TW) 2, performs a touch-and-go landing on the flight deck of USS *John C. Stennis* (CVN-74) in the Atlantic Ocean in 2019. *(US Navy photo by Mass Communication Specialist 3rd Class Ikenna Tanaka)*

- Obtain aircraft side numbers and pilot names from FDC/ready rooms.
- Maintain status boards with aircraft side numbers, event numbers, and pilots' names.
- Record the time of launches and landings.
- Record/update fuel states.
- Record pertinent remarks such as bolter, wave-off (foul deck and technique), hung/unexpended ordnance, divert/bingo, and any other aircraft information that may/will affect launch and recovery operations.
- Update aircraft lineup information during Case III operations.

Carrier-Controlled Approach (CCA)

- CCA controllers 'provide sequencing and separation to aircraft during launches and recoveries.'

CCA Officer/CCA Watch Officer

- Prior to the commencement of flight ops, identify any problems that may/will affect launch and recovery operations and formulate plans, whenever possible, to minimize the impact of the problems.

- Prior to Case II and III events, determine the Departure Reference Radial (DRR) instrument approach procedure and marshal radial.
- During flight operations, coordinate with Air Ops Watch Officer and Air Boss regarding recovery order, ramp time, deck conditions, emergencies, etc.
- Ensure that all relevant information about launch and recovery ops is disseminated to CCA, including type of departure/recovery (Case), instrument approach procedure, BRC, break/ramp time, DRR, airspace constraints, other scheduled flight ops, system or equipment casualties and malfunctions, environmental factors, etc.
- During flight operations, ensure that all aircraft conform to departure and recovery procedures and that adequate separation is provided between departing and recovering aircraft during Case II and III operations.
- Monitor aircraft and tanker fuel states, tanker refueling system status and coordinate refueling operations with Air Ops and Departure Control.

BELOW Lt John Mackowski, assistant Air Operations Officer, monitors fuel states for airborne aircraft in the Carrier Air Traffic Control Center (CATCC) aboard USS Harry S. Truman (CVN-75). *(US Navy photo by Mass Communication Specialist 2nd Class Kilho Park)*

CATCC Supervisor

- Assist the CCA Watch Officer in the performance of duties and responsibilities.
- Prepare CCA watch station assignments.
- Ensure that CCA is properly manned and ready for flight operations.
- Ensure that systems and equipment are evaluated, casualties and malfunctions are reported, and coordinate as necessary with maintenance personnel for appropriate action.
- Identify all airspace constraints that may affect launch and recovery operations.
- Review relevant information about scheduled flight operations including the Master Air Plan, tanking plan, COMMPLAN, Card-of-the-Day, EMCON conditions, etc.
- Monitor all aircraft fuel states.

Departure Control

- Maintain adequate separation and ensure safety of flight.
- Review the Air Plan and the tanking plan. Evaluate systems and equipment. Report casualties and malfunctions to the CATCC Supervisor.
- Identify all airspace constraints that may affect launch operations.
- Prior to commencement of flight ops, provide aircraft [with] any changes in flight composition, mission assignment, type of departure (Case), DRR, BRC, Position and Intended Movement (PIM), launch time, etc.
- Coordinate with CCA Watch Officer about all aspects of tanking operations, including tanker give, low-state or potentially low-state aircraft, changing weather conditions that may affect tanking operations, etc.

Marshal Control

- Maintain adequate separation and ensure safety of flight.
- Review the Master Air Plan.
- Evaluate system equipment communication status.
- Identify airspace constraints that may/will affect recovery operations.
- Coordinate with CATCC Supervisor for type of recovery (Case), expected BRC, expected marshal radial for fixed-wing aircraft and helicopters, expected final bearing, expected

type of approach, bolter holes, break/ramp time, first push time, DRR, etc.
- Ensure CCA Recovery (Marshal) Board is accurate and complete.
- Provide control instructions to aircraft that have commenced approach, when required.
- Issue vectors and/or speed changes to maintain separation.
- Monitor fuel states.

Approach Control

- Maintain adequate separation and ensure safety of flight.
- Review the Master Air Plan.
- Provide instructions, assistance and flight following to diverted/bingoed aircraft.
- Maintain count of aircraft launched and remaining to be launched.
- Provide relevant launch and recovery information to the planeguard helicopter, when on departure frequency.
- Conduct communication check with planeguard helicopter every 20 minutes during Case III operations (may be performed by Departure Control).

Final Control

- Maintain adequate separation and ensure safety of flight.
- Review the Master Air Plan.
- Evaluate system/equipment/communication status.
- Identify all airspace constraints that may/will affect recovery operations.

ABOVE A Naval Air Crewman (Helicopter) of the Helicopter Sea Combat Squadron (HSC) 8 gives a thumbs-up to an MH-60S Seahawk, also assigned to HSC-8, after landing on the flight deck of USS *Theodore Roosevelt* (CVN-71) during Pacific manoeuvres in 2019. *(US Navy photo by Mass Communication Specialist 2nd Class Anthony J. Rivera/ Released)*

- Coordinate with CATCC Supervisor for type of recovery (Case), expected final bearing, expected type of approach, bolter holes, first push time, etc.
- Provide each aircraft with precision or non-precision approach.

Visual Display Board (VDB) Operator

- Monitor approach frequencies and observe Approach Control radar display to ascertain aircraft recovery order and relative position.
- Maintain an accurate account of aircraft recovery order and relative position on the VDB.
- The VDB Operator should be manned, and maintaining an accurate lineup of airborne aircraft during Case II recoveries. This will help ensure a smooth transition to the Case III environment, if necessary.

Departure Board/ISIS Keepers

- Review the Master Air Plan.
- Evaluate equipment and communication status.
- Prior to the commencement of launch ops, record prelaunch information (e.g., event number, scheduled launch time, expected type of launch, expected DRR, expected BRC, ship's weather, altimeter, aircraft event numbers, side numbers and missions; tanker information; base information and comments, when required).

- After the commencement of launch ops, record BRC and DRR; monitor the departure button to obtain and record aircraft launch times and profile; and monitor the tanker button to obtain and record tanker fuel state, give and altitude, receiver aircraft fuel state, and the progress of the refueling operation.
- Coordinate with Departure Control, as required, to maintain an accurate and complete account of launch operations.
- After the completion of launch ops, communicate aircraft that launched to the Marshal Board/ISIS Keeper.

Marshal Board/ISIS Keeper

- Review the Master Air Plan.
- Evaluate equipment and communication status.
- Prior to commencement of recovery ops, record pre-recovery information: event number, expected type of recovery (Case), expected type of approach, expected final bearing, break/ramp time, aircraft side numbers (in expected recovery order), expected marshal radial, DME, altitude, EAT, approach/final button, and bingo or tank fuel state. After recording information, check accuracy of aircraft information by comparing with Air Operations Launch and Recovery status board. When aircraft begin to check-in with Marshal Control, monitor marshal button to obtain and record assigned recovery order, marshal radial, distance, altitude, EAT, approach/final button, fuel state, and any additional information regarding emergencies, malfunctions, etc.

Approach Board/ISIS Keeper

- Review the Master Air Plan.
- Evaluate equipment and communication status.
- Record final bearing/BRC and downwind heading; monitor approach/final buttons simultaneously, with a split headset, to obtain and record aircraft fuel state, approach status, profile and outcome.
- Coordinate with Marshal and Approach Control as required, to maintain an accurate and complete account of recovery operations.
- After completion of recovery operations, check accuracy of Air Operations Launch and Recovery Status Board.

BELOW The CATCC aboard USS Enterprise (CVN-65), the banks of screens showing aircraft state and position. (DoD/PH3 Carolla Bennett)

From the above list of duties, we can discern several overlapping themes. All the CATCC personnel are practically engaged with the fulfilment of the Air Plan, monitoring that plan against the unfolding airspace reality. They must all ensure the accurate recording of decisions and transfer of information between stations; a fluid communications choreography is at the heart of an effective CATCC. Note also the importance of fuel-monitoring processes. Modern jet aircraft are fuel-hungry beasts. As a general rule, naval ATCs are taught that a typical jet fighter uses fuel at approximately 100lb (45kg) per minute, and that the lower the altitude the greater the fuel consumption, thus on many occasions a jet will be virtually running on empty by the time it lands. Upon approaching the carrier, the pilot may give one of two verbal alerts to his fuel status. If he says 'minimum fuel', this alerts CATCC that the aircraft can have little or no delay in landing, although the situation is not severe enough to require that the aircraft is given priority over other immediate landings. If there are traffic conflicts or decisions to be made about priority, however, the 'minimum fuel' aircraft should be pushed to near the front of the queue. Should the pilot declare 'low or emergency fuel', this is a genuine emergency. He will report to the CATCC the amount of fuel remaining and the ATCs will clear the way for his landing or immediate refuelling by other F/A-18s. As we can see, if the relationship between fuel consumption and recovery procedure is not managed properly, then mere minutes can make the difference between an aircraft landing safely or ditching into the sea. To advise on fuel issues, and any other issues of aircraft damage and flying conditions, the CATCC room also includes representatives from each of the squadrons in flight.

Recovery process

Once the carrier aircraft have performed their mission, then it is time to head back to the carrier. 'Time' is the key word here. Although carriers are perfectly ready to accommodate operational modifications to schedules, in most cases the aircraft will have a scheduled cyclic land time, usually dictated by

ABOVE Aviation Boatswain's Mate (Equipment) 1st Class Brandon Benedict makes his final checks on an aircraft catapult prior to flight operations aboard USS *John C. Stennis* (CVN-74). *(US Navy photo by Mass Communication Specialist 3rd Class Kyle Steckler)*

the realities of fuel consumption. As the aircraft turns back, the pilot contacts the CSG Air Defense Controller (Red Crown) and alerts him to his approach. This is important, and we must remember that one of the roles of the warships that surround the carrier itself is to act as air defence pickets, destroying any approaching hostiles before they can attack 'Mother'. Red Crown then passes the communications over to Strike Control, and any relevant information to the recovery – aircraft condition (including fuel state), weather, predicted Case recovery etc –

RIGHT An EA-18G
Growler assigned
to the 'Vikings' of
Tactical Electronic
Warfare Squadron
(VAQ) 129 aligns itself
for a landing aboard
USS *Ronald Reagan*
(CVN-76) in 2009.
*(US Navy photo by
Mass Communication
Specialist 3rd Class
Torrey W. Lee/Released)*

is exchanged prior to the aircraft entering the Carrier Control Area (CCA) at 50nm (57.5km) from the carrier.

As the aircraft enters the CCA, Strike Control hands over the aircraft to the Marshal Control in the CATCC. The flight leader will inform the Marshal Control of his altitude, the aircraft with the lowest fuel state in the flight (in hours and minutes for helicopters and pounds weight for fixed-wing aircraft), the total number of aircraft in the flight, the type of PALS approach requested, and any other information that might affect the landing. In return, the marshal controller communicates essential approach information to the pilot, such as case recovery holding instructions (including holding altitude), weather conditions at the ship, altimeter settings and BRC and bingo information. He also establishes the initial sequencing and separation of aircraft.

Case I recoveries

The exact process of the recovery operation changes according to weather/visibility conditions, as defined by the Case system explained earlier. A Case I situation is naturally the most convenient recovery setup, with no significant restrictions upon visibility. The pilot notifies the Marshal Control that he has visual contact with the carrier with a 'see you' call,

and in these instances the Marshal Control can hand over the aircraft straight to Pri-Fly for landing guidance.

No later than 10nm (11.5km) out, the aircraft is given its required holding altitude, which it maintains as it flies into a left-hand holding pattern, meaning that the aircraft flies a long circle, 5nm (5.75km) in diameter around the carrier anti-clockwise. So that all participants have a common understanding of the position of the aircraft in the pattern flow, the flight circle is broken into four points: Point 1 is at the 3 o'clock position, almost directly overhead the carrier but leaning to the starboard side, then Points 2, 3 and 4 follow sequentially in 90-degree increments. Each squadron in the holding 'stack' must maintain its given altitude; the lowest altitude will be 2,000ft (610m) AGL and there will be minimum of 1,000ft (305m) between each squadron. When the aircraft have to perform altitude changes, which they will do as they progressively move down for landing, all climbs are performed between Points 1 and 3 of the holding pattern and descents between Points 3 and 1.

On the flight deck, aircraft may well be undergoing launch, and once the last aircraft has gone, or the aircraft in the holding pattern receive a 'Signal Charlie' call from the tower, the recovery process can now begin in earnest. The lower flight in the stack now breaks the holding pattern, flying out on a heading of roughly 210 degrees to the BRC. The other flights in the stack now logically shift their holding altitudes down to the next stage. An important consideration for Case I landings is that they are usually conducted under Zip Lip conditions, thus the pilots themselves must accurately determine when to

depart holding, fly to the initial [a point 3nm/5.6km/3.5 miles astern the ship at 800ft/240m, paralleling the ship's BRC] and break. The goal is to arrive in the groove just as the flight deck is made ready for recovery operations (ready deck). This is called breaking the deck and is a skill that must be mastered in order to maximize the efficiency of recovery operations.

(US Navy, 2014, 2-15)

As they depart holding, the aircraft drop down an altitude of 800ft (244m) outside of Point 3 and proceed to the initial, then continue inbound and fly just outboard of the starboard side, paralleling the BRC. The 'break' is a level, 180-degree turn performed in front of the ship, in which the aircraft drops down to 600ft (183m), lowers its landing gear, and swings back around the port side of the carrier, ready to then turn into the BRC again and fly in for the final landing.

It is crucial that the timing of the break is performed at the correct intervals, with the break interval set by the last aircraft in the landing pattern. Note that

No breaks will be performed more than 4 NM ahead of the ship. If you are unable to break before 4 NM, you will have to depart and reenter the pattern. To accomplish this, maintain 800 feet until 5 NM, then climb to 1,200 feet and execute a left-hand arc back to the initial. Tower must be notified of your intentions.

(US Navy, 2014, 2-15)

If more than six aircraft are arriving off the fantail at roughly the same time, the flight will be instructed to 'spin it', climbing and turning until the correct landing interval can be established.

Having made the break, the aircraft will then proceed to the '90' directly astern of the carrier, dropping the altitude to 450ft (137m), before then going to the '45' – directly lined up with the angled recovery deck – at 325–375ft (99–114m). Although this sounds simple in description, in reality the pilot will be working extremely intensively to make all turns with precision. Too long or too short a turn can spoil the landing relationship between an aircraft and its wingman, who is following relatively closely behind in preparation for his own landing. On the flight deck, they typically allow just 45 seconds for an aircraft to touch the deck, arrest, come to a complete stop and be wheeled out of the way for the next landing.

At about ¾-mile (1.2km) distance, the pilot will start to pick up the visual cues from FLOLS. Tim Hibbetts, a US Navy aviator, here

BELOW A Case I landing pattern. *(US Navy)*

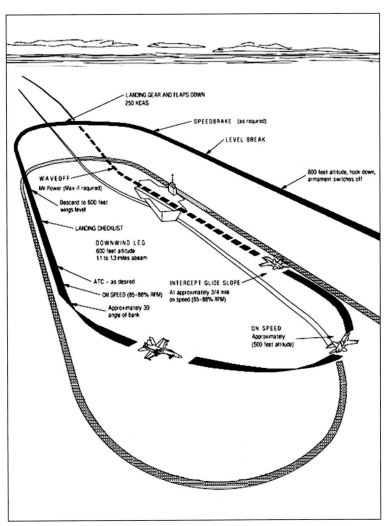

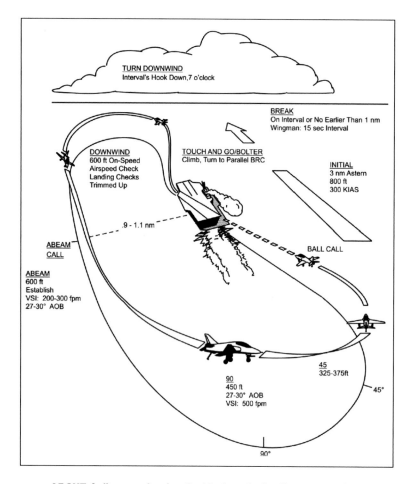

TURN DOWNWIND
Interval's Hook Down, 7 o'clock

BREAK
On Interval or No Earlier Than 1 nm
Wingman: 15 sec Interval

DOWNWIND
600 ft On-Speed
Airspeed Check
Landing Checks
Trimmed Up

TOUCH AND GO/BOLTER
Climb, Turn to Parallel BRC

INITIAL
3 nm Astern
800 ft
300 KIAS

.9 - 1.1 nm

ABEAM
CALL

BALL CALL

ABEAM
600 ft
Establish
VSI: 200-300 fpm
27-30° AOB

45
325-375ft

45°

90
450 ft
27-30° AOB
VSI: 500 fpm

90°

ABOVE A diagram showing the ideal carrier landing pattern, the aircraft making progressive descents and turns until it finally runs into the angled landing strip on the '45'. *(US Navy)*

explains the optical principles of FLOLS from the pilot's standpoint:

The Fresnel Lens Optical Landing System is going to show you – when everything is aligned – how high you are compared to the ideal. The green reference lights show where the ball should be and then it rises and falls based on your distance from the optimum glide path. Way out at ¾ of a mile, each of the five cells is about 30' high, so you'd have go 30' higher to show one cell of motion up. Once you cross the ramp, you only have to go up or down 2.4' to show a whole cell of motion. When you touch down, to put the hook in between the 2- and 3-wire, your eyes are going to be in an 18" high window. If the ball is at the top, you're going to sail over the wires. If it's at the bottom, it turns red and means you're dangerously close to striking the ramp and potential catastrophe.
(https://www.quora.com/What-is-it-like-to-land-on-an-aircraft-carrier/answers/5075475)

By focusing intently on the ball, the pilot will adopt both the correct glidepath and the right alignment with the centreline of the carrier, the latter essential for preventing the landing aircraft striking any of the many others parked on the

RIGHT Pri-Fly controls, looking aft of the ship. Personnel in these positions will keep track of aircraft during the approach to final recovery. *(Patrick Bunce)*

flight deck. But at the same time, the pilot must also make adjustments based on the movement of the flight deck and the effects of crosswinds. One interesting moment described by Hibbetts is when the aircraft hits the 'burble', an area of disrupted airflow about ¼–½-mile (0.4–0.8km) behind the carrier caused by the carrier's huge island cutting the air flow. Further problems are caused by warm air rising off the deck producing unwanted lift.

Well before all this is going on, the flight deck crew are themselves in flat-out activity. A full description of their duties during this phase would take a short volume in itself, but the following are key preparations and procedures:

- The arresting gear officer checks the status of the deck for recovery operations, ensuring that there are no obstructions, that all personnel are on station and that the arresting gear is functional. He notifies Pri-Fly when the deck is ready.
- The LSO Spotter/Talker makes sure that the platform is ready for recovery, turning on deck status lights and also establishing voice comms with the recovery stations or CATCC. (Comms between all the various elements of the flight deck personnel are tested prior to recoveries.) When the LSO is confident that all is ready, he reports 'Manned and Ready' to the Air Officer.
- The Air Officer completes a Recovery Checklist, which includes: Case recovery and time; confirmation of first ramp time with CATCC and the bridge; obtains expected BRC; announces at 15 minutes before landing 'Man all recovery stations'; determines the aircraft recovery status (numbers, type, fuel, unexpended ordnance etc).
- The Pri-Fly Arresting Gear Controller reports all recovery stations manned.
- The Recovery Officer (AGO) again makes sure that the landing area is clear, and that mechanical features such as waist catapults are properly configured for landings.

After the LSO reports 'Manned and Ready', the bridge gives clearance for landings to begin and lens and deck lighting is turned on (unless operational requirements dictate otherwise). A 'Land Aircraft' announcement is made. As

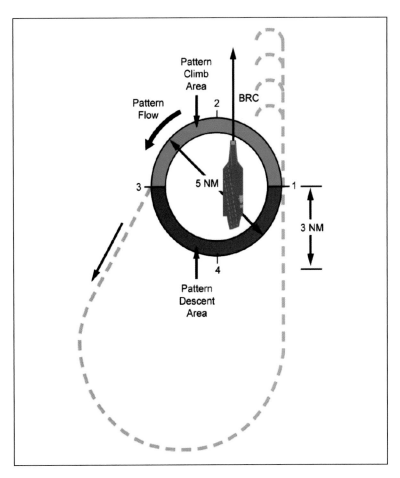

the aircraft approaches, the Air Officer now determines the aircraft type and directs that the arresting gear and lens be set, the former in terms of its arresting weight. The Primary Flight Arresting Gear Controller enters the aircraft type into the Arresting Gear Pri-Fly Operator flat panel and informs the Arresting Gear Engine Operator to verify the setting required for the next aircraft. There follows a complex but thorough cross-check system to ensure that the arresting gear is properly configured for the aircraft about to touch down.

At the same time, the Deck-Edge Operator checks that all the deck pendants are deployed properly, being taut and retracted, with the arresting gear in battery, while the Arresting Gear Engine Operators report arrestor gear engine settings. The IFLOLS Console Operator readies the IFLOL system, monitoring the equipment for any signs of malfunction. When all the arresting gear checks have been made, the Arresting Gear Officer changes the deck status light from red to green; if at any point he switches it back to red, this means that the

ABOVE A Case I overhead holding pattern. Note how a circular flightpath has specific climb and descent sections, in 180-degree arcs.
(US Navy)

deck is 'foul' and landings cannot proceed unless the problem is resolved and the light is switched back to green. (The light is switched to red the moment a jet touches down, and is only switched to green again when the next landing is approved.)

The moment is arriving for the aircraft to make its final touchdown. By this stage, the LSO Spotter/Talker has informed the LSO of the aircraft type and whether the gear, flaps and arresting hook are down, all this information conveyed with a simple 'Hornet, All Down!' He also tells the LSO that the arresting gear is set, the weight setting for the aircraft and whether the deck is clear or foul (depending on the deck light illumination); a sample phrase might be: 'Gear Set, Three Six Zero, Hornet, Clear Deck'.

During a Case I landing, the LSO input will be minimal in terms of communications, to maintain radio silence, but he monitors everything with laser-like focus, and can order the aircraft to 'wave-off' if the approach isn't satisfactory. Any wave-off is classed as a mandatory instruction, *ie* one that the pilot must obey. It might be on account of pilot error (see 'Grading the Landings' box), but it can also result from factors such as a fouled deck, excessive wind conditions or mechanical problems with the aircraft or arresting gear. If the wave-off command is given, the pilot will push the power to MRT, retract his speed brakes, maintain the landing altitude and fly flat over the flight deck, unless directed by the LSO or the Tower to make a starboard pass. After passing the ship's bows, the aircraft parallels the BRC, climbs up to 600ft (183m), and turns downwind to re-establish itself in the landing pattern. A 'touch-and-go' or 'bolter' is performed

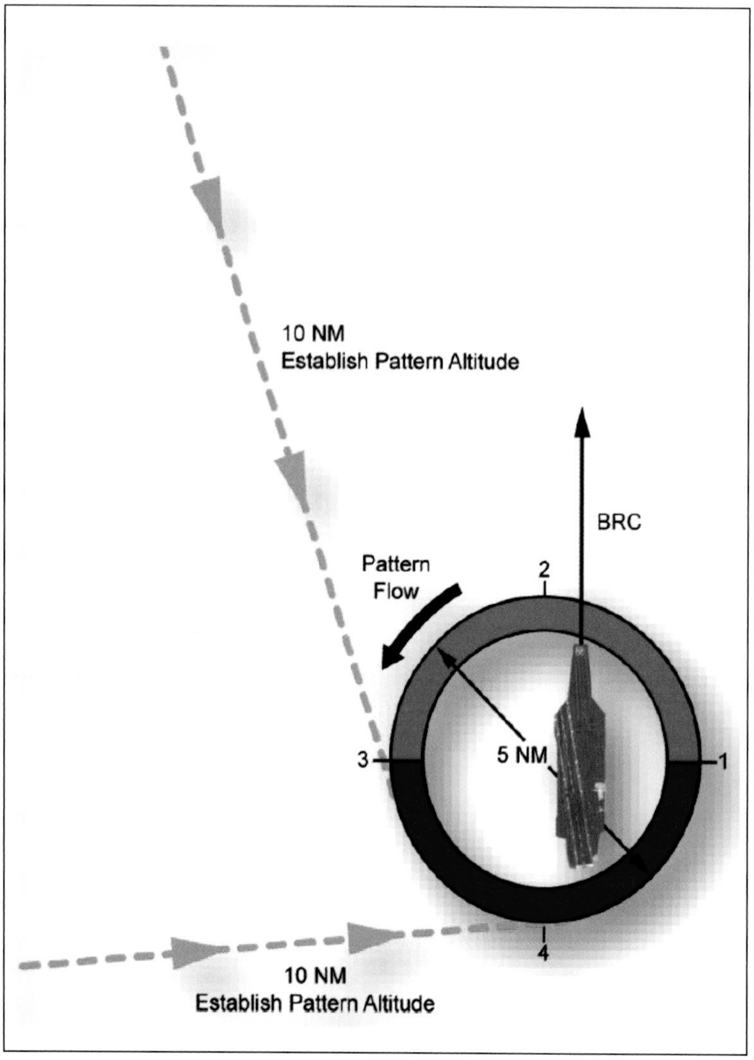

BELOW A Case I port holding pattern entry, with the holding altitudes established at 10nm (18.5km).
(US Navy)

10 NM
Establish Pattern Altitude

BRC

Pattern Flow

2

3 — 5 NM — 1

4

10 NM
Establish Pattern Altitude

GRADING THE LANDINGS

As well as performing a vital role in guiding an aircraft down on to the flight deck, the LSO is also responsible for grading each of the landings in terms of its quality. These grades are very much a matter of public record, as they are posted on what is known as the 'Greenie Board' in the carrier's ready room. Each landing is given a coloured sticker to indicate the landing status:

Green – OK: the landing was performed well, with no errors.
Yellow – Fair: the landing was satisfactory, but there were some minor errors.
Brown – No grade: landed, but with gross errors.
Red – Wave-off: the landing was refused because of approach errors, the pilot being sent around again.
Blue – Bolter: the aircraft's wheels touched down, but the pilot had to take off again because of failure to arrest.

The main objective of every carrier pilot is to keep a consistent line of green, with possibly the occasional yellow. Too many reds and blues can result in the pilot's naval aviation career coming to an end.

LEFT LSOs observe a Boeing F/A-18F Super Hornet assigned to VFA-11 touching down on the flight deck of USS *Harry S. Truman* (CVN-75), during flight deck certifications in the Atlantic Ocean. *(US Navy photo by Mass Communication Specialist 3rd Class Kristopher Wilson/ Released)*

LEFT An F/A-18F Super Hornet of Strike Fighter Squadron (VFA) 122, performs a touch-and-go – note the absence of arrestor hook – on USS *Nimitz* (CVN-68). *(US Navy photo by Mass Communication Specialist Seaman Keenan Daniels/ Released)*

when an aircraft has touched down on the flight deck, but fails to engage the arresting gear. Much like the wave-off, the pilot in this instance advances power to MRT, retracts the speed brakes and rotates up and off the flight deck.

All being well, however, the carrier pilot takes his aircraft down for a successful landing. The principle is basically that of maintaining correct power, ball relationship and flight deck adjustment all the way down until the wheels touch the deck and the arresting gear brings the aircraft thumping to a halt in about two seconds:

Carrier Arrestment*. Execute the approach exactly as a touch and go, flying the ball all the way to touchdown. When the aircraft touches down, advance the power to MRT and retract the speed brakes. Do not anticipate an arrested landing. Maintain MRT until the aircraft comes to a complete stop and the yellowshirt located at the 1 to 2 o'clock*

position signals for power back. The yellowshirt will then signal for brake release and a pull-back, followed by a stop signal and hook up signal. The pull-back allows for the wire to clear the hook. If the pilot applies the brakes during the evolution, the aircraft will tilt back, potentially damaging the tail section. Follow the yellowshirt's instructions/ commands.

(US Navy, 2014, 2-17)

Once the aircraft is down, then the flight deck crew will quickly move it to a parking area on the deck for post-flight procedures, such as removing unspent ordnance, refuelling (if required) or maintenance.

Case II landings

In Case II landings, the weather ceiling is below 1,000ft (305m) and 5nm (9.2km) visibility. One key factor that distinguishes Case II and

BELOW An SH-60B Seahawk assigned to the 'Saberhawks' of Helicopter Anti-submarine Squadron Light Four Seven (HSL-47) prepares to land aboard the USS *Abraham Lincoln* (CVN-72). *(US Navy photo by Photographer's Mate Airman James R. Evans/Released)*

III landings from Case I is that the level of communications between ship and aircraft is raised – especially at night and in severe weather, there is no Zip Lip.

A Case II is, as its number implies, half-way between a Case I and Case III. Indeed, official Navy manuals explain that for a Case II:

Case III procedures are used outside 10 NM and Case I procedures are used inside 10 NM, or after reporting 'see you.' This approach will be flown until the ship is in sight, at which point, the flight will contact tower and proceed inbound as if Case I. If the flight does not see the ship by 5 NM, the aircraft will be vectored into the bolter/wave-off pattern and instructions will be given for a Case III recovery.

(US Navy, 2014, 2-19)

Once the Marshal in the CATCC directs a Case II/III landing, the aircraft moves into a Case II/III marshal pattern holding fix, explained as follows:

Ideally, the holding fix will be on the 180 radial relative to BRC. Weather and airspace considerations may not allow for this. Generally, the holding radial will be within 30 degrees of the 180 radial. Aircraft will hold on the assigned radial at a distance equal to 1 NM for every 1,000 feet of altitude plus 15. In other words, the distance of the holding fix is determined by adding 15 to the assigned holding altitude in angels. For example, if instructed to hold on the 220 radial at angels 8, the fix would be determined as follows:

i. Distance = Angels + 15 = 8 +15 = 23

Therefore, hold on the 220 radial at 23 DME at 8,000 feet. The lowest altitude for assignment is 6,000 feet for turboprop and jet aircraft.

(US Navy, 2014, 2-19)

BELOW Two Aviation Boatswains Mates (Handling) direct aircraft on the flight deck of USS *Dwight D. Eisenhower* (CVN-69). Four colours of illuminated wands are used: amber, green, red and white, each specific to different deck personnel. *(US Navy photo by Mass Communication Specialist 3rd Class Kaleb J. Sarten/ Released)*

The holding pattern forms a six-minute left-hand circuit, with each aircraft in the stack separated by 1,000ft (304m) of altitude. Getting into the holding pattern, as always, requires a high degree of precision, the pilot strictly controlling his relationship to time and space. He has to be ready to make the approach at the Expected Approach Time (EAT) with just plus or minus 10 seconds of time allowance.

Approaches to landing on the carrier during a Case II situation are normally separated by one-minute intervals, as opposed to 30 seconds in Case I. During the approach, the pilot will set his aircraft at a speed of about 250 KIAS and a descent rate of 4,000ft/min (1,219m/min), reducing the rate of descent to 2,000ft/min (607m/min) at 5,000ft (1,524m). When he reaches 1,200ft (366m), the pilot levels off and, if the ship is in sight, reports a 'see me'. If he still can't see the ship by 10nm (18.5km), he makes an authorised descent to 800ft (243m), then if the ship still isn't visible at 5nm (9.2km), he notifies the Marshal for further instructions, vectors into the bolter/wave-off pattern and begins preparations for an instrument approach.

The Marshal now provides the pilot with key information about the landing conditions, including weather, expected EAT and any relevant diversion information. The pilot then continues his approach until the ship is finally in sight, at which point the Marshal switches control of the landing to the Tower and the pilot

approaches and lands in the same manner as a Case I landing.

Case III landings

A Case III landing is just about the most demanding standard manoeuvre a pilot can perform in aviation. Particularly on moonless nights, with poor weather mixed in, the pilot might have almost zero visual contact with the ship until his wheels touch the flight deck. The success of these landings depends squarely upon the pilot's ability to fly via instrumentation only, the ATC's communications with the aircraft and the automated landing systems fitted to both aircraft and carrier.

In Case III conditions, the pilot is directed into the Case II/III holding pattern explained previously; he also makes the same descent pattern, levelling off at 1,200ft (366m). During this time, the Marshal will have been calling out the aircraft's position, and also connecting the aircraft to the ACLS, which occurs at somewhere between 8 DME and 4 DME. Aircraft push times are separated by one minute. At the point of ACLS lock-on, the pilots are trained to compare the needles with bull's-eye (ACLS to ICLS) to ensure a good lock with the system. If there is a disagreement between the pilot's instruments and the approach controller's instruments, the controller will break the lock and the aircraft and ship will establish a new ACLS lock.

The pilot now takes the aircraft in steadily to touchdown, calling the ball at ¾-mile distance. The experience and technical demands of this experience are here recounted by Hibbetts:

The controller on the ship confirms that they've locked you up and tells you to fly 'needles' and you keep pressing in, resetting your RADALT to 400' to warn you that it's time to start looking for a ship. Looking through the HUD at nothing but instrumentation, you start breaking out of the clouds at about a mile, the ship suddenly looming right there where it should be. At about 300' above the water, they tell you, '¾ of a mile, on and on, call the ball'. You've been checking it out for a bit now, making sure that things look good. Sperry (the velocity vector) is out on the

BELOW A Case II approach profile, showing the sequential altitude and speed markers. *(US Navy)*

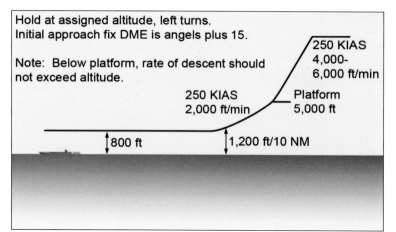

Hold at assigned altitude, left turns.
Initial approach fix DME is angels plus 15.

Note: Below platform, rate of descent should not exceed altitude.

250 KIAS
4,000-
6,000 ft/min

250 KIAS
2,000 ft/min

Platform
5,000 ft

800 ft

1,200 ft/10 NM

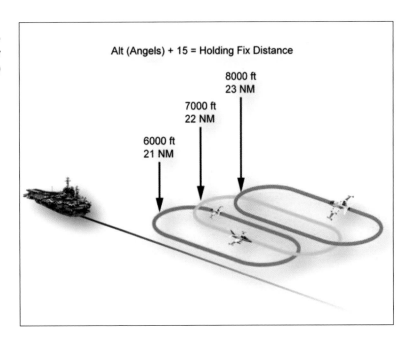

Alt (Angels) + 15 = Holding Fix Distance

8000 ft
23 NM

7000 ft
22 NM

6000 ft
21 NM

bow, but coming slowly to the landing area, the ball is centered up, needles are on and on, in the center of your display, inside the velocity vector when you're doing it right. You've already checked your fuel state and taken off a couple hundred pounds for the last few seconds since you noted it, '411, Hornet ball, 5.5'. So, you've told them your side number, your aircraft type, and your fuel state, in thousands of pounds. Everyone references that state for all the various triggers it will trip, such as when to tank, when to bingo somewhere else, when to rig the barricade. So, you're sounding as confident as you can on the radio and paddles reciprocates with an easy, buy-you-a-drink, 'Roger ball, 15 knots axial'. There are a number of specific calls he can make

BELOW The limited visibility of night operations is highly apparent in this image, which shows an F/A-18F Super Hornet just after take-off from USS John C. Stennis (CVN-74), somewhere in the Atlantic Ocean. (US Navy photo by Mass Communication Specialist Seaman Sarah M. Thielen/Released)

ABOVE An Aviation Ordnanceman folds a wing on an F/A-18E Super Hornet so the aircraft reduces the space it occupies on the flight deck of USS *Abraham Lincoln* (CVN-72). *(US Navy photo by Mass Communication Specialist Seaman Mohamed Labanieh/Released)*

to help you out if he starts seeing you do stuff and you're not recognizing it. No one else talks on the radio after the ship tells you to call the ball until about 45 seconds later, after you've trapped. The LSO owns the radio.
(https://www.quora.com/What-is-it-like-to-land-on-an-aircraft-carrier/answers/5075475)

All being well with the systems and procedures, the pilot should therefore be able to take the aircraft down accurately on to the flight deck for a safe arrested landing, even on the darkest of nights.

Carrier launches and recoveries are the meat and drink of the supercarriers – the entire purpose of their existence. The extraordinary efficiency and regularity with which they are carried out is testament to not only human ingenuity, but more than half a century of hard lessons learned. Accidents are not uncommon, and many pilots will personally know fellow air crew killed during flight operations. As quotidian as carrier air operations can become, they can never be taken for granted.

RIGHT An X-47B UCAS crosses the bows of the USS *George H.W. Bush* (CVN-77), the first aircraft carrier successfully to catapult launch an unmanned aircraft from its flight deck. *(US Navy photo by Erik Hildebrandt/ Released)*

Chapter Five

Major electronic and defensive systems

A supercarrier represents the ultimate target for potential aggressors. For this reason, the *Nimitz* and *Gerald R. Ford* carriers carry with them some of the world's most advanced naval navigational, surveillance and self-defence systems, in addition to those surrounding it in the CSG.

OPPOSITE **The bridge of the USS *John C. Stennis* (CVN-74), packed with GPS navigation systems and SATCOM communications.** *(US Navy photo by Mass Communication Specialist Thomas R. Pittman/Released)*

Explaining in detail all the key electronic systems found aboard an aircraft carrier would be a work of considerable scale, far beyond the scope of this single volume. Entire naval manuals running to many hundreds of pages are produced just on single departmental systems, and indeed individual pieces of equipment. Furthermore, the pace of change in naval technology is relentless, meaning that discussions about a piece of kit used in the here and now can be dated within a matter of years or even months. A big change in this regard is the recent decision of the US Navy, as with all the US armed services, to utilise more commercial-off-the-shelf (COTS) components as opposed to military specifications (MILSPEC) or government-off-the-shelf (GOTS) components.

With this caveat in mind, this chapter provides a survey of some of the most important pieces of electronics aboard *Nimitz*- and *Gerald R. Ford*-class carriers at the time of writing, at least as far as public access reference materials allow. Specifically, we focus our attention upon navigation, radar, electronic warfare (EW) and defensive suites. In the context of the latter, we also study the roles and responsibilities of the Combat Direction Center (CDC) or Combat Information Center (CIC) that handles the carrier's defensive functions, plus describe the specific weapon systems positioned around a modern supercarrier. As we will see, even without its air wing, the modern supercarrier remains a potent weapon platform in its own right.

BELOW The carrier island (this is that of *Dwight D. Eisenhower*) is the primary mounting platform for many of the carrier's antennae and sensors. *(Patrick Bunce)*

Navigation and surface search

The navigation systems utilised aboard a supercarrier are often those that guide many other US Navy surface vessels, as both rely upon the same set of information streams. The one advantage a supercarrier has is an availability of space, both for monitors and kit on the bridge and the related sensors dotted about the ship. Here we give an overview of the types of navigation systems usually found aboard.

During the author's tour of the USS *Dwight D. Eisenhower*, the navigation officer was keen to show me a classic sextant on the bridge, packed in a wooden storage box but at the ready. The officer was also eager to explain that regardless of the advanced systems used by carrier navigators, the age-old skills of navigating by clock, stars and sun are still taught and regularly reinforced. In 2016 a series of media stories broke the news that once again the US Navy was investing in training its sailors in celestial navigation, for the tactical reason that in a future high-tech war there is the possibility that knocking out GPS satellite navigation might be a first move by the enemy. There is also the fact that, much as with the GPS we follow in our cars, electronic systems can make errors; understanding how to sense-check GPS against celestial bodies is a good way of preventing potentially career-ending errors.

The number of what are referred to as 'non-electrical and non-electronic navigation aids' aboard a carrier is surprisingly large. It includes:

■ Magnetic compasses (fixed and portable).
■ Timepieces and chronometers (useful for indicating accurate navigational time).
■ Auxiliary navigation instruments, specified as sextants, stadimeters, protractors, binoculars, alidades, bearing and azimuth circles, hand-held and installed telescopes and clinometers.
■ Audible ship signal devices (bells, gongs and whistles), used for communicating navigation commands in conditions of restricted visibility.
■ Paper navigation charts – produced to high degrees of accuracy, modern charts are a failsafe way of orientation in unfamiliar waters.

Beyond these traditional methods of navigation, however, the modern supercarrier relies upon all the benefits of advanced navigational technology. In the category of 'Electronic Navigation Systems, Radio' the one on which all carriers rely is GPS, which steadily removed the need for the land-based OMEGA and LORAN systems used from the 1960s to the 1990s and the space-based Navy Navigation Satellite (TRANSIT). The primary GPS sensors used aboard US supercarriers until recently have been the WRN-6 Satellite Signals Navigation Set and the SRN-9 and SRN-19 Navy Navigation Satellite System (NAVSAT). At the time of writing, however, a process is under way to replace Navigation Sensor System Interface suites and standalone military GPS receivers (such as the WRN-6) with the new Global Positioning System-Based Positioning, Navigation, and Timing Service (GPNTS), developed by Raytheon. A press article summarises the advantages of this system as:

> The latest Selective Availability/Anti-Spoofing military GPS receivers; digital, nulling GPS anti-jam antennas, and redundant rubidium clocks for synchronized time and frequency. GPNTS is also the lead system for development and integration of maritime domain GPS receivers capable of receiving and using the new military only M-code signal. M-code capable GPNTS systems are expected to be available in 2020.
>
> (https://www.doncio.navy.mil/chips/ArticleDetails.aspx?ID=4618).

The US supercarriers have another tool in their navigational box in the form of Inertial Navigation Systems (INS). An INS generates positional, orientation and velocity information not through the input of external information, but via computers, motion sensors (accelerometers) and rotation sensors (gyroscopes), which basically perform an extremely advanced type of dead reckoning. The three key INS devices aboard the supercarriers are the AN/WSN-7 Inertial Navigation System, the AN/WSN-7A Ring Laser Gyro Navigation Systems and the AN/WSN-7B Ring Laser Gyrocompass. As an example of its capabilities, the AN/WSN-7 continuously calculates and indicates the

ship's position, attitude, heading and velocity in relation to the earth's rotation, and also has the virtue that it cannot be detected or jammed by enemy EW instruments.

In addition to the GPS and INS systems, the *Nimitz* carriers utilise surface-search radars, to provide additional navigation and to scan the seas for the position of other shipping and potential threats. Key commercial radars used have been the SPS-59 (LN-66), the Bridgemaster E (BME) and the Furuno 904. Another key surface-search radar type is the Northrop Grumman Norden Systems SPS-67V, operating at G-band. It delivers navigation, station keeping and general surface-search functions, while the AN/SPS-67(V)3 and (V)5 variants also provide a quick-reaction automated target detection. Raytheon's AN/SPS-73(V)12, an X-Band short-range, 2-D radar system, is fitted to several other *Nimitz*-class vessels, and performs similar surface-search/navigation/target-detection functions.

Air search radar

Air search radar systems are a crucial part of a supercarrier's defensive capabilities, protecting against air threats out to long ranges while also enabling the efficient vectoring of onboard aircraft, or the application of shipboard firepower, to deal with those threats. Looking at the *Nimitz*-class carriers, the major air search radar systems include the ITT SPS-48E and SPS-48G 3-D, operating at E/F-band; the Raytheon SPS49(V)5 on the C/D-band; and the Raytheon Mk 23 Target Acquisition System (TAS) on the D-band. The SPS-48-type radars have been the cornerstone of supercarrier air search for more than five decades. The AN/SPS-48E and G types can detect and track targets to 200nm (370km) distance and up to 69 degrees in elevation, providing target range, bearing and altitude information. Yet in August 2019 it was announced that the SPS-48-type

ABOVE **The US Navy works to ensure that traditional maritime skills stay alive. Here Quartermaster 2nd Class Javen Rogers uses a sextant to take a celestial reading from a weather deck aboard USS *John C. Stennis* (CVN-74) in the Atlantic Ocean, November 2019.** *(US Navy photo by Mass Communication Specialist Thomas R. Pittman/Released)*

BELOW **A traditional gimball compass on the flag deck of the USS *Dwight D. Eisenhower* (CVN-69).** *(Patrick Bunce)*

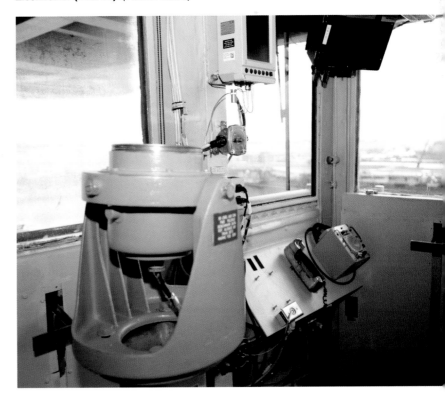

RIGHT The square AN/ SPS-48E 3D air-search antennae dominates the top of USS *Theodore Roosevelt* (CVN-71). To its left is a Mk 95 illumination radar for the Sea Sparrow. *(US Navy photo by H2 Tracy Lee Didas/Released)*

radar would likely be phased out in favour of Raytheon's new SPY-6V2, an active electronically scanned array air and missile defence 3-D radar previously fitted to *Arleigh Burke*-class destroyers as the AMDR (Air and Missile Defense Radar) system. AMDR is composed of 37 individual Radar Modular Assemblies (RMAs), each an active electronically scanned array radar block; the modularity of the system (blocks can be added or removed) means that it can be scaled up or down according to need. The S-band and X-band sensors, allied to a Radar Suite Controller (RSC), produce a system that is highly sensitive and very versatile – it can offer horizon search, precision tracking, missile communication, terminal illumination of targets, periscope detection and even electronic warfare attacks.

The *Gerald R. Ford* class of carriers has taken the air search radars in new directions. *Ford* itself has the DBR from Raytheon, formed by combining the X-band AN/SPY-3 multifunction radar with S-band Volume Search Radar (VSR) emitters, arranged into three phased arrays. The three X-band faces focus on low-altitude tracking and radar illumination, and the three S-band faces perform all-weather target search and tracking, all in a non-moving (ie non-rotating) system that has low-maintenance virtues.

The DBR offers a fast, broad-spectrum response to a highly complex combat airspace. Interestingly, however, the second of the *Ford* class – *John F. Kennedy* – will not receive the DBR but rather the Enterprise Air Surveillance Radar (EASR – also SPY-6). In this system, each EASR array is composed of nine RMAs in a modular arrangement, and together they can provide multiple capabilities simultaneously, including anti-air and anti-surface warfare, air traffic control and some EW.

Communications

In addition to a plethora of standard VHF/UHF radio communications, the supercarriers rely upon secure satellite communications (SATCOM) and fleet broadcast systems to transmit and receive messages among the CSG and across the world, linking the carrier with theatre, regional and national commands. There have been several broad architectures underpinning naval SATCOM. The primary network is provided by a combination of the Defense Satellite Communications System (DSCS), which runs off 14 DSCS-III satellites launched between the early 1980s and 2003, the Global Broadcast Service (GBS) network and the now-ageing Military Strategic and Tactical Relay (MILSTAR) satellites. Together these systems deliver high-bandwidth secure data transfer. The various antennae carried by the *Nimitz*-class carriers to access these networks include the WSC-3 (UHF), the WSC-6 (SHF) and USC-38 (EHF).

Another important comms system used by the supercarriers is the Challenge Athena (WSC-8), designed to transfer high-bandwidth data in a variety of forms – telephone, video conferencing, e-mail, radio, intelligence data and also commercial national television. The latest high-speed version is the Challenge Athena III.

SATCOM capabilities do not stay still. Currently there are two further SATCOM systems being placed into orbit, both of which will integrate with the carriers' comms. One is the Advanced Extremely High Frequency (AEHF) system, a network of six satellites (five have been launched at the time of writing) in geostationary orbit that will replace MILSTAR and will operate at 44GHz Uplink (EHF band) and 20GHz Downlink (SHF band). It will allow data rates of up to 8.192Mbit/sec, and is highly secure against interception and

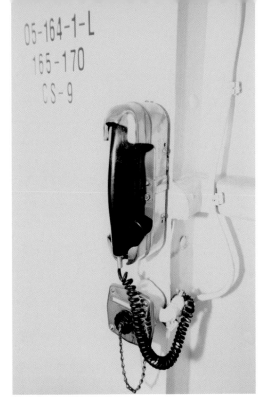

LEFT An internal communications phone aboard the USS *Dwight D. Eisenhower* (CVN-69), logically located next to a bull's-eye marker so the speaker can place himself to the caller. *(Patrick Bunce)*

BELOW The large radome at the top front of the USS *Dwight D. Eisenhower* (CVN-69) houses a SATCOM system, and behind it is the SPS-48E radar antenna. *(Patrick Bunce)*

jamming. The other new network is Wideband Global SATCOM system (WGS), produced as a collaboration between the US Department of Defense and the Australian Department of Defence. The data capabilities of this system are, according to promotional reports, formidable, with a single WGS spacecraft offering as much bandwidth as the entire existing DSCS constellation. The first launch of a WGS satellite was in 2007 and the final is planned for 2023.

Given the constant upgrading of data transfer bandwidths, the supercarriers of the *Gerald R. Ford* class will have communications capabilities that would have been the stuff of dreams to the first crew of the USS *Nimitz*. One notable feature about the new class that it is installed with a Globecomm-designed, multi-functional communications and entertainment system, with the first internet protocol (IP) video system in the US Navy fleet. The combination of powerful SATCOM and an internal fibre-optic network means that the crew will be able to live-stream high-resolution video content even while out on distant seas.

Air defence

Although the US supercarriers are potent in the extreme, no warship is invincible. In recent years, some defence analysts have claimed that the *Nimitz*- and *Gerald R. Ford*-class carriers are becoming increasingly vulnerable to new generations of Russian and Chinese anti-ship missiles, ballistic missiles and torpedoes, which have greater speed, stealth, evasion and explosive force than previous generations of weapons.

We now, therefore, turn our attention to the supercarriers' defensive systems. While we can assess each of the individual weapons in turn, we note that the US Navy has sought to bring the whole carrier defensive suite into a single, holistic operating system. This effort makes sense. If a carrier were to be faced with multiple incoming and fast-moving threats, swarming about the airspace, the last thing needed is lots of uncoordinated unilateral defensive actions, which might duplicate effort and waste critical survival seconds.

The first attempt at integration was the Naval Tactical Data System (NTDS), an early naval computer system that collected data from various sensors around the ship and processed it into a single battlespace picture. This was eventually replaced in the late 1990s by the Advanced Combat Defense System (ACDS), with either Block 0 or the software-improved Block 1 run into all the *Nimitz*-class carriers. The ACDS is a powerful automated command-and-control system for the carriers' defensive suites, but even that was eventually superseded by the Ship Self-Defense System (SSDS), installed aboard some *Nimitz*-class carriers (the first was USS *Dwight D. Eisenhower*) and as standard in the *Gerald R. Ford* class. The SSDS takes information from many different sensors simultaneously – AN/SPS-49 air-search radar, AN/SPS-48E air-search radar, DBR (SPY-3 and SPY-4), AN/SPQ-9B horizon-search radar, AN/SPS-67 surface-search radar, AN/SLQ-32 electronic warfare system, Centralized Identification Friend or Foe (CIFF) – depending on the configuration of the individual carrier. Using its powerful software algorithms, it then fully automates the fire-control process (although humans are in the loop), leading to very fast engage response times and a coherent response to multiple threats.

A good explanation of how this might work in practice comes from an article written in June 2019 for Navaltoday.com, which describes a test of the SSDS on board *Gerald R. Ford* conducted off California. The test simulated two incoming cruise missile threats:

The system incorporates Dual Band Radar (DBR), which searched for, located and tracked the targets. DBR then provided uplink and radar illumination to the Evolved Sea Sparrow Missile [ESSM] to support missile guidance. Raytheon's Cooperative Engagement Capability, or CEC, validated and processed the Dual Band Radar data for SSDS. The SSDS then processed the CEC data, classified the targets, determined the appropriate engagement ranges, passed launch commands to the interceptor missiles, and scheduled DBR support for the engagements. The ESSM engaged and defeated both targets using live and simulated interceptors.

(Navaltoday.com, 2019)

Such formidable defensive technologies, to which we can add those of the other ships in the CSG, means that the future survivability of the supercarriers remains high.

Combat Direction Center/ Combat Information Center

All the ship's defensive suites and systems, with the exceptions of basic weapons such as deck-mounted .50-cal machine guns (used for very close-in defence against small vessels), are handled from the carrier's Combat Direction Center (CDC), also known as the Combat Information Center (CIC); the latter title tends to have been superseded by the former.

The CDC has a broad swathe of responsibilities, but in summary it is there to protect the ship from all surface, air, sub-surface and EW threats. Under the direction of a Tactical Action Officer (TAO), the CDC has authority for weapons release at all times; a fast-incoming anti-ship missile will be moving far more quickly than the traditional chain of command allows.

The CDC is another crowded space on the carrier, with multiple computer stations each manned by crew responsible for individual

ABOVE US Navy sailors maintain an SLQ-32(V)4 shipboard electronic warfare antenna aboard the USS *George H.W. Bush* (CVN-77). *(US Navy photo by Mass Communication Specialist 3rd Class Tristan B. Lotz/Released)*

LEFT An Operations Specialist Seaman operates an advanced combat direction system console in the commanding officer's tactical plot room aboard the USS *Enterprise* (CVN-65), 2011. *(US Navy photo by Mass Communication Specialist Seaman Jared M. King)*

aspects of the ship's defence. Personnel in the CDC include (note that specific titles will alter depending on the carrier):

- ■ **CDC Watch Officer** – Monitors the overall surface and sub-surface threat picture.
- ■ **Air Defense Warfare Coordinator (ADWC)** – Monitors air threats, and takes responsibility for all the air defence weapon systems.

BELOW Operations Specialist 3rd Class Carlos Galicia monitors air contacts within radar range in the CDC aboard the USS *Theodore Roosevelt* (CVN-71). *(US Navy photo by Mass Communication Specialist 3rd Class Joseph S. Yu)*

- ■ **Strike** – These individuals monitor Mode 2 and Mode 4 IFF, classifying aircraft according to whether they are friendly or potential/ actual threats.
- ■ **Tactical Data Coordinator** – Ensures that there are secure and efficient data-links between friendly ships and aircraft.
- ■ **Sensor Operators** – Individuals who operate the various defensive sensors, maximising the returns.
- ■ **ID Operator** – Analyses the returns and provides data from them.
- ■ **Weapons Operators** – There are individual personnel responsible for each of the torpedo, missile and CIWS systems on board.
- ■ **EW Module Operators** – Monitor the EW threats and tracking emitters.
- ■ **Area Intercept Coordinators (AICs)** – Send out aircraft to distant threat interceptions, and maintain comms throughout any engagements.

In terms of how the CDC personnel classify and respond to threats, it is helpful to think of the carrier as at the centre of a series of concentric circles radiating outward, with each circle representing a radius of action. The outermost circle is the province of the carrier's air wing, which can position a Combat Air Patrol (CAP) or interception at about 160–180nm (300–330km) from the carrier. Moving inwards, the next defensive layer will be provided by the other ships of the CSG, which have a formidable array of their own defensive technologies. The exact distance relationship between the carrier and the CSG vessels varies according to the mission and potential threats, but typically the vessels will be either in visual range or just over the horizon. For incoming aerial threats, the next defensive circle will be covered by the Sea Sparrow Missiles, followed by the RAM system. Finally, close-up defence is the province of the CIWS and of the Mk 38 25mm Machine Gun System (MGS). Anything closer than that (such as small boats) will usually be handled by Marines or naval personnel operating machine guns and small arms from the side of the ship.

This illustrative picture of carrier defence is far from watertight, and has many possible instances of overlap and reversal, but it is a useful aid for visualisation. To add more detail to this picture, we will now revisit the circles of defence from the CSG ships inwards, looking at the specific weapon systems within each.

The CSG

The composition of a CSG is variable, but we can generalise with reasonable accuracy. At the heart of the group is the carrier itself, with its embarked air wing of 75–90 aircraft. The CSG will then typically include one or two *Ticonderoga*-class Aegis guided missile cruisers, armed with the Mk 41 Vertical Launch System (VLS) capable of firing Tomahawk cruise missiles (at long-range land targets) or RIM-66 Standard MR (medium-range) SAMs. Each ship also has RUR-5 ASROC anti-submarine missiles and RGM-84 Harpoon over-the-horizon anti-ship missiles.

Closer in to the carrier will be two to three guided missile destroyers of the *Arleigh Burke* class, designed specifically for anti-aircraft and anti-submarine warfare. These are formidably armed warships indeed, not only equipped with 5in guns and CIWS systems but also with the same Mk 41 VLS as the cruisers but firing an even wider spectrum of missile types, including the RIM-161 Standard Ballistic missile defence missile, the RIM-174 Standard Extended Range Active Missile (ERAM), the RIM-162 Evolved Sea Sparrow Missile (ESSM), plus a Harpoon missile launcher.

Finalising the combat picture, shadowing the CSG might also be one or two attack submarines, equipped not only with their torpedoes but also with more Tomahawk cruise missiles. The CSG will also include a combined ammunition, oiler and supply ship (AOE/AOR), to provide on-station logistical support.

Sea Sparrow

The RIM-7 Sea Sparrow has endured aboard the US carriers since it entered service in the 1970s, its relevance to modernity kept alive by a sequence of upgrades. The original NATO Sea Sparrow Missile System (NSSMS) is essentially the shipborne version of the semi-active radar homing AIM-7H air-to-air missile (AAM). The original *Nimitz*-class configuration of this missile was as the Basic Point Defense Missile System (BPDMS), which had eight RIM-

ABOVE An Aviation Ordnanceman sets 2.75in (70mm) rockets in an aircraft-mounted pod aboard the USS *Abraham Lincoln* (CVN-72). *(US Navy photo by Mass Communication Specialist 3rd Class Allayah Carr/Released)*

7E-5 Sea Sparrows fired from a Mk 25 launcher and guided by a manually trainable Mk 115 illuminator.

The early Sea Sparrow had definite limitations. It had a theoretical range of 10nm (19km), but because it was launched from a static position rather than an aircraft at speed and altitude, the missile often fell short of this range. Nevertheless, the Navy pushed on with refining both the missile and, equally important, its guidance and launcher systems. During the 1980s, the Mk 115 illuminator was replaced by the Mk 95 Continuous Wave Illuminator X-band radar, which had automated functions, and then the Mk 95 was in turn incorporated into the Mk 91 Guided Missile Fire Control System (GMFCS), integrating the missiles into the SSDS. Capabilities were also enhanced by the introduction of the Mk 23 Target Acquisition System (TAS), actually part of the Mk 9 GMFCS, a highly advanced detection, tracking, identification, threat evaluation and weapon assignment system, ideal for small, high-speed threats coming in either from low over the horizon or from high altitudes. Working out to ranges of 20nm (37km), it can track 54 targets simultaneously.

The next stage in the Sea Sparrow evolution was an improved missile and equally improved launcher unit. The missile was the RIM-7M. The key enhancement in

skimming missile types such as the Exocet, which had wrought such terrible damage on Royal Navy ships during the Falklands War of 1982. The launcher system for the missile now became the Improved Basic Point Defense Missile System (IBPDMS), the RIM-7M now launched from the eight-missile Mk 29 launcher unit. The IBPDMS was fitted to the *Nimitz* carrier fleet during the 1980s.

The missile itself continued its evolution during the 1990s with the RIM-7P. This time the missile's guidance system was extensively changed, allowing for the missile to be fired to a high altitude above the incoming threat, gaining greater range, and then directed down on to the target as it approached and the sensor returns grew stronger. This guidance alteration also had the tactical benefit that the missile could now be used in an anti-shipping role against small vessels.

The RIM-7P took the Sea Sparrow into the 2000s. Furthermore, from 2001, *Nimitz*-class carriers began to receive the Northrop Grumman SPQ-9B Surface Surveillance and Tracking Radar, to replace the Mk 23 TAS. This high-resolution, track-while-scan, X-Band, pulse-Doppler radar detects, tracks and targets both subsonic and supersonic sea-skimming missiles, the three-beam antenna providing for a very positive lock-on to the target.

ABOVE A RIM-7P NATO Sea Sparrow Missile launches from the USS *Abraham Lincoln* (CVN-72) during a combat exercise in the Pacific Ocean, August 2007. *(US Navy photo by Mass Communication Specialist 2nd Class Jordon R. Beesley/Released)*

this missile was the reduction of its minimum altitude to just 15m (49ft) or even less; the RIM-7E had a minimum altitude of about 30m (98ft). This facility, combined with a better proximity fuse, meant that the Sea Sparrow was now far more capable against sea-

RIGHT Sailors upload an AIM-7 Sparrow AAM to an F/A-18E Super Hornet attached to 'Fist of the Fleet' of Strike Fighter Squadron (VFA) 25 on USS *Abraham Lincoln* (CVN-72). *(US Navy photo by Mass Communication Specialist Seaman Mohamed Labanieh/ Released)*

Taking the Sea Sparrow story up to date, the very latest evolution of the type is the RIM-162 Evolved Sea Sparrow Missile (ESSM). The ESSM directly countenances the threat of the latest generations of supersonic anti-ship missiles, and is a major upgrade of the type, not merely a progressive evolution. Improvements to the missile include:

- Significant improvements in aerodynamics through fitting strakes that give it a 'skid-to-turn' capability.
- A more powerful Mk 143 Mod 0 solid fuel rocket, delivering a speed in excess of Mach 4 and a range of more than 27nm (50km).
- More sophisticated interception, being able to tap into the latest guidance systems (such as AN/SPY-1 and Active Phased Array Radar/APAR); the Block 1 missile uses terminal semi-active radar homing, while Block 2 has full active radar homing (meaning that the missile contains a radar transceiver that enables the missile to both find and track the target autonomously).

Aboard the supercarriers, the RIM-162D ESSM is launched from the Mk 29 launcher, in contrast to the fitting on many other US surface ships, which use either the Mk 41, Mk 48 or Mk 56 VLS.

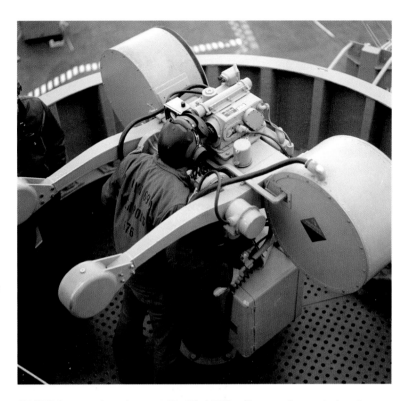

ABOVE A gunner's mate mans the Mk 115 Sea Sparrow fire-control system director during a RIM-7 missile firing exercise aboard the USS *Dwight D. Eisenhower* (CVN-69). *(US Navy)*

BELOW A RIM-162 Evolved Sea Sparrow Missile (ESSM) is launched from the aircraft carrier USS *Carl Vinson* (CVN-70), eventually reaching speeds of more than Mach 4. *(US Navy photo by Mass Communication Specialist 3rd Class Patrick Green/Released)*

RIGHT Sailors aboard the USS *Harry S. Truman* (CVN-75) download the RAM system aboard the *Nimitz*-class aircraft carrier. *(US Navy photo by Mass Communication Specialist 3rd Class Ann Marie Lazarek)*

BELOW A Mk 31 Rolling Airframe Missile (RAM) is launched from the aircraft carrier USS *Dwight D. Eisenhower* (CVN-69) during a Live Fire with a Purpose (LFWAP) event in September 2019. *(US Navy photo by Mass Communication Specialist 1st Class Tony D. Curtis/Released)*

RIM-116 Rolling Airframe Missile (RAM)

Both the *Nimitz*- and *Gerald R. Ford*-class carriers are fitted with the ESSM for medium-range air threats. When the threat comes closer, within 5nm (9km), a different missile system kicks into relevance – the RIM-116 Rolling Airframe Missile (RAM). The RAM is essentially a point defence weapon, designed to tackle anti-ship missiles or aircraft that have broken through the outer circles of protection. The 'RAM' part of its title relates to the way that the missile rotates in flight to give it gyroscopic stability, in much the same way that a rifle bullet is spun from a firearm.

The original Block 0 missile combined the rocket motor, fuse and warhead of the AIM-9 Sidewinder AAM with an infrared seeker based on that in the FIM-92 Stinger, plus passive radar frequency homing; when launched, the missile first tracks in on enemy radiation emissions before switching to the infrared homing for terminal guidance. The subsequent Block 1 type permitted infrared-only homing (useful if the attacking missile has no onboard radar). The latest Block 2 has upgraded the missile even further, improving its manoeuvrability through a four-axis independent control actuator system, plus enhancing the rocket motor, passive radio frequency seeker and infrared seeker.

The RAM comes packaged in the Mk 49 Guided Missile Launching System (GMLS) and the Mk 144 Guided Missile Launcher (GML), which holds 21 missiles, the whole system defined as the RAM Mk 31 Guided Missile Weapon System (GMWS). One important point is that it does have its own integral sensors prior to the missiles being launched, hence the entire system is linked into the SSDS or the AN/SWY-2 Ship Defense Surface Missile System (SDSMS). Overall, the RAM is a reassuring presence aboard the carriers, as in some tests it has produced a kill rate of greater than 95%.

Phalanx CIWS

The Phalanx Close-In Weapon System (CIWS, pronounced 'sea-whiz') is a highly successful defensive component, seen defending the decks of all manner of ships across the world's navies. Despite its power and capability, it is essentially a weapon of last resort, designed to destroy anti-ship missiles, enemy aircraft and even (depending on the configuration of the system) fast-moving surface threats within its effective range of up to 2.2 miles (3.5km), should longer-range defensive missile systems have failed an earlier intercept.

In basic description, the CIWS is a 20mm rotary-barrel cannon (six barrels in a Gatling-gun arrangement, electrically powered), slaved to a Ku band fire-control radar and automated fire-control system that will send out a wall of armour-piercing tungsten penetrator rounds with pinpoint accuracy at a rate of up to 75 rounds per second (burst length is a continuous 60 or 100 rounds). Both the gun, rotating mount, its ammunition supply and its radar are united in a single self-contained unit, making it convenient to mount to the decks and platforms of supercarriers. The key to its success is that it combines all the detection, tracking, threat assessment and kill functions within that 'closed-loop' unit, with an ultra-fast reactivity that

BELOW The CIWS weapon station has its own Ku band fire control radar and automated fire-control system. *(Patrick Bunce)*

can respond to proximate threats within fractions of a second. The fire-control radar both tracks and targets the threat while also monitoring the path of the outgoing stream of projectiles, fine-tuning the latter until they come on target.

The US Navy and its carriers have acquired the CIWS in various block stages, each with upgraded capabilities. The Block 0 was the first generation, which was designed primarily to combat low-altitude anti-ship cruise missiles, but had little capability to tackle anything faster or more evasive, or threats emerging within more complex littoral environments. The subsequent Block 1 upgrade in 1988 featured a new search antenna with improved acquisition, especially against high-altitude targets, plus a larger ammunition capacity, a faster rate of fire, greater firing calculation processing power and improved elevation. Block 1A then ramped up the processing power even further with the High Order Language Computer (HOLC), which, with its improved fire-control algorithms, made the system better at countering manoeuvring targets. Then in 1999 came the Block 1B Phalanx Surface Mode (PSUM). The big change here was that it added a Forward-Looking Infrared Radar (FLIR) sensor, which meant the CIWS could now engage low and slow or hovering aircraft and surface craft. Furthermore, to improve the CIWS's efficacy in both night and day engagements, it has a thermal imaging Automatic Acquisition Video Tracker (AAVT) and stabilisation system. Notably, the FLIR capability of the Phalanx can be linked to the RIM-116 RAM, to aid the latter in target acquisition. Other Block 1B improvements include the Optimized Gun Barrel (OGB) package, with 78in (2,000mm) barrels instead of the Block 0/1 60in (1,500mm) barrels, the new

MK 38 25MM MACHINE GUN SYSTEM (MGS)

Designed specifically for countering small surface vessels, the Mk 38 is a single-barrel 25mm air cooled, semi- and fully automatic machine gun system, fitted to CVNs but also many other US Navy vessels. One of its virtues is its versatility. It can be trained, elevated and fired either manually by a human operator, or remotely; it is fitted with an electro-optical sensor, a fire-control system and an auto-tracking facility. With an effective range of 2,500yd (2,286m), it has single-shot or burst mode, with a maximum cyclical rate of 180 rounds per minute.

LEFT Another weapon system aboard the *Nimitz*-class carriers is the Mk 38, a 25mm machine gun system (MGS), installed for ship self-defence to counter Fast-Attack Crafts and Fast Inshore-Attack Crafts. *(Patrick Bunce)*

barrels delivering an improved dispersion pattern while also being thicker and more durable. The Block 1B can also fire the new Enhanced Lethality Cartridge, which provides a 50% increase in penetration mass.

Anti-torpedo systems

As explained in Chapter 2, the very structure of a US supercarrier makes it hard to sink, either by anti-ship missiles or by torpedoes. Modern torpedoes, however, are immensely destructive, utilising the incompressibility of water to generate crushing destructive pressures beneath a ship's hull. For this reason, while the carrier relies heavily on the anti-submarine capabilities of its own helicopters and the other ships/helicopters of the CSG for underwater defence, it also has its own integral anti-submarine systems.

The core torpedo countermeasures system used aboard the *Nimitz*-class carriers is the SLQ-25A 'Nixie', a passive, electro-acoustic system that decoys incoming acoustic homing torpedoes away from the carrier. It deploys an Acoustic Device Countermeasures (ADC) device beyond the carrier, towing it via a tow/signal-transfer coaxial cable. The ADC generates an acoustic signal to decoy the hostile torpedo away from the ship. The subsequent AN/SLQ-25B includes improved deceptive countermeasures capabilities, a fibre-optic

display local area network (LAN), a torpedo alert capability and a towed array sensor. It also includes the Launched Expendable Acoustic Decoy (LEAD), which is deployed from the Mk 137 launcher, part of the Mk 36 decoy system.

In recent years, the Nixie system has been supplemented by the Anti-Torpedo Torpedo Defense System (ATTDS), part of the broader Surface Ship Torpedo Defense (SSTD) system. The SSTD was fitted aboard *Dwight D. Eisenhower*, *Harry S. Truman*, *George H.W. Bush*, *Nimitz* and *Theodore Roosevelt*, and works in theory as follows. The ATTDS essentially consists of two components: 1) Torpedo Warning System (TWS) and 2) Countermeasures Anti-Torpedo (CAT). An official US Navy document from 2016 explains the two systems in detail:

TWS is being built as an early warning system to detect, localize, classify, and alert on incoming threat torpedoes and consists of three major subsystems:

■ The Target Acquisition Group consists of a towed acoustic array, tow cable, winch, power supply, and signal processing equipment. Data from the array and the ship's radar system are processed into contact tracks and alerts to be forwarded to the Tactical Control Group. The Navy intends for the array to be capable of both passive and active sonar operations.

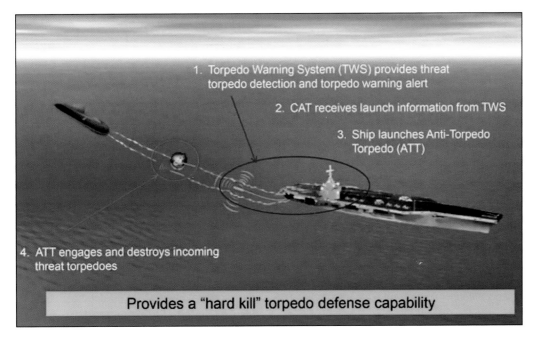

1. Torpedo Warning System (TWS) provides threat torpedo detection and torpedo warning alert

2. CAT receives launch information from TWS

3. Ship launches Anti-Torpedo Torpedo (ATT)

4. ATT engages and destroys incoming threat torpedoes

Provides a "hard kill" torpedo defense capability

LEFT A diagram showing the CVN's active torpedo defence, although there are some technical issues with the system that might lead to its being replaced. *(US Navy)*

■ The Tactical Control Group consists of duplicate consoles on the bridge and Combat Direction Center (on CVNs) that displays contacts, issues torpedo alerts to the crew, and automatically develops CAT placement presets using information sent from the Target Acquisition Group. The operator uses these displays to manage the threat engagement sequence and command CAT launches.

■ The Ready Stow Group will consist of the steel cradles housing the CATs. The permanent system consists of four steel cradles and associated electronics, each housing six anti-torpedo torpedoes (ATTs) at different locations (port/starboard and forward/aft on CVNs).

■ CAT is a hard-kill countermeasure intended to neutralize threat torpedoes and consists of the following:
  ♦ The ATT is a 6.75-inch diameter interceptor designed for high-speed

LEFT An anti-torpedo torpedo (ATT) weapon is fired from a launcher deck aboard the aircraft carrier USS *Dwight D. Eisenhower* (CVN-69). *(US Navy photo by Mass Communication Specialist 3rd Class Kaleb J. Sarten/ Released)*

and maneuverability to support rapid engagement of a threat torpedo.

♦ The All-Up Round Equipment consists of a nose sabot, ram plate, launch tube, muzzle cover, breech mechanism, and energetics to encapsulate and launch the ATT.

♦ A Stored Energy Propulsion System powers the tactical CAT. A battery-powered electric motor CAT exists for test purposes only. Engineering Development Model-2 is the current hardware version of the CAT.

(DOT&E, 2018, 223)

In operational use, the TWS sensor system detects the incoming torpedo, the information is relayed to the CAT, which is then launched from the ship and steers itself to intercept the threat. In 2019, however, a report from the Pentagon's Office of the Director of Operational Test and Evaluation found that the system was unreliable, with the TWS giving false positions and the CAT showing inconsistency in torpedo interception and kills. The future of the ATTDS is therefore unclear at the time of writing. In practical terms, for the future, the carrier fleet is more likely to rely upon the anti-submarine capabilities of external assets or of helicopters, rather than its own defensive systems.

BELOW A sailor aboard the USS Dwight D. Eisenhower (CVN-69) inventories ordnance on the flight deck of the aircraft carrier during an ordnance transfer with USS John C. Stennis (CVN-74). *(US Navy photo by Mass Communication Specialist 1st Class Tony D. Curtis/Released)*

Decoy systems

The US supercarriers can draw upon a range of kinetic options for defeating incoming aerial, surface or underwater threats. Yet as we have seen in the carriers' anti-torpedo defences, decoy alternatives can be deployed. One of the key pieces of deck-mounted decoy equipment on the *Nimitz*-class carriers is the BAe Systems Mk 36 Super Rapid Blooming Off-board Countermeasures (SRBOC) Chaff and Decoy Launching System. The Mk 36 consists of six Mk 137 launcher tubes, each of 5in (130mm) diameter, set in two parallel rows, with four of the tubes set at a 45-degree angle and the other two at 60 degrees. When the system is triggered by an incoming missile threat, it launches one of three types of decoy munitions from the tubes, with the purpose of creating false data sets to draw the missile away from the ship. The decoy munitions are:

■ SRBOC – chaff to deceive RF-emitting missiles/radars.
■ NATO Sea Gnat – like SRBOC, but with greater range and a larger chaff payload.
■ TORCH – generates heat signatures to deceive infrared-seeking missiles.

The *Nimitz*-class carriers also have their own EW suite aboard – the SLQ-32(V)4. The system has two units fitted, one to port and one to starboard, feeding their information to a common computer. On threat detection, the system can either trigger the activation of the Mk 36 decoy system, or it can engage in active radar jamming.

The exact composition of the EW suites aboard the *Gerald R. Ford* class is largely concealed from public view. The *Nimitz* class, however, is the beneficiary of the Surface Electronic Warfare Improvement Program (SEWIP), thus it is likely that the *Gerald R. Ford* will be also. A Navy document, updated in 2017, provides the technical details of SEWIP:

SEWIP Block 1 provides enhanced EW capabilities to existing and new ship combat systems to improve anti-ship missile defense, counter targeting and counter surveillance capabilities. The upgrade addresses obsolescence mitigation through introduction of electronic surveillance enhancements (ESE) and Improved Control and Display (ICAD) as well as incorporation of adjunct receivers for special signal intercept including specific emitter ID (SEI) and high gain/high sensitivity (HGHS). The SEI and HGHS capability provides improved battlefield situational awareness. [. . .]

SEWIP Block 2 provides enhanced Electronic Support (ES) capability by means of an upgraded ES antenna, ES receiver and an open combat system interface for the AN/SLQ-32. These upgrades are necessary in order to pace the threat and improve detection and accuracy capabilities of the AN/SLQ-32. The SEWIP Block 2 program is designated as an ACAT II program. The SEWIP Block 2 Program achieved full rate production in September 2016.

SEWIP Block 3 will provide electronic attack (EA) capability improvements required for the AN/SLQ-32(V) system to keep pace with the threat. This block upgrade will provide a common EA capability to all surface combatants outfitted with the active variant of the AN/SLQ-32. [. . .]

SEWIP Block 4 is a future planned upgrade that will provide advanced electro-optic and infrared capabilities to the AN/SLQ-32(V) system.

(US Navy, 2017, np)

From these explanations of the Block evolution of SEWIP, it is clear that in an age of 'hybrid warfare', in which data, information and sensors are weapons in their own right, the supercarriers will receive considerably upgraded EW capabilities. Given the nature of emerging threats, EW personnel and systems are likely to be fully engaged, regardless of their location in the world.

Chapter Six

Carrier logistics

The operational capability of a US supercarrier stands or falls on its logistics. Only the proper management of both onboard supplies and of replenishment operations ensures that the carrier can take full advantage of its nuclear endurance.

OPPOSITE The USS *Theodore Roosevelt* (CVN-71) pulls alongside the Military Sealift Command (MSC) fleet replenishment oiler USNS *Big Horn* (T-AO-198) during an under-way replenishment in October 2013. *(US Navy photo by Mass Communication Specialist 2nd Class Sean Hurt)*

(227kg) of hamburger meat and 800lb (363kg) of vegetables are consumed. To provide the 6,000 or so crew with bedding requires an onboard supply of 14,000 pillowcases and 24,000 sheets. These items, plus the tens of thousands of uniform elements, means that the laundry personnel process about 5,500lb (2,500kg) of items every day. Every week, the carrier's barber shop performs about 1,500 haircuts, with all the requirements for hair products and cut-hair disposal. Every year, the ship's onboard post office processes 1 million pounds (450,000kg) of mail.

These figures purely relate to the personal life of the sailors on board. When we factor in major operational logistics, the figures keep spiralling upwards. Although the ship does not need conventional fuel for its nuclear reactors, it certainly does need prodigious quantities of aviation fuel – it has onboard storage for 3.3 million gallons (12.5 million litres). Extrapolating from public domain sources, furthermore, a *Nimitz*-class carrier can hold some 9 million pounds (4 million kg) of ordnance. A 6-million-pound (2.7-million-kg) ammo replenishment aboard the USS *John C. Stennis* in early 2015

The floating logistical footprint of a US supercarrier is dizzying, with bare statistics impressive enough to command immediate respect. Every single day, for example, the ship's catering services prepare and deliver some 18,000–20,000 meals, and have onboard food storage facilities to maintain that pace for about 60 days. In one day alone, some 500lb

required some 1,400 crane loads to lift from the Naval Magazine (NAVMAG) Indian Island to the ship, delivered over a period of three days. We must also factor in the tens of thousands of parts required to keep aircraft airworthy.

The superlatives of these immense ships keep stacking up. In this chapter, therefore, we look into how these feats of naval logistics are accomplished, and some of the major systems aboard that make life at sea for months on end viable for thousands of crew.

Supply

As explained previously one of the chief advantages of nuclear energy as a maritime powerplant is that the carrier can remain at sea almost indefinitely (at least within the decades of fuel endurance and other maintainability issues). A key point of strain that this fact imposes upon the ship and the crew is the issue of resupply. As capacious as the ship's onboard storage facilities are, the fact remains that unrelenting consumption means resupply is a recurring and necessary event.

There are two processes of Underway Replenishment (UNREP) by which the ship can be resupplied at sea:

- Ship-to-ship connected replenishments (CONREPs).
- Ship-to-ship vertical replenishments (VERTREPs).

In addition to UNREPS, the carrier can also be resupplied by in-port pickups and by long-distance carrier onboard deliveries (CODs). We will look at each of these in turn.

Ship-to-ship connected replenishments (CONREPs)

In a CONREP, the carrier receives resupply from a Military Sealift Command (MSC) oiler or auxiliary ship, typically sailing directly alongside the carrier and physically connected to the carrier via a fuel coupling or resupply rig. Note that it is possible to perform a CONREP with the auxiliary vessel astern, but by sailing alongside there are numerous advantages: the ships can together maintain a greater constant speed; one auxiliary ship can resupply two ships simultaneously (one either side);

BELOW Illustrating the challenge of UNREP manoeuvres, heavy seas slap against the fast combat support ship USS *Sacramento* (AOE 1) as it transfers fuel and cargo to the aircraft carrier USS *Carl Vinson* (CVN-70), using multiple STREAM rigs. *(US Navy photo by Photographer's Mate 2nd Class Inez Lawson/ Released)*

also dry goods and fuel can be transferred simultaneously, rather than fuel only.

A CONREP requires a great deal of precision, in both timing and seamanship. Rendezvous coordinates are agreed in advance, the location and timing fitting around the carrier's operational commitments and the geopolitical realities of the international waters. The vessels must also agree a course of sailing, as the replenishment can take several hours. Once they meet, the ships will sail parallel to each other at a close distance – about 160–180ft (49–55m). Course holding must be tight at all times, although weather conditions can make the replenishment impossible (conditions above Sea State 5 usually prevent a CONREP). Because of the sheer size of a carrier, plus the wake it creates, the auxiliary ship faces more challenges with keeping course. At a replenishment speed of, say, 12 knots, just a single degree of course variation will result in the ship shifting 20ft (6m) sideways per minute. To ensure that the ships stay at a constant distance apart, therefore, a laser rangefinder is used to measure the gap, as Quartermaster 1st Class Efrain Torres of the USS *Theodore Roosevelt* (CVN-71) explains:

We use a laser rangefinder that pinpoints how far the other ship is from us. It's like binoculars, it sends a laser that hits the other ship and tells us how far away it is.

Then the laser rangefinder reports it back to the conning officer and the officer of the deck in the pilot house.

The quartermaster also reports all changes in course and speed up to the ship's senior commanders, the information displayed on a status board on the bridge.

The physical process of transferring goods from ship to ship is accomplished by the use of a Standard Tensioned Replenishment Alongside Method (STREAM) rig. There are various types of STREAM rig, but the principle uniting them all is a tensioned spanwire (or multiple spanwires) affixed between the two ships, this providing a means by which to support fuel transfer pipes or cargo winches. (The initial set-up of the spanwire is accomplished by shotlines fired between the ships.) Once connected, and as long as the two ships can maintain a steady and parallel course, very large transfers can be performed. Aviation fuel transfers of more than 1 million gallons, for example, are common, with multiple fuel lines (up to six) running between the replenishment ships and the carrier.

Vertical Replenishment (VERTREP)

Vertical Replenishment (VERTREP) is the process of transferring cargo to the carriers via helicopter, the helicopter arriving either from

RIGHT An Aviation Boatswain's Mate (Fuel) monitors an Aviation Lube Oil (ALO) transfer aboard USS *Dwight D. Eisenhower* (CVN-69). *(US Navy photo by Mass Communication Specialist 3rd Class Kaleb J. Sarten/ Released)*

FUEL AND CARGO RAS

The following is a US Navy description of the technical procedures for utilising the STREAM rig for both fuel and cargo transfers between ships:

When utilizing the STREAM rig for FAS [fueling at sea] operations a tensioned spanwire is suspended between the two ships. A series of hose saddles are attached to the spanwire by trolleys. The actual transfer hoses are then suspended in between the saddles. The receiving end of the hose rig is tipped with a coupling. A variety of fueling couplings may be used to ensure compatibility between the delivery and receiving ships. The most common is a probe fueling coupling. The probe may be used in the transfer of either DFM or JP-5 products. The probe itself has a latching mechanism that holds it in the receiver by spring force. The receiver is mounted on the receiving ship by a swivel arm. The swivel arm allows the receiver to move throughout the full working range of the receiving station, ensuring proper alignment prevents the probe from unseating. The probe assembly will unseat from the receiver when a 2,500 lb. line pull is applied. The receiver also has a manual release lever, which is the desired way to release the probe upon completion of the fuel transfer.

During RAS [replenishing at sea] the STREAM transfer rig utilizes a tensioned wire highline suspended between two ships. The exact type of STREAM rig is dependent on the kind of cargo. In all rigs, cargo to be transferred is connected to a trolley, which rides on the highline. The trolley is moved between the ships by inhaul and outhaul winches located on the delivery ship. When using a STREAM rig with all tensioned wires, the wire rope outhaul is fairled through a SURF (Standard Underway Replenishment Fixture) block and attached to the outboard side of the trolley. The SURF is located on the receiving ship. A ram tensioner, located on the delivery ship, applies highline tension ensuring constant load support regardless of ship separation or motion. However, if ship separation becomes too great the amount of wire on the winch drum may be exceeded. A stream rig can handle loads up to 8,750 lbs. under ideal conditions.

(https://fas.org/man/dod-101/sys/ship/unrep.htm)

ABOVE An Aviation Boatswain's Mate (Handling) 2nd Class *HE OR SHE??* uses a tractor to move a jet on the flight deck of the aircraft carrier USS *Abraham Lincoln* (CVN-72). Many of the vehicles run on JP-5 aircraft fuel. *(US Navy photo by Mass Communication Specialist Seaman Mohamed Labanieh/ Released)*

LEFT An Aviation Ordnanceman 3rd Class moves cargo from the US Postal Service on the flight deck of USS *Abraham Lincoln* (CVN-72) during an UNREP with the fast combat support ship USNS *Arctic* (T-AOE 8) in September 2019. *(US Navy photo by Mass Communication Specialist 3rd Class Jeremiah Bartelt/ Released)*

a shore installation or another ship. VERTREP is typically used for moving ordnance, food, supplies and spare parts. Its advantages when compared to CONREP lie mainly in its flexibility. Performing a VERTREP naturally does not require that a supply ship is steaming parallel, or even close, to the receiving ship, although in reality the two vessels will often adopt a close and sympathetic course to speed up the rate of transfer between the ships.

For a major VERTREP involving one or two helicopters, the receiving ships should ideally be stationed about 380–980yd (350–900m) upwind of the supply ship, which allows the helicopters to fly with their loads into the wind, but then return to the supply ship in a lighter state with a tailwind. For every additional helicopter employed, an extra 220yd (200m) of distance should be added.

Although a CONREP is an invaluable transfer tool, the complex requirements of maintaining the physical connection between the ships is demanding on time and manpower. VERTREP breaks the need for this physical connection, and the helicopters can also make transfers at long distance. Through VERTREP, furthermore,

the carrier can receive supplies without obliging itself to sail on one particular course for an extended period of time, and it can also steam at a greater speed than would be possible with a CONREP. Exploring the disadvantages, however, VERTREP can be limited by adverse weather conditions (wind, heat, humidity) and also by the range of the particular helicopter; added to the latter is the fact that the hovering and lifting-off manoeuvres performed by the helicopters during VERTREP guzzles fuel at a heavy rate. Moreover, VERTREP operations can tie up the flight deck, restricting other air operations, and there is also a slightly increased risk of sensitive loads (*eg* missile components) being damaged in the drop to the deck.

With extremely light loads that can be carried internally, or for transferring personnel, VERTREP helicopters can make a physical wheels-down landing on the carrier flight deck. More commonly, however, the helicopters make their deliveries via loads underslung beneath the helicopter in cargo nets. The helicopters pick up their loads at source, fly to the carrier, then are guided in to the VERTREP receiving station by flight officers. The cargoes are lowered as gently

as possible on to the flight deck, where they are unhooked and processing begins as the aircraft flies off. Performed with efficiency, the VERTREP can bring goods in at a rapid rate, certainly as fast as the supply personnel can move the

Major UNREPS are dynamic events aboard the supercarriers, classified as 'all-hands evolutions'. The critical factor is that the supplies are moved very quickly from Receiving Stations and onwards to the staging areas or storerooms. Any build-up of clutter around the ship, but especially on the flight deck, poses a physical danger to crews, and especially increases the risk of FOD from the rotor downwash of subsequent VERTREPS.

The two key people in the planning of an UNREP are the carrier's Executive Officer (XO), who has overall planning authority, and the Supply Officer, who takes charge of all movement, storage and maintenance of onboard supplies. Many other departments can be involved in the UNREP planning, but the Air Department and Weapons Department have particular importance: during CONREP transfers, the Weapons Department personnel take charge of the transfer of materials to the ship, whereas during VERTREP the Air Department has the responsibility. Note, however, that once the Air Department or Weapons Department personnel disconnect the slung load from the helicopter, then responsibility for that load passes over to the Supply Department.

The deck of a supercarrier has multiple earmarked Receiving Stations, which are quite simply designated spaces where supplies can be received on board. Typically, the receiving stations are located at hangar deck level, with the exception of the VERTREP station which is usually on the aft flight deck. The receiving stations are co-located with the ship's elevators, with three of the elevators lowered for CONREPS while one of the aft elevators remains raised for VERTREP flights. When the elevator is full of stores, or has reached its maximum weight allowance, it is lowered down to the hangar deck, the supplies are offloaded and the elevator returns to flight deck level.

From Receiving Stations, the goods will then progress to Sorting Stations. Because UNREPS can be so fast-paced (the ship might be taking on board more than 100 tons of cargo an hour), there is no time for considered stock accounting at the point of delivery. So, at the Sorting Stations, the cargo is separated by type and storage destination. Official Navy guidelines on this process state that the Sorting Stations can be established anywhere, as long as their location isn't blocking a passage for moving the goods onwards. Then come the Strike Stations. These stations are located at access points where the material is moved below decks, and thus includes ammunition elevators, hatches fitted with electric hoists and any other transfer point. It is vital that this work is performed very quickly, as a ship with open hatches is extremely vulnerable to battle damage. Indeed, the personnel at all the stations pretty much work in unrelenting fashion to get the supplies on board, moved quickly and stowed away.

RIGHT An engineering team build a jet engine aboard the aircraft carrier USS *Abraham Lincoln* (CVN-72). The carriers' self-sufficiency demands that they transport hundreds of thousands of aviation parts. (US Navy photo by Mass Communication Specialist 3rd Class Allayah Carr/Released)

goods from the Receiving Stations to the Sorting Stations and Strike Stations (see feature box).

In-port replenishment

In-port replenishment sounds deceptively simple compared to UNREP, but it still needs meticulous planning if it is to be done effectively. Much depends on the port at which the carrier will take on the supplies. If that port is a US Navy installation, then dockside procedures and facilities are likely to be precisely configured for the requirements. In foreign ports, however, the procedures and facilities might dictate special procedures, not least in relation to port navigation, anchoring arrangements, dockside lifting equipment, manpower required, security and many other considerations. Making clear prior arrangements is crucial, as any problems during the replenishment can result in the ship missing crucial time landmarks in its operational schedule.

Carrier Onboard Delivery (COD)

Carrier Onboard Delivery (COD) specifically refers to the use of carrier-capable aircraft bringing supplies or personnel directly on board. It differs from VERTREP in that the aircraft are usually part of the carrier's own air wing and that the aircraft always perform full arrested landings.

While helicopters have in the past been used for COD, the main instruments of the mission are the C-2A Greyhound and, recently, the Osprey MV-22, known in the COD role as CMV-22B. As explained in Chapter 4, the cargo load capabilities of these two aircraft are considerable, and they provide a regular supply lifeline for the carrier crew, especially relating to personal supplies such as mail from home.

Food and water

Some of the opening statistics of this chapter outline the logistical challenge of providing a crew of more than 5,000 personnel with at least three meals a day. In one day at sea, for example, the ship's crew can consume 1,600lb of chicken, 160 gallons of milk, 30 cases of cereal and 350lb of lettuce, based on figures given for USS *Harry S. Truman*. This ship has 17 galleys and 114 personnel to serve up over 18,000 meals a day. The walk-in freezer storage space alone is around 11,000sq ft (1,000m^2) in area.

While the food storage, organisation and cooking procedures involved with this volume of meals are in themselves impressive, we also need to take into account the massive volume of fresh water required to cook many of the meals, plus provide the ship's crew with drinking water and water for sanitation, personal hygiene, general cleaning and engineering.

The *Nimitz*-class carriers are fitted with four water distillation plants, producing in total about 400,000 gallons (1.5 million litres) of fresh water daily, from seawater pumped aboard, meaning that the ship is quite free of external water supplies. The distillation plants utilise heat produced by the nuclear reactors, transmitting that heat to the influent seawater through heat exchangers. The heat exchangers (a series of metal tubes or plates enclosed in a metal casing) separate the heat source fluid (steam) from the fluid that receives the heat (seawater), at the same time providing as much thermal contact through the metal surfaces as possible. The products are clear drinking water and what is known as 'brine', concentrated seawater and its organic contents. This brine is disposed of back into the sea, and is an appreciable emission – the total daily H$_2$O 'flow' of 400,000 gallons is vastly exceeded by a brine flow of 6,800,000 gallons (25 million litres).

The new *Gerald R. Ford* class of carrier does not use distillation methods of purification, but rather has a reverse osmosis (RO) desalination system. RO plants separate fresh water from seawater by passing the latter through semi-permeable membranes, which retain matter and non-potable substances, allowing fresh water to pass through. The substances that are retained by the membranes form the brine. The downside of RO is that 'shipboard RO plants produce lower-purity fresh water than distilling plants, with total dissolved solids (TDS) concentrations two orders of magnitude greater than distilling plant distillate' (Environmental Protection Agency, 1999, 3). However, they avoid the scaling issues of distillation systems, which have to undergo rigorous citrus cleaning in port every five to seven years.

Ordnance

The storage and movement of ordnance on the supercarrier is one of the most sensitive of processes involved. 'Ordnance' covers a surprisingly large variety of weaponry, in turn subdivided by their component parts. It includes: bombs of all sizes, from 250lb (113kg) to 2,000lb (907kg), with multiple

BELOW A Master-at-Arms 3rd Class secures ordnance aboard *USS Dwight D. Eisenhower* (CVN-69) during an ordnance transfer with the *USS John C. Stennis* (CVN-74). *(US Navy photo by Mass Communication Specialist Seaman Joseph T. Miller/Released)*

fusing and tail-kit options; missiles for both aircraft and onboard defence, including air-to-air, air-to-ground, anti-ship, the hazard of these munitions including the fuel and rocket components; torpedoes, either for the shipborne defence systems or for helicopter deployment; pyrotechnics, such as decoy flares; cannon ammunition; gun and fuel pods. Ensuring that all these are properly built, moved and armed, and also de-armed if returned from a mission unused, is a critical safety requirement involving a very strict observance of the procedure.

The ordnance aboard a supercarrier is buried deep within a below-decks network of magazines, the number of which varies somewhat depending on the carrier. During the author's tour of the USS *Dwight D. Eisenhower*, an ordnance officer explained the system of magazines aboard that particular carrier:

Every magazine has its unique thing. Some of them will have different types of bombs, some of them will have rockets, some of them will have missiles. Some of them will include items that we don't like to store together, so we separate and segregate them. We have 33 magazines that we are using right now to store parts and bombs and missiles. We keep, for example, small-arms ammunition separate from the bombs. Certain types of ordnance have their limitations on what we can store with it. Other magazines will have the parts and we'll move ordnance as required into the assembly area so that everything that we need to assemble a bomb is moved to the same spot.

We have ten weapons elevators that we can use to move the ordnance throughout the magazine series, so we can get ordnance to the build areas. In the build areas we have assembly tables set up, pneumatic hoists. They [ordnance personnel] will take a 'shape', [an individual ordnance component], put it on the table, and assemble it as ordered, and then send it up.

The magazines are fully air conditioned – we keep things at a certain temperature, because ordnance doesn't like a lot of heat. We have magazine sprinkler systems and different types of alarm in each space – temperature alarms, flooding alarms, alarms

that tell us if the sprinkler system kicked
off – and all that is monitored separately. We
have 'rovers' who will rove these magazines
throughout the day to check the status
manually for several levels of failure.

It is a 24-hour operation. Throughout
the day we are moving the ordnance
around and getting it up to the flight deck
for the airplanes and the flight deck crew.
At night, that's when everything really
happens because that's when we get the
order sheets. We get the order sheets in
the afternoon, so late afternoon and early
evening is when the folks down in the
magazines are busy pulling stuff. Ordnance
Control has ordnance accountants and stock
control, so it's a first-in, first-out system – the
older stuff goes out first, which might be
buried somewhere in the magazine. They'll
dig it out and move it to the assembly
area, so it's like assembling the pieces of a
custom car.

The primary bomb-build magazine is where
the basic explosive casing of the ordnance
is combined with tail kits and nose kits/fuses
to create the working device, the ordnance

ABOVE Sailors assigned to Weapons Department attach a replenishment
pennant to an ordnance storage case on the flight deck of the USS *Harry S.
Truman* (CVN-75). *(US Navy photo by Photographer's Mate Airman Ricardo J.
Reyes/Released)*

BELOW An ordnance hoist in one of the USS *Dwight D. Eisenhower's* (CVN-
69) magazines. *(Patrick Bunce)*

RIGHT The bomb assembly table is designed to allow 360-degree rotation of the ordnance during the assembly process. *(Patrick Bunce)*

personnel building the devices according to the ordnance load plan. As indicated in the testimony above, it is somewhat akin to a vehicle assembly area, albeit with far more rigorous procedures. In the room there is a bomb table – a long metal bench with frames for holding individual bombs up to 2,000lb (907kg) in weight in each slot. The bombs

are lifted from pallets on to the table using a pneumatic hoist, where the components are installed. When a collection of ordnance is ready, it is raised up to the flight deck for loading aboard the aircraft.

The act of arming individual aircraft with the right ordnance is a matter of close coordination between the aircraft handling group, ship's ordnance group and air wing ordnance personnel. A status board is maintained and updated, listing all the ordnance being moved and its assigned aircraft. The flight deck is the area where the ordnance typically is finally armed, just prior to the aircraft being launched. Doing this on the flight deck is an obvious safety choice; the material effects of a major explosion will usually be significantly less on an open flight deck than in the confined spaces below decks.

There are designated arming and de-arming areas on the flight deck. The arming areas tend to be just in front of the JBDs, once the aircraft is about to take off. De-arming areas are reached by careful taxiing of the aircraft to the designated area, ideally an open location where the accidental launch of a missile would enable that weapon to fly out to sea. Particular caution is taken when dealing with a 'hung' weapon, *ie* one that the pilot has attempted to deploy in action, but which has failed to drop or launch.

RIGHT Arming wires aboard USS *Dwight D. Eisenhower* (CVN-69); the wires keep some types of ordnance in a safe condition until release or manual arming. *(Patrick Bunce)*

Arming protocols are strictly followed, as once armed the weapon is 'live' and ready for use. US Navy guidelines are as follows for this stage:

Weapons/bomb racks/launcher arming functions to be performed after engine turnup are defined in the individual store loading manual/checklists. Final arming of forward-firing weapons shall be conducted in the arming area just prior to launch. All evolutions authorized in the rearming area may be accomplished after engine turnup and prior to taxi. Those evolutions authorized to be accomplished only in the arming area shall be conducted as follows:

1. *The Air Gunner or a designated Air Wing Ordnance Coordinator shall supervise all arming evolutions.*
2. *Assigned Air Wing Arming Coordinators shall be positioned on the bow and waist catapults during launch to oversee all aircraft final arming.*
3. *The CVW Ordnance Officer shall assign arming crews.*

(US Navy, 2007b, 7-13)

Conversely, when the aircraft return to the ship, the pilot informs the flight marshal of any unexpended/hung ordnance on the approach, and the Air Officer announces the details over the flight deck communications system, so that personnel can prepare themselves for the de-arming task. Depending on the urgency or nature of the de-arming, the weapons can be de-armed before engine shutdown, although ideally the aircraft should be in an engine shutdown and clear of the aircraft recovery area. De-arming is closely supervised by the Air Gunner or an Air Wing Ordnance Coordinator.

Before moving away from our insight into the magazines and weapon handling, we should note a key technological change between the *Nimitz* class and *Gerald R. Ford* class. The former's weapon elevators are capable of moving 10,500lb (4,762kg) of ordnance at a speed of 100ft/min (32m/min). The *Gerald R. Ford* class, however, has been fitted with the Advanced Weapons Elevators (AWEs), which are operated via electromagnetic, linear synchronous motors,

ABOVE A US Navy-approved Raymond forklift in an ordnance magazine aboard the USS *Dwight D. Eisenhower* (CVN-69). Note how the surrounding stored bombs are all without fins and nose kits. *(Patrick Bunce)*

BELOW Advanced Weapon Elevator (AWE) operators on the *Gerald R. Ford*. The AWEs should eventually have a 33% increase in sortie generation rate compared to the *Nimitz*-class elevators. *(US Navy photo by Mass Communication Specialist 2nd Class Liz Thompson/Released)*

Weapon Movement The presence of airborne weapons outside of designated magazines greatly increases the danger to the carrier should a fire or explosion occur. The greater the quantities of weapons involved, the greater the risk. To minimize this risk, only that quantity of weapons required to sustain operations shall be transferred to the hangar or flight deck. With exception to actual loading evolutions, weapons on skids/trucks shall be positioned fore and aft and continuously attended. Airborne weapons shall be positioned in such areas as to be readily available to afford adequate time for safe aircraft loading. Staging areas for assembled weapons shall be restricted to those areas that:

1. Are convenient to jettison locations.
2. Have at least two clear routes of access.
3. Are covered by sprinkler system or manned fire hoses.
4. Are located as far as practicable from fueling stations and LOX carts.
5. Are manned and have provisions for physically securing weapons.

The priorities that shall be utilized in locating staging areas for weapons include the following:

1. Flight deck outboard of island.
2. Hangar deck.
3. Sponsons.

Staging areas shall be used for ready service only, not for protracted stowage nor for extending the total weapons stowage capacity of the ship. All weapons in staging areas shall be on mobile trucks/skids. All ordnance jettison ramps will be exercised daily prior to flight operations involving ordnance. Jettison ramps in the ordnance staging area will be rigged at all times that ordnance is present. All other ramps will be rigged when required as determined by the Air Gunner. The aircraft elevators may be used to supplement and expedite transfer of weapons from the hangar deck to the flight deck. Coordination between the ordnance handling officer and the aircraft handling officer is necessary.

(US Navy, 2007b, 7-11)

RIGHT Stored ordnance and a bomb assembly table aboard the USS *Dwight D. Eisenhower* (CVN-69). The blue bombs are dummy training ordnance. Note the tail kit over on the right.

(Patrick Bunce)

moving 24,000lb (10,886kg) of ordnance at 150ft/min (46m/min). This theoretically means an increase in sortie generation rate of 33%, although at the time of writing the AWEs are struggling with a variety of technical issues which have yet to be resolved.

Fuel

Aviation fuel is the operational lifeblood of an American supercarrier. Both the *Nimitz*- and *Gerald R. Ford*-class aircraft carriers transport more than 3 million gallons (11.3 million litres) of JP-5, the standard aircraft fuel type. Managing the logistics of aviation fuel in its passage from storage tanks to aircraft requires an elaborate engineering system structured into the Aviation Fuels Operational Sequencing System (AFOSS).

Aviation fuel storage aboard the carriers is arranged by two different types of fuel tank – storage tanks and service tanks. Storage tanks provide the simple bulk storage of the JP-5 in its untreated state. Service tanks, by contrast, contain a fuel ready for use within the aircraft. In line with operational demand, the fuel is transferred from the storage tanks to the service tanks, passing through various filtration and

quality processes to ensure that the JP-5 is ready to use in precision aircraft engines.

Before any of this can happen, of course, fuel needs to be taken on board, either through an UNREP (see page 156) or portside. When at sea, CVN carriers refill from multiple starboard-side filling connections, which are situated outboard of the hangar deck, set on fuelling

ABOVE An ordnance elevator brings munitions up to the flight deck from the magazines deep below. *(US Navy photo by Photographer's Mate Airman Christopher Molinari/Released)*

LEFT The fleet replenishment oiler USNS *Kanawha* (T-AO 196) maintains a parallel course alongside USS *John C. Stennis* (CVN-74) to conduct a fuelling-at-sea in the Atlantic, October 2019. *(US Navy photo by Mass Communication Specialist 3rd Class Jarrod A. Schad/ Released)*

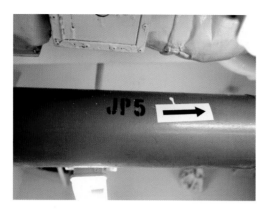

RIGHT One of the JP-5 fuel transfer pipes aboard a CVN. (Patrick Bunce)

AVIATION FUELLING PROCEDURES – NAVAIR 00-80T-120

Fuel Loads

Requirements are published in the Air Plan. The Air Operations Officer shall authorize changes in published fuel loads.

1. Fuels Control Petty Officer relays fuel requirements to fueling crew leaders and fuel crewmen on the 4JG sound powered phones and/or flight deck communication circuits.
2. The AVFUELS Control Talker maintains aircraft fuel loads on the AVFUELS status sheet. The status sheet includes the type of aircraft, side number, start and final fuel load. The fueling crew leaders report to the AVFUELS Control Talker when fuel requirements have been met.
3. A fueling crew shall consist of a crew leader manning the 4JG at the fueling station, and a minimum of one nozzle operator per hose in use. A PQS-qualified fuels flight deck supervisor shall be available on deck to coordinate fueling operations and also acts as a safety petty officer.
4. Aircraft are refueled per the Air Plan. The Fuels Control Talker maintains accountability for fuel billing by recording on the fuel checker card the amount of fuel on board prior to fueling, after fueling, and the amount issued.

Fueling Stations

1. After the service pumps are started and piping is pressurized, turn on the de-fuel pump.
2. Open fueling station supply valves per AFOSS.
3. Connect ground wire from ship to aircraft.
4. Remove refueling adapter cap, connect nozzle to aircraft, place the toggle switch to the 'on' position and commence the fueling operation.
5. Upon completion of fueling and de-fueling aircraft, close fueling station per AFOSS.
6. JP-5 refueling/de-fueling in port may be accomplished with the approval of the commanding officer or his designated representative.

(US Navy, 2008a, 8-8)

sponsons, all located in elevator ramp recesses. During UNREP, two or three filling connections are typically used, but during dockside replenishment, the carrier can also use additional filling connections on the port side to refuel from fuel barges. As the fuel comes on board, it is passed down to the storage tanks via a transfer system, which consists of multiple transfer pumps located in pump rooms that also contain centrifugal purifiers for cleaning the fuel. These purifiers, however, are bypassed during transfer operations except when service tanks are being filled. (The transfer system is responsible for all movement of the fuel around the ship, not just from the filling points to the storage tanks.)

The onboard fuel has to pass through several stages of cleaning before it reaches its ready-to--use state. The fuel is typically allowed a period of settling, which encourages foreign bodies and water content within the fuel to sink to the bottom. The system also includes a 'stripping' component – this recovers lost tank volume while maintaining clean fuel for issue. The stripping system cleans the fuel of contaminants by recirculating it through a bank of filters/separators, and the service tanks also contain their own filtration and separation system. A US Navy document here explains the efficiency and process of fuel cleaning:

Filters are designed to remove 98% of all solids and 100% of all entrained water from the fuel passing through them. This is accomplished in a two-stage operation by two separate filtering media installed within the filter shell. The first stage consists of a bank of COALESCING elements, surrounded by a hydrophobic screen, that performs the function of removing solids and coalescing water. Coalescing means the bringing together of fine particles of entrained water to form large droplets that then fall out of the fuel by gravity. The second stage consists of a bank of SEPARATOR elements that perform the function of repelling the coalesced water droplets that were too small to fall out by gravity.

(US Navy, 1993, 8-6)

To determine the quality of the fuel in the tanks, personnel from the Aviation Fuels Division

(V-4) will perform regular 'soundings'. These are performed by using sounding tapes, which are 50ft (15m) steel tapes graduated in feet and inches and fitted with a plumb bob via a snaphook on the bitter end. The tape is coated in a water-indicating or fuel-indicating paste and it is then wound down into the tank via a sounding tube, the plumb bob keeping the tape taut. The presence of water droplets or the colour-change of the pastes gives the operators information about the level and quality of the fuel in the tanks.

For the fuelling of aircraft, fuel is pumped up from the service tanks to the JP-5 fuelling stations above. Typically an aircraft is refuelled shortly after recovery, to maintain it in a ready state. If necessary, however, aircraft can be defuelled using the CLA-VAL hose reels, which extract the fuel to a defuelling main, from which it is sent back to a designated storage tank.

The logistics of maintaining life aboard a supercarrier are far greater than this single chapter can encompass. The priorities of food, water, ammunition and fuel are obviously fundamental – classed as the basic needs of an operational aircraft carrier. Beyond these, however, is a whole world of minor and not-so-minor challenges. Although it is part of a wider naval support network, and takes regular resupply, a supercarrier to a large extent strives to be a self-contained entity, carrying everything it needs to sustain itself far from shore for months at a time. That it is able to do so is a remarkable feat of logistical engineering.

ABOVE Sailors assigned to Carrier Air Wing (CVW) 3 inspect an auxiliary fuel tank aboard the USS *Dwight D. Eisenhower* (CVN-69). *(US Navy photo by Mass Communication Specialist 3rd Class Devin Alexondra Lowe/ Released)*

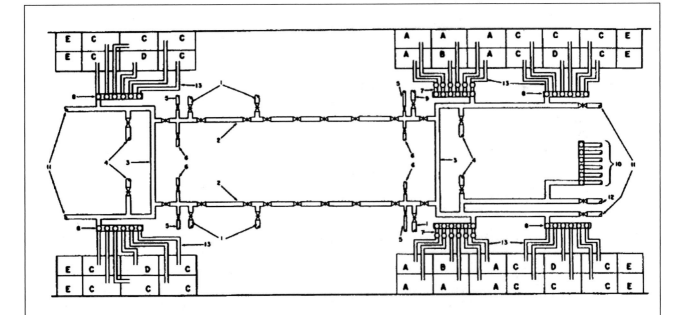

A diagrammatic representation of the JP-5 filling and transfer system typical aboard a CVN. *(US Navy)*

A. JP-5 or ballast
B. JP-5, ballast, or overflow
C. JP-5
D. JP-5 or overflow
E. JP-5 service
1. Downcomers
2. Transfer main
3. Transfer-main branch headers
4. Transfer-pump suction headers
5. Transfer pump discharge
6. Stripping pump discharge
7. Double-valved manifold
8. Single-valved manifold
9. Defuel main
10. Double-bottom tank fill lines
11. Transfer-main branch headers (to other storage tanks)
12. Transfer-main branch header (to peak tank)
13. Storage-tank fill and suction lines

Chapter Seven

Daily life and operations

We have now arrived at a solid understanding of the major constituent parts of a supercarrier, and how those parts work together to deliver air missions. To complete our picture, we delve into the daily life of a carrier a little deeper, relying as much as possible on the words of crew members, derived from interviews conducted aboard the USS *Dwight D. Eisenhower*, but also from a selection of US Navy archive material. By doing so, we discover carriers as truly *living* entities, homes at sea for thousands of people.

OPPOSITE Aviation Ordnanceman Airman Taylor Yost communicates with other crew members on a sound-powered telephone in the hangar bay of USS *Theodore Roosevelt* (CVN-71). *(US Navy photo by Airman D.J. Schwartz/Released)*

167
DAILY LIFE AND OPERATIONS

Command authority

We start at the very top of the command tree, with the ship's captain. What is readily apparent about a carrier captain is not just the breadth of the responsibility – every shade and hue of management responsibility is on his shoulders, human, tactical, strategic and diplomatic – but also the range of knowledge required, both of flight and of naval operations. The captains and XOs are therefore typically ex-US Navy pilots with extensive carrier operations under their belts, added to which is an immense investment in self-learning, diverse postings and ship commands.

The captain of the USS *Dwight D. Eisenhower*, Captain Kyle P. Higgins, USN, is one such example. Having graduated from the US Merchant Marine Academy in 1990, he subsequently served as a Third Mate aboard SS *Cape Nome* during Operation Desert Shield, before becoming a Naval Flight Officer in September 1992. His first years in naval aviation were spent as an A-6E Bombardier/Navigator with the VA 52 'Knightriders' aboard USS *Kitty Hawk* (CV-63), before transitioning to ES-3As in the VQ 5 'Sea Shadows' deploying aboard USS *Constellation* (CV-64). In September 2000 he again moved aircraft type, flying in the EA-6B Prowler with VAQ 130, during which time he undertook combat missions in Operation Iraqi Freedom aboard USS *Harry S. Truman* (CVN-75).

He then served as Commanding Officer of the 'Yellow Jackets' of VAQ 138 in 2008 and as XO of USS *John C. Stennis* (CVN-74) in 2013. Higgins was also the Commanding Officer of the US Seventh Fleet Flag Ship, USS *Blue Ridge* (LCC-19) in 2016. Rounding off his naval aviation and command experience (he has accumulated more than 2,300 flight hours and 790 arrested landings), his shore tours include attending the Naval Postgraduate School to gain a Master of Science Degree in Space Systems Operations. He also served on Commander, Electronic Attack Wing, US Pacific Fleet (COMVAQWINGPAC) staff as a Requirements Officer and Chief Staff Officer, plus commanded Provincial Reconstruction Teams Parwan and Uruzgan, Afghanistan, from October 2009 to November 2010, where he operated jointly with the Government of Afghanistan. He completed an OPNAV staff tour as Director, Fleet Readiness, in November 2017.

In an interview with the author, Captain Higgins gave some context to his experience and background, explained how he arrived at his position and also described the relationship between him and his XO:

It doesn't happen just by experience, and it doesn't happen just by chance. It happens because we make it happen. We go through the process of learning. This is the vast difference between the Executive Officer of an aircraft carrier and the captain – we are separated by about seven years. I've been doing this kind of work since 2012. . . . When we send a junior captain (the XO) here, to work with a senior captain, he learns how the ship works. So the XO works that second deck piece, and manages the day-to-day, making sure that it contributes to the overall goal of the ship, whatever that goal might be. The captain, on the other hand, has been in his shoes. I've done that job on another ship [USS John C. Stennis] in different times and a different set of circumstances. I happened to have a maintenance period for mine, so I learned a different side of our business. And it was dry dock maintenance, so I learned how to make that type of relationship work with the external entities coming onboard. [. . .]

We know how to run squadrons – we are very good at that. We have done that our whole lives. Usually a squadron consists of about 200 people and 12 aircraft, but I have commanded squadrons of just four aircraft. That's a tyranny of small numbers – if one aircraft goes down you've lost 75% of your operational capability. You also usually have two aircraft in maintenance at any one time. [. . .] But running a ship is very different. Technically the responsibilities are just the same – being in command is being in command. But it does get very specific on certain things on ship's captains, especially if you are fortunate enough to be in the air wing and embark on the ship. [. . .]

An important stage in my career was when I stepped into what they call a 'deep draft', when I was given the opportunity to lead a ship [USS Blue Ridge] as commanding officer. My personal crew size was about 650 sailors, and then I had Seventh Fleet staff on top of that, so I had another 350–360 sailors. So overall my ship held about 1,000 sailors. [. . .] So I

learned how to run a ship that way. Then I went to the Pentagon and learned some 'Big Navy', and how the Pentagon works and how we make decisions at a senior level. Then I was fortunate enough to screen for command here.

ABOVE The band **Vertical Horizon perform on the flight deck of USS *Harry S. Truman* (CVN-75) as part of a Navy Entertainment tour.** *(US Navy photo by Mass Communication Specialist Seaman Emily M. Blair/Released)*

LEFT Guests tour the aircraft carrier USS *Theodore Roosevelt* (CVN-71) during the Norfolk Naval Station Fleet Fest. Family involvement in the life of the carriers is very much encouraged. *(US Navy photo by Mass Communication Specialist Seaman Apprentice Wyatt L. Anthony)*

In command, Captain Higgins is an ultimate focal point for the flow of information around the ship. He explained how the captain connects with the departments beneath him:

I have 20 direct reports – I have 20 different departments. Each ship is slightly different, but most of us have all the same functions, but it's a matter of how they are built. We decided to have independent departments. Each one has its very own specific function and process. For example, the medical folks are straight from medical, not dental – there's a whole dental department which deals with the dental side. [. . .] We have intelligence – there's a whole department devoted to that. We have Combat Systems, which deals with not just the ship's self-defense systems and how they operate, but they deal with radios, they deal with internal communications, they deal with satellite communication circuits, the computer networks – just a variety of things. As those things functionally go up and down, they advise me on what is available, how much is available, and when it can be available. And we work very closely with the admiral's staff to make sure that it is done properly.

We have an entire operations department that runs current and future operations. They see what we are doing on the day-to-day – they use that schedule to look into the future and with their staff counterpart they say that 'future ops are going to look like this'.

The navigation team is exactly what it

sounds like, but it's not as simple as going from Point A to Point B like the merchant marine. The merchant marine goes from port to port and everything in between is money. The Navy doesn't work that way. We are in port, and then we do things, and those things equate to time, and that time has consequences, such as sea space and protecting the ship, and a whole load of other factors we have to take into account. We have to be somewhere on a timeline. For flying isn't free. Flying means wind. You've got to find the wind and you've got to stay in the wind, so it's all time-based decision-making.

The Air Department runs all of the air operations from day to day – future and current. 'Future' involves looking at planned maintenance – if I've got to take this piece of machinery down for long term or short term, what does that mean for catapults? If one of them has to come down for maintenance which one should come down first, and what am I doing next, and how important is it to the launching of the airplanes? If we take the wrong catapult down at the wrong time that could cause a traffic jam on the roof. Now I've just burned everyone with doing something different when we could have planned it better. [. . .] Supply department, engineering, reactor etc. – they all play into this.

The picture painted by Captain Higgins is one of inclusivity and teamwork. Later in the interview, he explained that the sole purpose of an aircraft carrier is to 'launch and recover aircraft', and that *everyone* aboard the ship supports that aim, regardless of their role or rank. Thus, as he described, the mess department might see its responsibility purely as providing the crew and air wing with food, but ultimately the contribution that makes to nutrition, health and morale directly feeds into the efficiency of the air operations. It is an image of a single, holistic team.

Another insightful, high-level perspective on the qualities of the carrier team comes from Vice Admiral Mike Shoemaker, who in 2018 (when the interview that follows was conducted) was Commander, Naval Air Forces (CNAF), exercising responsibility for all US Navy air units.

He was asked by a Navy press officer: 'Today in 2018, compared to when you came in, what do you think of the sailors and aviators that make up Naval Aviation?' His reply, here related at length, focuses our attention more on the qualities of the air wing itself, and the intelligence, education and proper planning that feed into combat missions, both on shore and at sea:

In the visits I have made around the fleet in my three years here, I continue to be incredibly impressed by our people. They're the key to everything we do, and retaining quality folks is key. We've done a pretty good job of that. I talk to young maintainers on the flightline [. . .] and it's inspiring to see what they're doing to recover readiness, the creativity, how they've worked amongst different squadrons to learn from each other and to think out of the box in terms of ways to improve readiness and the quality of maintenance and the training that they get. The way they work together is incredible. I was at the Fleet Readiness Center in Lemoore, and I saw one of the young mechanics in there, manufacturing parts. He showed me the blueprints he got from industry, and he's making parts that are not in the stock system anywhere. Not just legacy Hornets, these are Super Hornets as

well. He was excited to show me how he can use this machine and turn out parts, in some cases ones that don't exist. That kind of innovation is really exciting and we see it all the time. I spend a lot of time at our Boots on the Ground events talking to young Sailors and Marines. And you can't not walk away from those events completely impressed with their creativity, innovation, drive and work ethic. I'm very excited about where our young maintainers are across the force, and they grow into our seasoned chiefs and master chiefs who we must have to run Naval aviation.

ABOVE Interior Communications Electrician 1st Class Mark Gauthia, a Chief Petty Officer (CPO) selectee assigned to USS *George Washington* (CVN-73), spray-cleans baskets during a volunteer event at the Virginia Peninsula Foodbank. *(US Navy photo by Mass Communication Specialist 2nd Class Anna Van Nuys/ Released)*

LEFT An Aviation Electronics Technician 2nd Class conducts maintenance on an MH-60S Seahawk helicopter, assigned to Helicopter Sea Combat Squadron (HSC) 9, in the hangar bay of USS *John C. Stennis* (CVN-74). *(US Navy photo by Mass Communication Specialist 3rd Class Mitchell Banks/ Released)*

ABOVE The final
section of main mast
is installed on the
USS *George
Washington* (CVN-73)
at Huntington Ingalls
Industries Newport
News Shipbuilding,
15 March 2019, during
the carrier's RCOH.
*(US Navy photo courtesy
HHI by Matt Hildreth)*

I look at the junior officers [JOs], and
I hear the stories from the strike group
commanders about what they're doing on
deployment. I look back to what we were
doing on my first deployment. Although we
weren't flying in combat, or flying over places
like Iraq and Syria, I do know that what they
have to do on those missions, in terms of
balancing the rules of engagement, ensuring
they have positive ID on the targets they're
supposed to hit, and then understanding
what their weapons are going to do and
estimating any potential collateral damage,
and working with folks on the ground who
may not be speaking great English, and I

watch how they pull all of that together –
lieutenants flying together over Iraq and Syria
– and they continue to execute flawlessly.

When I was a strike group commander,
during OIF [Operation Iraqi Freedom] in
Afghanistan, I'd sit through the debriefs
and I'd listen to the JOs walk through their
thinking on missions, of how they'd do
everything they could short of dropping a
bomb – until it was their last resort – to
meet the ground commander's intent.
I could not be more proud. I think it's
a testament to our training system, the
way we train starting at CNATRA [Chief
of Naval Air Training] through our FRSs

RIGHT Vice Admiral Richard W. Hunt, commander of US Third Fleet, crosses the 'rainbow sideboys' during an arrival aboard the USS *Abraham Lincoln* (CVN-72). *(US Navy photo by Mass Communication Specialist 3rd Class Lex T. Wenberg/Released)*

[Fleet Replacement Squadron] to fleet training, and really to the standardization that we have across the force. We have our air combat training continuum, which allows us in every community to track a junior officer's progress, through different qualifications, all the way up to where he or she is now instructing other junior officers. If you see a guy or gal who is a Level 3 or Level 4 qualified in a certain community or platform, you know exactly what that means. I think that's been one of the greatest strengths for Naval Aviation. We've gone through the Comprehensive Review and the Strategic Review, I look at some of the lessons learned there, and I keep falling back on Naval Aviation's standardization and that air combat training continuum. Those are programs that we must continue to embrace and execute across the force.

Shoemaker's comments illustrate how the combat capability flying off the decks of the CVNs is just the sharp end of a long training and technical spear, reaching right back on to land and training establishments such as the CNATRA. Following a primary training phase taken by all aviators, a naval pilot trainee can then go into one of six Student Naval Aviator training pipelines – Strike, Rotary, Maritime, Tiltrotor, E-2/C-2 and E-6. CNATRA also conducts four Naval Flight Officer (NFO) training pipelines – Strike Fighter, Airborne Early Warning (AEW), Maritime Patrol (MPR) and Take Charge and Move Out (TACAMO).

RIGHT An Electrician's Mate 3rd Class performs safety checks on electronics for members of the board of inspection and survey (INSURV) in the hangar bay of the USS *Dwight D. Eisenhower* (CVN-69). *(US Navy photo by Mass Communication Specialist 3rd Class Kaleb J. Sarten/Released)*

Watchstanding

All the roles performed on board a supercarrier involve a high degree of self-management and a diligent approach to procedure. One duty that requires reinforced nerves and an almost immunity to panic is that of acting as Officer of the Watch, up on the navigation bridge and officially in charge of manoeuvring the ship and managing the surrounding team, as the direct representative of the captain's orders. The emotions involved, and the tasks required, was well explained by Lt. J.G. Colleen M. Wilmington of the USS *Nimitz* in 2017:

You get the fear in the pit of your stomach a lot that you'll mess something up. Then you have the anxiety that you'll do something wrong or you'll upset someone, but that all has to go on inside. On the outside you have to be the one who's calm, cool and collected. When I give out orders, when I try to figure out where the ship is going to turn after a recovery, I can't let fear and anxiety come out in my voice. I can't necessarily get angry at someone, because then if I get angry at them they might start to second guess themselves. I need everybody to do their job, so you have to learn how to compartmentalize all those feelings and deal with them after watch.

I'm qualified on the bridge, from helm safety officer all the way through officer of the deck. I am the primary boat officer for this ship. I'm the locker officer, I also stand anti-terrorism watch and I recently qualified as non-nuclear EOOW [Engineering Officer of the Watch].

One of the basic general orders is to take charge of this post and all government property. For me, on any watch that I'm taking, government property includes each one of us, which means that when I take that role in any of my positions, my job is to fulfill the duties of that particular job while having overarching watch of everyone that stands with me.

BELOW An Interior Communications Electrician 2nd Class operates the ILARTS aboard USS *Dwight D. Eisenhower* (CVN-69) during an ordnance transfer with USS *John C. Stennis* (CVN-74).

The Officer of the Watch is not the only individual on the bridge at this time acutely aware of their heavy responsibilities. Another is the person assigned to perform Quartermaster of the Watch, as here explained by Quartermaster 3rd Class Stephanie Gortarez, also of the *Nimitz*:

I stand Quartermaster of the Watch. We are assistance [sic] to the navigator making sure that the ship stays in safe waters. When we make our reports, our shipmates are counting on us to be accurate and precise in those reports to ensure the safe maneuvering of the ship. We can't afford to be lackadaisical on watch because not only is our watch team relying on us, but the entire ship is relying on us.

Even though it's hard with everyday life, it's just making sure that you get enough sleep, because you have to stay awake; you have to stay vigilant and always keep an eye out for other people or anything around us. Sure you're tired at 1:30 in the morning, but that doesn't mean that you can go sit in the corner and go sleep; you have to pay attention. It's so important we have eyes on everything. If we miss one thing that can mean the loss of people's lives, and nobody wants that.

Drilling for disaster

Daily life for the sailors and air crew of a supercarrier naturally depends on both the roles that they perform and the circumstances of the ship. Everything from the time they wake up (and how many hours of sleep they get) through to the types of challenges they will face can shift from day to day and from place to place. When not in combat, however, the combat mindset is continually maintained through drills. A case in point is emergency procedures. Aboard the USS *George Washington* (CVN-73), for example, the drills confront a range of potential threats, not just from the actions of a state-level adversary. Damage Controlman 1st Class Mark Carroll, leading petty officer of the damage control division and duty fire marshal of duty section 10 explained:

It is important for sailors to participate in fire drills to gain experience, and that allows us to be prepared for the real deal. The drills the ship's fire marshal prepares allow us to prepare for any scenario that may arise. By running drills, this allows us to gain familiarity with the ship's layout and equipment, and can give us a good understanding that causalities can happen anywhere at any time. Another benefit to doing drills is so we can become familiar with all damage control equipment, and be comfortable in its utilization. When the real deal happens, that practice allows us to use our equipment without skipping a beat. All sailors need to do to get the most out of each drill is to actively participate. Staying motivated and engaged during the drills and asking questions to the leadership can allow everyone to have a good understanding of what's going on at all levels. A big, important aspect that most sailors probably do not hold in high regard is the drill debriefs with [the Damage Control Training Team]. By listening to the drill debriefs, it can allow sailors to understand how to improve their technique and procedures, and even get tips on how to do something better. These drill debriefs can allow us to see what we need to improve on and if sailors take these things to heart, it can allow them to grow in their respective positions and improve in all facets.

ABOVE **A stretcher in a casualty station aboard the USS *Dwight D. Eisenhower* (CVN-69). In an environment of unyielding metal, injuries are a daily occurrence.** *(Patrick Bunce)*

In days when low-level terrorist threats or psychiatric episodes also have to be taken into account, the ship's crew also drill for violent small-arms incidents aboard the carrier, as explained by Master-at-Arms 1st Class, Susan Olander, the training leading petty officer for the security department:

Active shooter drills are imperative for our sailors, not just security, but all hands. As active shooters are more prominent, it is important for our response forces to be ready to handle any situation. We try to keep the drill scenarios as real as we can. By practicing plausible scenarios, it brings home the reality of just how fast any situation can become an active shooter situation. If sailors weren't prepared to respond to active shooters, both response forces and ship's crew, they would find themselves essentially lost. This decreases our ability to stop the threat quickly and increases the opportunity for catastrophe. Treat every scenario as real and respond as if it were the real thing. Not treating a drill as the real thing can dampen the effect. Therefore, our response forces will not treat the real event appropriately.

Active shooter training is conducted annually. Paying attention to the material and stopping to think 'what would I do?' is an excellent way to prepare yourself. Always having an escape route, or quickly identifying potential weapons to defend yourself is an easy way to place yourself in the proper mindset.

In addition to drilling for localised or minor incidents, however, carrier crews also undertake drills for the most extreme of circumstances – the sinking of the ship. This eventuality is highly unlikely; the carrier's numerous waterproof compartments, emergency response systems and defensive capabilities put many barriers in the way of the ship slipping beneath the waves. Yet the Navy has learned to assume nothing.

The process of abandoning ship starts with the decision of the commanding officer, then the Tactical Action Officer (TAO) broadcasts that decision over the 1MC shipboard announcement system. In the same broadcast, the TAO provides the crew with important information that has a bearing on their survival, eg distance to nearest land, threat levels on that land, wind direction and speed, water

BELOW Sailors assigned to USS *Gerald R. Ford* (CVN-78) get their vitals taken before donating blood during an Armed Services Blood Program (ASBP) drive at Huntington Hall. *(US Navy photo by Mass Communication Specialist Seaman Zachary Melvin/ Released)*

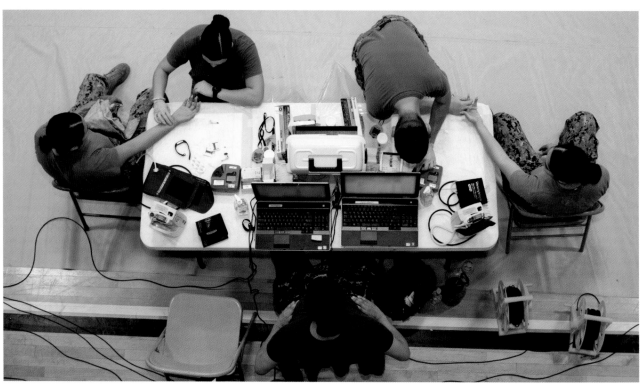

MK 8 LIFE RAFT

US Navy aircraft carriers use the Mk 8 inflatable life raft, each of which can hold 50 people. The lifeboats are affixed to the catwalks on the starboard and port sides of the ship, and they are either deployed manually by the crew or they automatically inflate when submerged 10–40ft (3–12m) underwater. The rafts contain extensive survival equipment, including the following:

- desalinator
- 50 bottles of fresh water
- food rations for each passenger
- a pressure relief valve retainer
- two storage bags for collecting rain water
- a torch
- six torch batteries
- a fluorescent sea marker canister
- signalling mirror
- sponge
- survival knife
- whistle
- drinking cups
- fishing kit
- first-aid kit.

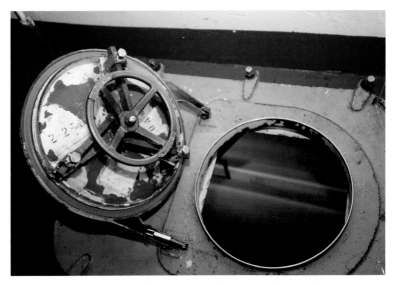

temperature, presence of friendly vessels and so on. The sailors then muster with their departments on the flight deck and in the hangar bay, then proceed to the ship's lifeboats.

Note that when in their lifeboats, a chain of command still prevails. The senior ranking sailor acts as the officer in charge (OIC), although if a chaplain, corpsman, nurse or doctor is the most senior person, he or she must pass the OIC position to the next highest rank. Following an abandon-ship drill in May 2018, Senior Chief Boatswain's Mate Scott Simpson, the USS

ABOVE Movement about a supercarrier requires some degree of strength, dexterity and flexibility, particularly when transiting through tight floor hatches. *(Patrick Bunce)*

LEFT Aviation Electronics Technician 3rd Class Joseph Mitchell measures the resistance in a circuit card aboard USS *Abraham Lincoln* (CVN-72). *(US Navy photo by Mass Communication Specialist Seaman Mohamed Labanieh/ Released)*

Abraham Lincoln (CVN-72) deck department's Leading Chief Petty Officer, explained:

BELOW Machinery abounds in almost every space around a supercarrier. Here we see one of the pumps used to turn the rudder in aft steering. (Patrick Bunce)

The order to abandon ship is to save lives. But it's easy to make the incorrect decision when panic overtakes your thought process. These decisions are usually a result of a lack of training or not thinking clearly. We hope this would never happen, but if it did, we need sailors to stay calm and remember their training.

Working days

When a carrier is out to sea with the air wing embarked, and particularly if the ship is involved with an exercise or combat operations, the pace of life is frenetic. Visitors to such a vessel often note the sheer level of noise involved, the ship having more in common acoustically and dynamically with a major industrial facility than a merchant vessel. Captain Higgins explained that everyone on the ship, regardless of how buried they were in the bowels of the vessel, would know when aircraft launches and recoveries were taking place, the activity transmitted through roars, structural rumbles, shaking and the crack of arrestor cables striking impact pads.

On the flight deck, naturally, there is a whirl of purposeful activity. Aviation Boatswain's Mates (Handling) (ABH) – the yellowshirts, for example – are directly responsible for the handling and manoeuvring of aircraft as well as the safety of all personnel during flight operations. Aviation Boatswain's Mate (Handling) 3rd Class, Melanie Cluck, from Palm Springs, California, of the USS _Nimitz_ (CVN-68), explained:

At first being a yellowshirt was scary, but now that I have some confidence I would say there is a sense of pride. On the flight deck we are not only responsible for directing aircraft but also for directing people. Normally anyone who needs guidance on the flight deck looks for a yellowshirt. Safety of all the personnel on deck is a big part of our job as well. So we don't only need to know our job, but everyone else's as well. You have to be able to really get control of your aircraft and understand the pilot. It's a gut feeling that you develop during your training, if you feel you need to slow the aircraft down you can, and you start to learn when exactly to turn it. We have hundreds of hand signals we can use to take control of the aircraft on deck. The people in the pilot seats are officers so you have to be professional and every motion you make has to be crisp and precise to prevent accidents.

On the USS *Dwight D. Eisenhower*, Aviation Boatswain's Mate (Equipment) Airman Quay Salter also sees the critical importance of clear actions:

Our primary mission of launching and recovering aircraft really depends on ABEs [Aviation Boatswain's Mate (Equipment)] and the catapults. We have to have our minds focused on the operation every second, and be ready for anything that needs to be done. Maintenance checks are weekly and done nearly every day or every other day. There is a lot of preventive maintenance and corrective maintenance that is performed on the catapults. It takes time to learn all the positions for a topside qualification, but all of the training runs together so you can keep learning and learning. It takes roughly 2–3 months of training to become topside qualified. The most important thing to remember while on the flight deck is safety. You have to be aware of your surroundings and mindful of where the jets are turning so you aren't caught off guard by a jet blast when it's turning.

Smooth collaborative effort is the cornerstone of the flight deck operations, as Bow Catapults Group Supervisor, Chief Aviation Boatswain's Mate (Equipment) Eleazor Rojas (also of the *Dwight D. Eisenhower*) explained:

Working up here requires a lot of teamwork. What we do is a crucial part of the mission, because without us Ike [the moniker for the Dwight D. Eisenhower] couldn't receive the jets to continue to support forces on the ground. Everyone working here knows that, and these sailors work hard under serious pressure and sometimes tough environmental conditions to get the job done without complaint.

Below decks

Although the flight deck is the most high-profile of the carrier's spaces, the activity that takes place there is matched by less glamorous, but no less essential, duties further down in the ship. Out at sea, for example, there

ABOVE The supercarriers work to cater for the spiritual needs of all crew members. Here Lt Cmdr David Kim, a chaplain aboard the USS *Gerald R. Ford* (CVN-78), leads a service in the ship's chapel. *(US Navy photo by Mass Communication Specialist Seaman Zachary Melvin/Released)*

is the endless requirement to make sure that the whole crew has their laundry done regularly and efficiently. Aboard the USS *George H.W. Bush* (CVN-77) laundry is owned by the carrier's Supply Department, which looks after the clothing of 4,500 sailors. The personnel who operate the laundry are actually on temporarily assigned duty (TAD) from other departments and divisions for a period historically known as food/logistics service attendance (FSA).

BELOW Ladders descending into one of the ordnance magazines aboard the USS *Dwight D. Eisenhower* (CVN-69). *(Patrick Bunce)*

Electronics Technician 3rd Class, Maria Diaz, described the process:

I've been working down here about two weeks. I'm originally from combat systems, CS-32. Basically, we pick up the laundry, wash it, dry it, and bag it. It's pretty straightforward work. We take in a lot of bags every day, and we have a night shift as well, so they take in plenty, too. Because we take in so many bags, we have to keep the loads organized. Ideally, we keep it one bag to a cart, though we can mix everything together with chiefs' laundry because all their stuff is stenciled and easy to collect and put back.

ABOVE Quade 'Quake' Milum, of the famous Harlem Globetrotters basketball team, played a game with sailors on the flight deck of USS *John C. Stennis* (CVN-74) during a Navy Entertainment sponsored visit. *(US Navy photo by Mass Communication Specialist 2nd Class John Hetherington/Released)*

Aviation Boatswain's Mate (Handling), Airman Tatiana Parraguevara, explained the machinery used to handle such loads:

Each washer has three slots which rotate out so we can fit more in. Each slot can hold up to 32 pounds, and that's just on this machine. The bigger machines can hold up to 66 pounds. We also have smaller, home-sized machines for VIPs, O-5 [a US Navy pay grade] and above, and master chiefs. I've been down here about four months. We don't have enough people in my division, so we have to rotate them out. But I like it down here, so I volunteered to get extended.

BELOW Culinary Specialist Seaman Larina Thompson prepares dessert in the aft galley of the USS *Abraham Lincoln* (CVN-72). The cooks aboard the carrier have to prepare food ranging from mass meals for the crew to fine dining for visiting dignitaries. *(US Navy photo by Mass Communication Specialist 3rd Class Jeremiah Bartelt/Released)*

There is also the matter of feeding the thousands of sailors. The food service division is responsible for providing nutritious meals to sailors aboard the USS *Abraham Lincoln*, not just in the steady and predictable conditions of port, but also during the managed chaos of a rapid deployment. '*Abraham Lincoln* must be ready to deploy at any moment,' said Chief Culinary Specialist Levy Obana. 'Supplies must be appropriately stocked to ensure operational mission readiness.' In total, the division will have to prepare meals for some 2,100 enlisted sailors in port, but more than 4,200 enlisted sailors when under way, an expansion that requires the opening of a second mess deck for the crew with a separate menu. In addition, the chiefs' mess and wardroom have menus for 300–360 chiefs and officers, and the number of meals requiring preparation will grow with the deployment of the air wing.

NAVSUP MENU PLAN

The Naval Supply Systems Command (NAVSUP) provides a menu plan to all ships in the US Navy fleet on a rotating 21-day cycle, and this menu is divided into two versions – at-sea or in-port. The use of the cycle menu is explained in NAVSUP's *Food Service Operation* Handbook:

A cycle menu works best for general messes. Cycle menus save time and allow an easier and more thorough analysis than menus written weekly. Cycle menus provide more accurate forecasting for ration costs, requisition requirements, and daily food preparation. In deciding on the most desirable cycle length, the variety and frequency of resupply, the number of duty sections, and the CS watch schedule should be taken into consideration. An odd-numbered day cycle allows each watch section the opportunity to prepare the entire cycle menu. Every attempt will be made to offer a selective menu. Selective menus offer one or more options for each meal category. Ideally, each menu should offer two or more entrées, side dishes, vegetables and desserts. A variety of beverages and breads will also be available.

(NAVSUP, 2010, 1-15)

The NAVSUP menus are designed around very specific nutritional balancing. Meals must consist of two starches, two vegetables and three main entrée items. Although the menus are pre-scheduled, the ship's staff responsible for implementing them must be ready to adapt to spur-of-the-moment changes. The menus don't change with the seasonal availability of food but are issued to commands by region.

BELOW USS *Gerald R. Ford* **(CVN-78) has invested in state-of-the-art gym equipment, to assist with maintaining crew fitness during long deployments.** *(US Navy photo by Mass Communication Specialist Seaman Zachary Melvin/ Released)*

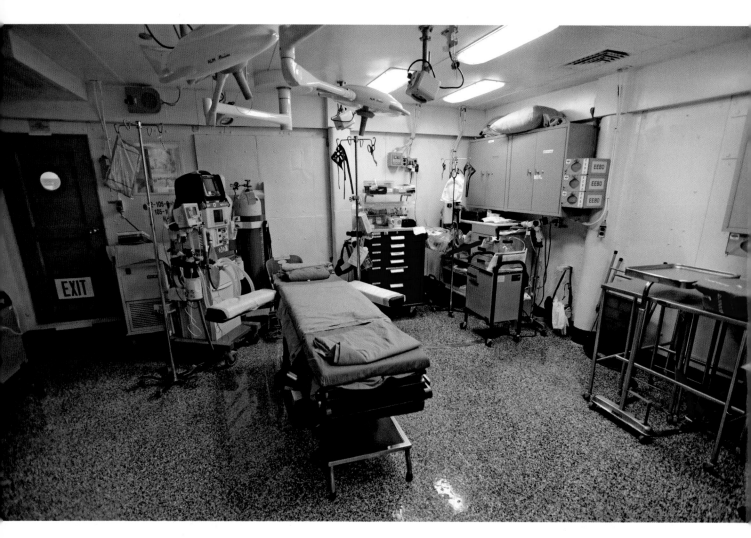

ABOVE One of the emergency treatment rooms in the Medical Department of USS Dwight D. Eisenhower (CVN-69).
(Patrick Bunce)

Levy Obana said:

Ensuring that our department has enough product to support both menus necessitates proper planning and accurate record of inventory. As required by the TYCOM, Abraham Lincoln, an operational carrier, is required at all times to have enough supplies to sustain the entire ship's staff for 30 to 45 days. Food provides more than just sustenance to sailors. It provides them energy to go back to work satisfied. As cooks and food service workers, our mission is to provide quality service and a variety of nutritious meals. Every member of our team works hard to make this possible.

The duties of the supercarrier's crew undergo a significant change when the ship puts in for a major period of dockside maintenance. The most significant of these is the RCOH, which typically takes about three years. During this period, some members of the crew (eg flight deck crew) might find that their duties are dialled down in intensity, or they are heavily repurposed. For example, Chief Aviation Boatswain's Mate (Equipment) Robert Lightner, of the *George Washington*, explained:

Our job as ABEs here during RCOH is different than when we are out at sea, because we are not launching and recovering aircraft and we are not really working on any of our own equipment. We are spread out all over the ship on various PM [preventative maintenance] teams helping to get George Washington out of the shipyard on time. After we are done with RCOH, we will have all new and updated equipment, which will help the longevity of the ship for years to come and be able to launch aircraft anywhere in the world to defend our country.

RIGHT An aviation engineer inspects an afterburner in the jet shop aboard the USS Theodore Roosevelt (CVN-71). *(US Navy photo by Mass Communication Specialist Seaman Bill M. Sanders/Released)*

For mechanically minded individuals, however, an RCOH can be one of the busiest times of their service. A case in point are the Electrician's Mates (EM), whose role during the RCOH is explained by Chief Electrician's Mate Leodolpho Romera II, a Chief Petty Officer in *George Washington*'s electrical division:

The EM's job in the yard is really broad. Basically everything that you touch that's powered by electricity is being maintained by electricians. We keep the lights on. We handle electrical distribution and take care of the load centers, which are the hubs that distribute the electrical power coming from the generators, along with things like power panels, fuse boxes, overhead lighting, and outlets.

From electricians to aviators, cooks to radar specialists, ordnance handlers to captain, the US supercarriers are ornate human enterprises, the thousands of individual human stories and roles making up a fighting whole. The future of carriers and their place in America's continuing power projection is a current hot topic in defence circles, although in fairness the destiny of carrier aviation has attracted its fair share of question marks since its inception. Given what carriers can perform, from almost any region of the world's oceans, however, it is currently hard to envisage what could replace them for both strategic and tactical power. With the advent of the *Gerald R. Ford* class, it is apparent that the age of the supercarrier will be with us for many decades to come.

RIGHT An Interior Communications Electrician 3rd Class assigned to the Air Department aboard USS George Washington (CVN-73) sorts tank level indicators (TLIs). *(US Navy photo by Mass Communication Specialist 3rd Class Trey Hutcheson/Released)*

Bibliography and further reading

BELOW F/A-18s and an E-2 Hawkeye sit on the flight deck of the USS *Theodore Roosevelt* (CVN-71) as it transits the Pacific Ocean in January 2020, the core of a Carrier Strike Group deployment to the Indo-Pacific region. *(US Navy photo by Mass Communication Specialist Seaman Alexander Williams/ Released)*

DOT&E (Director, Operational Test and Evaluation) (2018). 'Surface Ship Torpedo Defense (SSTD) System: Torpedo Warning System (TWS) and Countermeasure Anti-Torpedo (CAT)'. Available at: https://www.dote.osd.mil/pub/reports/ FY2017/pdf/navy/2017sstd_tws_cat.pdf.

Doyle, Michael R., Douglas J. Samuel, Thomas Conway and Robert R. Klimowski (n.d.). 'Electromagnetic Aircraft Launch System – EMALS'. Naval Air Warfare Center, Aircraft Division.

Elward, Brad (2010). *Nimitz-Class Aircraft Carriers*. Osprey Publishing.

Environmental Protection Agency (1999). 'Distillation and Reverse Osmosis Brine: Nature of Discharge'. Available at: https:// www.epa.gov/sites/production/files/2015-08/ documents/2007_07_10_oceans_regulatory_ unds_tdddocuments_appadistillation.pdf.

Friedman, Norman and A.D. Baker III (1983). *U.S. Aircraft Carriers: An Illustrated Design History*. Naval Institute Press.

Inspector General, US Department of Defense (October 2007). 'Non-Skid Materials Used on Navy Ships'. Department of Defense Inspector General. Available at: https://media.defense.gov/2007/ Oct/30/2001712599/-1/-1/1/NSM%20 Final%20Report%20TAD-2008-001.pdf.

Ireland, Bernard and Francis Crosby (2015). *The World Encyclopedia of Aircraft Carriers and Naval Aircraft*. Southwater.

Navaltoday.com (5 June 2019). 'USS *Gerald R. Ford* Ship Self-Defense System Aces Dual-Target Test'. Available at: https://navaltoday.com/2019/06/05/uss-gerald-r-ford-ship-self-defense-system-aces-dual-target-test/.

NAVSUP (January 2010). *Navy Food Service Operation Handbook*. Naval Supply Systems Command.

NAVSUP (US Naval Supply Systems Command) (2010). *Navy Food Service Operation Handbook*. Naval Supply Systems Command.

RAND (2005). *Modernizing the U.S. Aircraft Carrier Fleet: Accelerating CVN 21 Production Versus Mid-Life Refueling*. RAND Corporation.

RAND (2006). *Leveraging America's Aircraft Carrier Capabilities: Exploring New Combat and Noncombat Roles and Missions for the U.S. Carrier Fleet*. RAND Corporation.

US Navy (1989) *Aviation Storekeeper C*, NAVESTRA 10396. Naval Education and Training Command.

US Navy (1990). *Aviation Boatswain's Mate E 3 & 2*. Naval Training Command.

US Navy (1993). *Aviation Boatswain's Mate F*, NAVEDTRA 14003. Naval Education and Training Professional Development and Technology Center.

US Navy (1997). *Naval Ships' Technical Manual Chapter 588 Aircraft Elevators*, S9086-T3-STM-010/CH-588R1. Commander, Naval Sea Systems Command.

US Navy (1999). OPNAVINST 8000.16 Volume II, Ch.6.5 'Conventional Weapons Handling Procedures Afloat (CV and CVN)'. Chief of Naval Operations Instructions.

US Navy (September 1999). *Naval Ships' Technical Manual Chapter 420 Navigation Systems, Equipment and Aids*, S9086-NZ-STM-010/CH-420R1. Commander, Naval Sea Systems Command.

US Navy (2001). *Aviation Boatswain's Mate H*, NAVEDTRA 14311. Naval Education and Training Professional Development and Technology Center. Available at: https://www.globalsecurity.org/military/library/policy/navy/nrtc/14003_fm.pdf.

US Navy (2005). *Aircraft Carrier Flight and Hangar Deck Fire Protection: History and Current Status*. Naval Air Warfare Center Weapons Division.

US Navy (2007a). *NATOPS Landing Signal Officer Manual*, NAVAIR 00-80T-104. Naval Air Systems Command.

US Navy (2007b). *CV NATOPS Manual*, NAVAIR 00-80T-105. Commander, Naval Air Systems Command.

US Navy (2008a). *CVN Flight/Hangar Deck NATOPS Manual*, NAVAIR 00-80T-120. Naval Air Systems Command.

US Navy (2008b). *Flight Deck Awareness: Basic Guide*. Naval Safety Center.

US Navy (2010). 'Chapter 3 Mk 7 Aircraft Recovery Equipment and Barricade Systems', from *Aviation Boatswain's Mate E 3 & 2*. Available at: http://navyaviation.tpub.com/14001/css/Chapter-3-Mk-7-Aircraft-Recovery-Equipment-And-Barricade-Systems-71.htm.

US Navy (2011). *Air Traffic Controller (AC)*, NAVEDTRA 14342A. Center for Naval Aviation Technical Training (CNATT).

US Navy (2014). *Flight Training Instruction: CV Procedures (UMFO) T-45C*, CNATRA P-816. NAS Corpus Christi, TX: Naval Air Training Command.

US Navy (2016). *NATOPS General Flight and Operating Instructions Manual*, CNAF M-3710.7. Commander, Naval Air Forces.

US Navy (2017). 'Surface Electronic Warfare Improvement Program (SEWIP)'. Available at: https://www.navy.mil/navydata/fact_display.asp?cid=2100&tid=475&ct=2.

US Secretary of the Navy (2002). Patent US6575113B1, 'Cooled Jet Blast Deflectors for Aircraft Carrier Flight Decks'. US Patent Office. Available at: https://patents.google.com/patent/US6575113B1/en.

ABOVE The USS *Harry S. Truman* (CVN-75) is here seen from the flight station of a Patrol Squadron (VP) 4 P-8A Poseidon maritime patrol and reconnaissance aircraft during an anti-submarine warfare mission over the Atlantic Ocean, 30 November 2019. *(US Navy photo by Mass Communication Specialist 2nd Class Juan S. Sua/Released)*

Index

Office of Naval Research (ONR) 71
Operation Desert Shield 168
Operation Enduring Freedom 24
Operation Iraqi Freedom 20, 24, 168, 172
Operation Southern Watch 83
Ordnance (See also Bombs, Missiles and Torpedoes) 158-163
arming protocols 161
guidelines for safe movement 162
'hung' weapons 160
magazines 158, 161, 163
ordnance hoist 159
weapon handling 47, 161, 174

Pentagon 169
Personnel 7, 58-69, 157
aerographer's mate 50
air gunner 161
air wing officers 15
arming coordinators 161
AVFUELS control talker 164
aviation boatswain's mates 59, 77, 95, 97, 113, 121, 152-153, 178, 180, 182
aviation engineer 183
aviation ordnancemen 47, 65, 83, 124, 137, 150, 153, 161, 167
bay petty officer 75
chaplain 179
culinary specialists 158, 180
deck petty officer 75
electricians/electronics technicians 76, 171, 174, 177, 180, 183
fire controlmen 142
food/logistics service attendant (FSA) 179
fuels control petty officer 164
gunner's mate 139, 147
helmsman 32, 34
leading chief petty officer (LCPO) 75
leading petty officer (LPO) 75
machinists 80
master-at-arms 158, 176
Medical Training Team 44
Officer of the Watch 174-175
operations specialist 136
Quartermaster of the Watch 34, 131, 175
ship's complements 10-11, 15-16, 20-21, 36
supply officer 156
temporary assigned duty (TAD) 179
tactical action officer (TAO) 135
Powerplants 39
nuclear reactors (PWRs) 7, 17-18, 20-21, 24, 26, 39, 41, 46, 157
reactor compartments 31, 38-39
steam turbines (conventional) 15-19
Primary Flight Control (Pri-Fly) (control tower) 32, 46, 50, 59, 66-70, 89, 103, 116
ADMACS 69, 72
DSIMS 71-72
Flight Deck Management System (FDMS) 71
port-facing positions 68
Primary flight control personnel
ADMACS operator 69
Air Boss (Air Officer) 32, 60, 66, 68, 103, 107, 161
air spotter 67
forward spotter 69
gear personnel 66
Mini Boss (Assistant Air Officer) 68, 103
tower supervisor 69
Production figures 10, 12, 16, 25
Propulsion 39
power turbines 39, 41
propellers and shafts 25, 38, 41

Radar systems 19-20, 22, 26, 32, 35, 133, 137
air search 131-132
AMDR 132
dual band (DBR) 135

EASR 132
fire-control 143
FLIR 142
surface-search 131
RCOH (Refuelling and Complex Overhaul) 21-22, 25, 32, 39, 42, 45, 170, 172, 182-183
Repair lockers 63
Roles 20
Combat Air Patrol (CAP) 136
Command Search and Rescue (CSAR) 96
Royal Navy 102, 138
aircraft carriers 13

Safety and operating procedures 41, 46, 178-179
Second World War 6, 9-12, 15
Allied victory 10
Sensors 32, 43, 142
Ship Characteristics Board (SCB) 12
Ship Signal Exploitation Space (SSES) 45
Shoemaker, Vice Admiral Mike 170, 173
Soviet Union 11
Statistics and specifications 6, 10, 16, 20-21, 30-31, 50
displacements 7, 10-11, 14-16, 20-21
performance 19
range 7
sorties flown 7
weight 14
Steering 38, 41-42, 178
pumps 178
rudders 41-42, 178
Steps and ladders 37, 179
Submarines 18, 20, 137
Supplies and replenishment 149-165
carrier onboard delivery (COD) 90, 151-158
in-port replenishment 157
ship-to-ship connected replenishments (CONREPS) 151-154, 156, 163
ship-to-ship vertical replenishments (VERTREPS) 151-152, 154-156
STREAM rig 152-153
underway replenishments (UNREPS) 151, 1553, 156, 163

Theatres of operation 18
Middle East conflicts 18
Pacific 10
Vietnam War 18, 20
Torpedoes 134, 137, 144-146
Truman, President Harry 15

UAVs 124
Boeing MQ-25A Stingray (CBARS) 91
Northrop Grumman X-47B UCAV 91, 124
Upgrades, overhauls and refits 12-14, 26
costs 14
CVN-21 programme 26
sub-modifications 12
USS Nimitz major overhaul periods 23
US Air Force (USAF) 11
US Department of Defense 134
US Marine Corps Fighter Attack (VMFA) squadrons 86
US Navy
Military Sealift Command (MSC) 27, 149
Seventh Fleet 6, 25, 168
Boxer Amphibious Ready Group 6
Ronald Reagan Carrier Strike Group 6
Third Fleet 173
US Navy aircraft carriers
CVN-81 27
CVN-82 27
USS Abraham Lincoln (CVN-72) 21, 24-25, 31, 41-42, 47, 51, 65, 76, 85, 87, 94, 99, 120, 124, 138, 142, 153-154, 156, 173, 177-178, 180, 182
USS America (CVA-66) 17
USS Carl Vinson (CVN-70) 9, 21, 25, 27, 51, 100, 151

USS Coral Sea (CVB-43) 10, 14
USS Constellation (CVA-64) 17, 168
USS Dwight D. Eisenhower (CVN-69) 7, 22, 25, 27, 29, 32-34, 36-38, 41, 43-45, 47, 51, 54, 63, 69-73, 76-77, 89, 96, 101, 103, 128-129, 133, 140, 144-146, 152, 158-162, 165, 167, 173-175, 179, 182
USS Enterprise (CVAN-65) 17, 19-21, 27, 112, 135
USS Enterprise (CVN-80) 27
USS Essex (CV-9) 10
USS Forrestal (CVA-59) 16
USS Franklin (CV-13) 10, 13
USS Franklin D. Roosevelt (CVB-42) 10
USS George H.W. Bush (CVN-77) 21, 25-26, 32, 42-44, 50, 54, 91, 124, 135
USS George Washington (CVN-73) 21, 25, 41, 49, 51, 64-65, 87, 101, 150, 170-172, 175, 182-183
USS Gerald R. Ford (CVN-78) 27, 32, 35, 53, 61, 63, 161, 176, 179, 181
USS Harry S. Truman (CVN-75) 21, 23, 25, 41, 43, 51, 56, 59, 66, 74, 80, 110, 119, 140, 142, 157, 159, 168-169
USS Independence (CVA-62) 16
USS Intrepid (CV-11) 12
USS John C. Stennis (CVN-74) 7, 21, 24-25, 34, 51, 59, 67, 70, 109, 113, 123, 127, 131, 146-147, 150, 155, 158, 163, 168, 171, 174
USS John F. Kennedy (CVA-67) 17-18, 21
USS John F. Kennedy (CVA-79) 27, 30, 132
USS Kitty Hawk (CVA-63) 17, 168
USS Langley (CV-1) 10
USS Midway (CVB-41) 10, 13-14
USS Nimitz (CVN-68) 21-23, 25, 27, 32, 51, 78, 83, 90, 97, 119, 134, 143
USS Oriskany (CV-34) 12-14
USS Ranger (CVA-61) 16
USS Ronald Reagan (CVN-76) 6, 21, 25-26, 32, 90, 92, 95, 97, 134, 155, 157
USS Saratoga (CVA-60) 16, 18
USS Theodore Roosevelt (CVN-71) 21, 25, 27, 51, 82, 111, 131, 167, 169, 183
USS Ticonderoga (CV-14) 12
USS United States (CVA-58) cancelled 15
USS Yorktown 11
US Navy aircraft carrier classes
Enterprise 6
Essex 10-15, 18
Forrestal 6, 16-18
Gerald R. Ford 6-7, 26-27, 30, 36-37, 39, 41, 50, 52, 127, 132, 134, 147, 157, 161, 183
Independence 10
Kitty Hawk (Improved Forrestal) 17-18, 20
Lexington 10
Midway 10-12, 14-15
Nimitz 6-7, 9, 20-21 et seq.
Ronald Reagan 25
Theodore Roosevelt 25
Ticonderoga 12, 23
United States cancelled 15-16
Yorktown 10
US Navy ships
Arleigh Burke class destroyers 132, 137
USNS Arctic (T-AOE-8) 153-154
USNS Big Horn (T-AO-198) 149
USNS Kanawha (T-AO 196
USNS Matthew Perry (T-AKE 9) 155
USNS Mount Baker (T-AE 34) 27
USS Blue Ridge (LCC-19) 168-169
USS Boxer (LHD-4)
USS George Washington (SSBN-598) 20
USS Nautilus (SSN-571) 18
USS Normandy (CG-60) 23
USS Sacramento (AOE 1) 151
US Postal Service 153

Vertical Horizon band 169